So, Anyway . . .

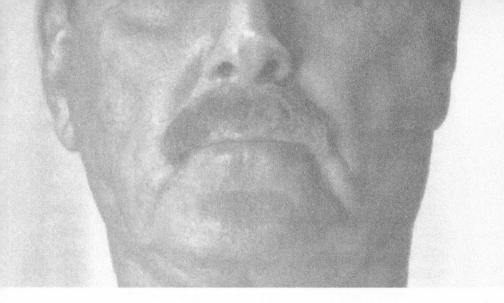

JOHN CLEESE

So, Anyway...

CROWN
ARCHETYPE

New York

All rights reserved.
Published in the United States by Crown Archetype, an imprint of
the Crown Publishing Group, a division of Random House LLC,
a Penguin Random House Company, New York.
www.crownpublishing.com

Originally published in Great Britain by Random House Books, an imprint of
Random House Limited, London.

Crown Archetype and colophon is a registered trademark of
Random House LLC.

Extracts from sketches written by John Cleese and Graham Chapman
copyright © John Cleese and The Graham Chapman Estate used by kind
permission of David Sherlock and The John Tomiczek Trust.

Library of Congress Cataloging-in-Publication Data
Cleese, John.
  So, anyway . . . / John Cleese. — First edition.
     pages cm
  Includes bibliographical references and index.
  ISBN 978-0-385-34825-6 (alk. paper)
  1. Cleese, John. 2. Comedians—Great Britain—Biography. 3. Motion picture
actors and actresses—Great Britain—Biography. I. Title.
  PN2598.C47A3 2014
  792.702'8092—dc23
  [B]

                      2014037869

ISBN 978-0-385-34824-9
eBook ISBN 978-0-385-34825-6

Printed in the United States of America

Jacket design: Richard Ogle
Jacket photographs: (front) Andy Gotts / Celebrity Pictures; (back) "Frost on Sunday"
TV the Class Sketch with John Cleese, Ronnie Barker, and Ronnie Corbett. 1970. Rex/
ITV; "And Now For Something Completely Different" John Cleese, 1971. Rex/Everett
Collection; Monty Python parrot sketch, 1971 AF Archive / Alamy; Cambridge Circus
New Revue at the Lyric Theatre. 1963 Rex/Phillip Jackson/Associated Newspapers;
Monty Python's Flying Circus, 1969 AF Archive / Alamy; All other photos courtesy
of John Cleese.

Photograph on page iii: Business Wire via Getty Images

10 9 8 7 6 5 4 3 2

First U.S. Edition

TO DAD
AND FISH

So, Anyway . . .

I

I made my first public appearance on the stairs up to the school nurse's room, at St. Peter's Preparatory School, Weston-super-Mare, Somerset, England, on September 13, 1948. I was eight and five-sixths. My audience was a pack of nine-year-olds, who were jeering at me and baying, "Chee-eese! Chee-eese!" I kept climbing the steps, despite the feelings of humiliation and fear. But above all, I was bewildered. How had I managed to attract so much attention? What had I done to provoke this aggression? And . . . how on earth did they know that my family surname had once been Cheese?

As Matron "Fishy" Findlater gave me the customary new-boy physical examination, I tried to gather my thoughts. My parents had always warned me to keep away from "nasty rough boys." What, then, were they doing at a nice school like St. Peter's? And how was I supposed to avoid them?

Much of my predicament was that I was not just a little boy, but a very tall little boy. I was five foot three, and would pass the six-foot mark before I was twelve. So it was hard to fade away into the background, as I often wished to—particularly later when I'd become taller than any of the masters. It didn't help that one of them, Mr. Bartlett, always referred to me as "a prominent citizen."

In addition, as a result of my excessive height, I had "outgrown my strength," and my physical weakness meant that I was uncoordinated and awkward; so much so that a few years later my PE teacher,

Captain Lancaster, was to describe me as "six foot of chewed string."
Add to that the fact that I had had no previous experience of the feral
nature of gangs of young boys, and you will understand why my face
bore the expression of an authentic coward as "Fishy" opened the
door and coaxed me out towards my second public appearance.

"Don't worry, it's only teasing," she said. What consolation was
that? You could have said the same at Nuremberg. But at least the
chanting had stopped, and now there was an expectant silence as I
forced myself down the stairs. Then . . .

"Are you a Roundhead or a Cavalier?"

"What?"

Faces were thrust at me, each one of them demanding, "Roundhead or Cavalier?" What were they talking about?

Had I understood the question, I would almost certainly have
fainted, such a delicate little flower was I. (And perhaps I should
explain to the more delicately nurtured that I was not being asked
to offer my considered views on the relative merits of the opposing
forces in the English Civil War, but to reveal whether or not I had
been circumcised.) However, my first day at prep school was not a
total failure. By the time I got home I had learned the meaning of
two new words—"pathetic" and "wet"—though I had to find Dad's
dictionary to look up "sissy."

Why was I so . . . ineffectual? Well, let's begin at my beginning.
I was born on October 27, 1939, in Uphill, a little village south of
Weston-super-Mare, and separated from it by the mere width of a
road which led inland from the Weston seafront. My first memory,
though, is not of Uphill but of a tree in the village of Brent Knoll,
a few miles away, under whose shade I recall lying, while I looked
through its branches to the bright blue sky above. The sunlight is
catching the leaves at different angles, so that my eye flickers from
one patch of colour to the next, the verdant foliage displaying a host
of verdant hues. (I thought I would try to get "verdant," "hues" and

"foliage" into this paragraph, as my English teachers always believed that they were signs of creative talent. Though I probably shouldn't have used "verdant" twice.)

Of course, I'm not *sure* it is my first memory; I'm sure I used to *think* it was; and I *like* to think it was, too, because it would make sense, baby me lying in a pram, contentedly watching the interplay of the glinting verdant foliage and its beautiful hues.

One thing I do know for certain, though, is that shortly before this incident with the tree, the Germans bombed Weston-super-Mare. I'll just repeat that . . .

On August 14, 1940, German planes bombed Weston-super-Mare. This is verifiable: it was in all the papers. Especially the *Weston Mercury*. Most Westonians were confident the raid had been a mistake. The Germans were a people famous for their efficiency, so why would they drop perfectly good bombs on Weston-super-Mare, when there was nothing in Weston that a bomb could destroy that could possibly be as valuable as the bomb that destroyed it? That would mean that every explosion would make a tiny dent in the German economy.

The Germans did return, however, and several times, which mystified everyone. Nevertheless I can't help thinking that Westonians actually quite liked being bombed: it gave them a sense of significance that was otherwise lacking from their lives. But that still leaves the question *why* would the Hun have bothered? Was it just Teutonic *joie de vivre*? Did the Luftwaffe pilots mistake the Weston seafront for the Western Front? I have heard it quite seriously put forward by older Westonians that it was done at the behest of William Joyce, the infamous "Lord Haw-Haw," who was hanged as a traitor in 1944 by the British for making Nazi propaganda radio broadcasts to Britain during the war. When I asked these amateur historians why a man of Irish descent who was born in Brooklyn would have such an animus against Weston that he would buttonhole Hitler on the matter, they fell silent. I prefer to believe that it was because of a grudge held by

Reichsmarschall Hermann Goering on account of an unsavoury incident on Weston pier in the 1920s, probably involving Noël Coward and Terence Rattigan.

My father's explanation, however, makes the most sense: he said the Germans bombed Weston to show that they really do have a sense of humour.

Whatever the truth of the matter, two days after that first raid we had moved to a quaint little Somerset village called Brent Knoll. Dad had had quite enough of big bangs during his four years in the trenches in France, and since he was up to nothing in Weston that was vital to the war effort, he spent the day after the bombing driving around the countryside near Weston until he found a small farmhouse, owned by a Mr. and Mrs. Raffle, who agreed to take the Cleese family on as paying guests. I love the fact that he didn't *mess around*. We were out of there! And it was typically smart of him to find a farm, where, at a time of strict rationing, an egg or a chicken or even a small pig could go missing without attracting too much attention.

Mother told me once that some Westonians privately criticised Dad for retreating so soon. They apparently felt it would have been more dignified to have waited a week or so before running away. I think this view misses the essential point of running away, which is to do it the moment the idea has occurred to you. Only an obsessional procrastinator would cry, "Let's run for our lives, but not till Wednesday afternoon."

Back to the tree. I revisited the farm many years later, and, just as I thought I remembered, there was a huge chestnut tree in the middle of the front lawn, under which I might easily have lain in a pram. In 1940 the farmhouse had been one of a row of houses of medium size strung along a road, with fields opposite; it didn't look very farm-like from the front, but when you walked up the drive and got to the back of the house you saw there was a proper farmyard, with mud and chickens and rusty farm equipment and ferrets in cages and rabbits in wooden hutches.

And it was this location that provides my second memory. (It must come after the first because in it I am now standing up.) I was bitten by a rabbit.

Or rather, I was nibbled by a rabbit, but, because I was such a weedy, namby-pamby little pansy, I reacted as though I'd lost a limb. It was the sheer unfairness of it all that so upset me. One minute, I was saying, "Hello, Mr. Bunny!" and smiling at its sweet little face and funny floppy ears. The next, the fucker savaged me. It seemed so gratuitous. What, I asked myself, had I done to the rabbit to deserve this psychotic response?

The more pertinent question, though, is: why was I such a *wuss*? And the obvious answer is that it's because I was the only child of older, over-protective parents. I have a memory (No. 3) to support this. I'm now about three and am in the Red Cow Inn, the hub and beating heart of Brent Knoll. Somehow I bang my hand, and just before I burst into tears, I hold it up to my father and howl, "Daddy, look! I've hurt my precious thumb!" This, to my astonishment, gets a big laugh. Is my thumb *not* precious, I wonder? Dad certainly thinks it is. When the occasion demands, he always says, "Oh, you've hurt your precious ——— [fill in applicable body part]."

I hesitate to criticise Dad, because what sanity I have I owe to his loving kindness. But there's no doubt that he did pamper me, and such early coddling was one of the reasons I embarked on a wussy lifestyle. Throughout my schoolboy days I never felt very manly, or strong, or virile, or vigorous, or healthily aggressive. At school I avoided playground "gangs," because I didn't understand why anyone would want to behave like that. I loved ball games, but was always appalled at how rough, for example, rugby looked, even at the safe distance I kept while pretending to play it. When I was seventeen, my assistant Clifton College housemaster, Alec MacDonald, finally took me to task for funking tackles. Describing my efforts as "dancing around like a disabled fairy," he ordered me to watch while he gave a demonstration of how to tackle properly. He asked a member of the first XV, Tony Rogers, to run at him. He closed in on Rogers, and then went in hard, just as Rogers tried to sidestep him. The result was that the top of Mr. MacDonald's head came into sharp contact with Rogers' right hip. Mr. MacDonald was unavailable for teaching later that afternoon; indeed he did not reappear for forty-eight hours. When he did, I was too cowardly to remind him that he had specifically told me that "if you go in hard, you never get hurt." So when I see international rugby teams lumbering out at Twickenham, I look at them with awe, but also with a sense of being genetically disconnected from them. I was not born to be butch, and I have accepted my innate unmanliness without complaint. Besides, it seems to me that cowards very seldom cause trouble, which is probably why there is a history of them being shot by people who do.[1]

None of this, incidentally, is to say that my infant wussiness was in any way admirable. But while I was undeniably a gutless little weed there was an upside: at least I didn't display the habitual mindless aggression of some young males. Better a wuss than a psycho, I say, and I am proud that I have never been able to force myself to watch cage fighting.

If part of my weedy outlook on life came from my father's pampering, a fair proportion was down to my complicated relationship with my mother. And in this context another early memory comes to mind. I am lying in bed, falling asleep, when a noise causes me to turn and see shadows moving on the half-open door of my bedroom. They are shadows of my parents fighting. Dad has been coming into my room and Mum has started attacking him, pummelling him with

---

[1] The most perceptive definition of a coward is Ambrose Bierce's: "One who in a perilous emergency thinks with his legs." This trait seems to me such a wise response to danger that it explains why generals want cowards dead; if they weren't, the concept of just plain running away would catch on so fast that the top brass would be out of a job overnight—or at least, would have to do some fighting themselves, which is not part of their job description.

a flurry of blows which he is trying to fend off. There is no sound—I sense they are both trying not to wake me—and the memory has no emotion attached, although it is very clear. Just the shadows which last a few seconds and then . . . silence. As I write this, my throat tightens a little. The level of violence I'm describing is low: there are no shillelaghs or chainsaws here, just lower-middle-class fisticuffs, with no prospect of Grievous Bodily Harm, as English law calls it. Nevertheless, my beloved dad, a kind and decent person, is being attacked by this unknowable creature who is widely rumoured to be my mother.

Young children have so little life experience that they inevitably assume that what happens around and to them is the norm. I remember that when my daughter Cynthia was very young she was surprised to discover that some of her friends' fathers did not work in television. So it would have been hard for me to describe my relationship with my mother as problematic because I had no idea what the word "motherly" conveyed to most people. Dad once described to me how, during the First World War, he had witnessed a wounded soldier lying in a trench and crying out for his mother. "Why on earth would he cry for her?" I wondered. When, over the years, I began to hear friends tell me that their mother was their best friend, someone with whom they routinely discussed their daily life, and to whom they looked for emotional support, I simply thought, "How wonderful that must be . . ."

Please do not think that I am loftily labelling her a "bad mother." In many ways she was a good mother; sometimes a very good mother. In all day-to-day matters she was extremely diligent: preparing good meals, making sure I was properly clothed and shod and warm and dry, keeping the house neat and clean, and fiercely protective of me. Under light hypnosis, I once recalled a German air raid, with the sound of the bombers not far away, and Mother throwing herself on top of me, under a big kitchen table. If it was a false memory, it's still what she would have done.

From a practical point of view, then, she was impeccable. But she was also self-obsessed and anxious, and that could make life with her very uncomfortable indeed.

Mother (left) and me.

A clue to her self-obsession, I always felt, was her extraordinary lack of general knowledge. On one of her visits to London in the late '80s, a salad was prepared for lunch which contained quails' eggs. She asked what kind of eggs they were and I explained that they were moles' eggs, and that when we wanted them, we would go up to Hampstead Heath very early in the morning, as moles laid them at the entrance to their burrows during the night, collect the eggs and make sure we ate them the same day before they had time to hatch. She listened with great attention, as my family's jaws sagged, and said she thought them "delicious." Later that day she caught a mention of Mary, Queen of Scots. She recognised the name and asked me who this was. With my family listening, I pushed the envelope a little, telling her that Mary was a champion Glaswegian darts player who had been killed in the Blitz. "What a shame," she said.

I was being a bit naughty, of course, but I also wanted to prove to my family the truth of a comment I had made earlier about Mother, which they had not accepted on first hearing. I had told them that *she had no information about anything that was not going to affect her life directly in the immediate future;* and that consequently she possessed no general knowledge—and when I said no general knowledge, I didn't mean very, very little. Naturally they had thought I was exaggerating.

And the reason for this was not that she was unintelligent, but that she lived her life in such a constant state of high anxiety, bordering on incipient panic, that she could focus only on the things that might *directly affect* her. So it goes without saying that she suffered from all the usual phobias, along with a few special ones (like albinos and people wearing eye patches). But she also cast her net wider. In fact, I used to joke that she suffered from omniphobia—you name it, she had a morbid dread of it. It's true that I never saw her alarmed by a loaf of bread or a cardigan or even a chair, but anything above medium size that could move around a bit was a hazard, and any reasonably loud sound startled her beyond reason. I once compiled a list of events that frightened her, and it was quite comprehensive: very loud snoring; low-flying aircraft; church bells; fire engines; trains; buses and lorries; thunder; shouting; large cars; most medium-sized cars; noisy small cars; burglar alarms; fireworks, especially crackers; loud radios; barking dogs; whinnying horses; nearby silent horses; cows in general; megaphones; sheep; corks coming out of sparkling wine bottles; motorcycles, even very small ones; balloons being popped; vacuum cleaners (not being used by her); things being dropped; dinner gongs; parrot houses; whoopee cushions; chiming doorbells; hammering; bombs; hooters; old-fashioned alarm clocks; pneumatic drills; and hairdryers (even those used by her).

In a nutshell, Mother experienced the cosmos as a vast, limitless booby trap.

Consequently, it was never possible for her really to relax, except perhaps for the times when she sat on the sofa knitting while Dad and I watched television. But even then she was active, knitting away against time. I noticed years ago that when people (myself definitely included) are anxious they tend to busy themselves with irrelevant activities, because these distract from and therefore reduce their actual experience of anxiety. To stay perfectly still is to feel the fear at its maximum intensity, so instead you scuttle around doing things as though you are, in some mysterious way, short of time. But although Mother kept herself busy in countless and pointless ways, it did not alleviate her worrying: her pervading sense that she was keeping nameless disasters at bay only by incessantly anticipating them, and that one moment's lapse in this vigilance would bring them hurtling towards her. I once proposed to Dad that we should purchase a large hamster wheel for her, so that she would find it easy to remain active all day, instead of having continually to invent non-essential activities like polishing cans of peas, or stacking cups, or sewing borders on handkerchiefs, or boiling knitting needles, or weeding the carpet.

Her own approach was to write her worries down on a piece of paper, so that there was no chance she would forget one, thus unleashing it. After Dad died, I would drive down to Weston to visit her and she would greet me with a cup of coffee and a very long list of worries which she had been compiling during the previous weeks, and we would sit down and discuss each worry in turn at some length: what it was about, and why it mattered, and how likely it was to happen, and what she could do to forestall it, and what we could do if it did actually happen, and whether we would know what to do if it didn't . . . and after we'd processed six or so, she'd make me another cup of coffee and we would continue working till bedtime. And if we hadn't got through them all by then, we'd leave the rest for breakfast. It took me decades to realise that it was not the analysing of her worries that eased them; it was the continuous contact with another person that gradually calmed her.

Why Mother should have been quite so anxious I simply don't know, but the net effect was to make her difficult. Actually, "difficult" is not quite fair. There was only one thing that she wanted. Just one. But that one thing was her own way. And if she didn't get it, that upset her. And she was prettily easily upset; in fact I think it's fair to say she had a real facility for it; and when something did upset her—and there was a *very* limited supply of things that, in the final analysis, didn't—she would throw a tantrum, or several tantra, of such inconceivable volume and activity that there must have been times when Dad yearned for the relative tranquillity of the trenches in France.

But Mother would never have seen herself as a tyrant: her trick was to rule through weakness. Whereas Dad might *prefer* to sleep with a window open, Mother *had* to have it shut, because she *just couldn't cope* with the alternative. Sadly, there was no choice, so negotiation was never an option, although Dad once confided to me that she had been much more flexible before they'd got married.

It was only in later years that I began to see just how alarmed Dad really was by the tantrums. While he talked occasionally about the need "to keep the little woman on an even keel," his faux-amused casualness was intended to conceal his fear, for when Mother lost her temper, she really lost it: her rage filled her skin until there was no room left for the rest of her personality, which had to move over till things calmed down a bit. The phrase "beside oneself with anger" could have been coined in Weston-super-Mare.

Mother could be quite charming and bright and amusing, but that was when we had visitors. Once they had gone, her sociability began to fade. This meant that there was nearly always tension in the Cleese household because when mother was not actually angry it was only because she was not angry *yet*. Dad and I knew that the slightest thing—almost anything—would set her off, so constant placatory behaviour was the name of the game.

It cannot be coincidence that I spent such a large part of my life in some form of therapy, and that the vast majority of the problems I was dealing with involved relationships with women. And my ingrained habit of walking on eggshells when coping with my mother dominated my romantic liaisons for many years. Until it began to fade, women found me very dull. My own unique cocktail of overpoliteness, unending solicitude and the fear of stirring controversy rendered me utterly unsexy. Very, very nice men are no fun. I once wrote a sketch based on my younger self (for the 1968 show *How to Irritate People*), in which I tried to show just how infuriating this desire to be inoffensive can be:

> JOHN CLEESE: I'm afraid I'm not very good company tonight.
>
> CONNIE BOOTH: No, it's me. I'm on edge.
>
> JC: No, no, no, you are marvellous, really super! It's me.
>
> CB: Look, let's forget it.
>
> JC: I'm not good company.
>
> CB: You are.
>
> JC: I'm not. I've been fussing you.
>
> CB: It's all right.
>
> JC: I have been fussing you. It's my own fault, you told me last time about fussing you too much.
>
> CB: Please!
>
> JC: Look, am I fussing you too much?
>
> CB: A bit.

Although there was little real emotional communication between us, my mother and I had our moments of closeness, almost all of them when we laughed together. She had quite a sharp sense of humour—and as I got older I discovered to my surprise that she also laughed at jokes that were rather dark, if not quite black. I remember on one occasion listening to her as she methodically itemised all the reasons why she didn't want to go on living, while I experienced my usual sense of glum failure at my powerlessness to help. Then I heard myself say, "Mother, I have an idea."

"Oh? What's that?"

"I know a little man who lives in Fulham, and if you're still feeling this way next week, I could have a word with him if you like—but only if you like—and he can come down to Weston and kill you."

Silence.

"Oh God, I've gone too far," I thought. And then she cackled with laughter. I don't think I ever loved her as much as I did at that moment.

SO, ANYWAY . . . there we were in the Raffles' house, pretty safe from German bombs, with a ringside view of a Somerset farmer's life, milking cows and fattening pigs and executing chickens. It was a very small farm, and the only surprising thing was that Mr. and Mrs. Raffle didn't speak English. I don't mean that they spoke another language; they didn't speak anything that could be recognised as a language. They clearly understood each other's noises, though, and we sensed that while they didn't like each other much, their limited vocabularies precluded unnecessary disagreements. How Dad negotiated our rent with Mr. Raffle I don't know. He probably used pebbles, although it's possible that the Raffles' young son, who was picking up some English at kindergarten, acted as interpreter.

Mr. Raffle owned two sheepdogs, so it was a bit of a surprise when we discovered that he had no sheep. Dad thought he kept the dogs so that people would think he owned sheep; Mother thought they might be cowdogs. I liked them—they were friendlier than the rabbits, although they did spend a lot of time staring into the rabbit hutches. As for the rabbits, I've never worked out why the Raffles actually bothered to keep any, since they had ferrets to catch them in the wild. I can only assume that, having caught them, they liked to keep them fresh and close by until a quick snack beckoned. That could explain why my attacker sank its fangs into me: it was not going to go quietly.

Sadly, just as I was beginning to name all the animals, and to get to know the little village of Brent Knoll, the Cleese family moved to Devon, to a little cottage in Totnes. Then, for no apparent reason, we moved back to the Raffles', then back to Devon (to Horrabridge, where I saw a spider so big I could hear its footsteps), then back to Brent Knoll, and then, immediately after VE Day, to Burnham-on-Sea, where we lived in three different houses in three years, before arriving in Weston-super-Mare (again) in 1948 so that I could attend St. Peter's Preparatory School. In all, we moved eight times in my first eight years.

I was too young to be part of a discussion on the subject, so I can only guess why we moved so often. From a practical point of view, constant relocation caused few problems because it never involved Dad having to change jobs. As an agent (or salesman) with the Guardian Assurance Company, he had been assigned a territory in the West Country which he drove around, selling mainly life insurance, but also a lot of Storm and Tempest cover to farmers. Because he was known to be such a decent chap, a lot of the life insurance came to him via personal recommendations from Somerset bank managers and solicitors: they knew he was competent and honest, and would not try to sell their clients more cover than they needed. This meant he always sold more life insurance than any of the other Guardian agents, but in a rather leisurely way, never driving off before 9:30 a.m., nor returning after 4:30 p.m. His secret was that, because of his contacts, he never needed to make "cold calls"; and provided he lived in the middle of Somerset, it didn't much matter where, as the distances were so small.

If the demands of Dad's job don't explain the constant moves, his worries about money might. As an insurance agent, his earnings peaked at £30 a week in the early '50s. Given that miners and most footballers got £10, it was not a bad salary and I certainly never sensed that we lacked for anything. Moreover the Cleese family never contemplated buying "expensive things." They weren't on our radar. For example, it literally never occurred to me that we might go abroad for our holidays; or that we might buy a car that was new; or that we would have anything for our Christmas lunch other than chicken.

Father (right) with small child.

Nevertheless such outlandish thoughts must have occurred to my father, who was kind and generous and would have loved to have provided us with a more gracious lifestyle of the kind he had enjoyed while working in India, Hong Kong and China in the early '20s. £1,500 per annum, however, didn't stretch very far, and although he hid his financial anxieties very well, I did begin to notice that, now and then, he'd go out of his way to save money on a purchase. Mother noticed, too, and we would look at each other as he extolled "surprisingly inexpensive" stylish Yugoslavian sports jackets, or top-class Libyan shoes, or premier quality Albanian ham that he had bought knowing full well that they would soon lose shape, or prove unwearable, or taste very odd indeed. It's not unreasonable to assume, therefore, that most of our moves were motivated by the hallucination that they would help cut costs.

But they may also have had an unintended side effect. Research has shown that constant relocation in childhood is often associated with creativity. It seems that the creative impulse is sparked by the need to reconcile contrasting views of the world. If you move home, you start living a slightly different life, so you compare it with your previous life, note the divergences and the similarities, see what you like better and what you miss, and as you do so, your mind becomes more flexible and capable of combining thoughts and ideas in new and fresh ways. There's also another way creativity can develop: if important people in your life, especially parents, have different ways of viewing the world, you find yourself trying to understand what they have in common, and how they contrast, in an attempt to make sense of their conflicting views. On the other hand, if your parents have a harmonious relationship and you grow up in one place where people share the same attitudes as those around them, you are unlikely to be innovative, or even to want to be. I doubt whether there's a special creativity faculty at Iowa State University.

So, creatively, I was doubly blessed: constant relocation *and* parental disharmony. Add to these two gifts the well-established fact that many of the world's greatest geniuses, both artistic and scientific, have been the product of serious maternal deprivation, and I am forced to the conclusion that if only my mother had been just a little more emotionally inadequate, I could have been HUGE. I could have been musically gifted, and talented in the visual arts, and an outstanding dancer, and an inventor, and a published poet, instead of being good, within very limited parameters, at writing and acting comedy. Oh well.

Despite these early years spent charging around the West Country, I have only a few scattered memories other than the Raffles' farm and the Horrabridge spider. I remember, for example, being out on a walk with Dad, and hearing a rumbling sound, and looking up and seeing the sky fill with large planes, flying towards the Continent. This was one of our daytime raids, Dad explained. We were winning the war so we didn't have to fly at night any more. Once, Dad and I talked to a nice young American airman who let me get up into his Jeep, where I scraped my precious ankle. On another occasion Dad drove us to the hills behind Weston, where we looked at a German plane that had crashed in a field. It was smaller than I expected. There were lots of sightseers, but they were very quiet.

Best of all were the Sundays when Dad would take me to Brent Knoll railway station. Here we were allowed up into the signal box, and the signalman would let me move the big levers that changed the points. Then we would go down on to the platform where there would be a huge wickerwork hamper full of racing pigeons, and the stationmaster would let me open the lid wide, and the pigeons would fly up and away, in a tightly knit flock, high into the sky, where they would circle round and round three times—always three times—before heading north to their homes in Widnes and Warrington and Wigan. It was the most exciting and beautiful experience.

The only direct effect the war had on our lives came when my parents received news that our furniture had been destroyed. The day we first moved to the Raffles', my parents had moved it into storage in a warehouse owned by Lalonde's, the well-known Westonian auctioneers, and now an incendiary bomb had overcooked it. It wasn't very posh furniture, of course, and in a way the Bosch did us a favour, because now we could move house with much greater ease, passing between various kinds of furnished accommodation unencumbered by very much in the way of belongings.

I notice that a lot of my early memories are connected with the war, but this is simply because such moments stood out so starkly from my normal, everyday experience. Months passed in the Somerset and Devon countryside without my being even vaguely aware of the conflict. In fact, I now realise how glad I am that I grew up in small West Country villages, surrounded by verdant foliage and emerald hues. I associate all this with a kind of quiet contentment, of effortless, calm mindfulness that I can seldom recapture in cities. Reading years ago what the psychologist Abraham Maslow had to say about "peak experiences," I recognised that these moments nearly always occur in repose, and in my case are never connected with work. Wordsworth wrote of his favourite flowers:

> For oft, when on my couch I lie
> In vacant or in pensive mood,
> They flash upon that inward eye
> Which is the bliss of solitude;
> And then my heart with pleasure fills
> And dances with the chrysanthemums.

When I recall moments of perfect, timeless happiness they include: sitting in a deckchair in the garden of my house in Holland Park, gazing at two Burmese kittens doing cabaret; looking at Vermeer's painting of Delft in The Hague, and allowing it to affect me; playing with a baby kangaroo in Sydney; listening to John Williams playing the guitar; cruising down the middle Rhine, sipping Moselle; eating fish and chips with my wife at Geale's two nights ago; or lying on the grass in the sun, and having my "inward" eye conjure up images of Dick Cheney being waterboarded. Again, none of them seem to be connected with work or, indeed, any kind of striving. Explain that to Terry Gilliam.

2

My last recollection of the Brent Knoll era is of being visited by a rather short, quiet and elderly man called John Cheese. He was my dad's dad, and enjoyed a reputation for being the white sheep of his family: apparently he had disapproved so strongly of his father and brothers that he had left home as soon as he was able, and moved miles away to Bristol to dissociate himself from them. Quite what his family got up to was never spoken of. I believe they were bakers, but that may have been a cover story they used to allow them to be up all hours of the night.

My grandfather must have been in his seventies when I first met him. In those days that was a considerable age and I remember him walking rather slowly with the aid of a stick as he, Mother and I made our way along the Somerset lanes. He was a very formal man— restrained and careful and sedate—though he exuded a kind and gentle air. In fact he looked just like Doctor Dolittle and although I liked being around him, and recall how courteous he and Dad were to each other, I don't remember having much actual fun with him. He had one little joke in his repertoire: he would tell of a pet peacock that flew over the wall into a neighbour's garden and laid an egg. Did the egg belong to the peacock's owner or the neighbour? When we'd guessed he would remind us that pea*cocks* didn't lay eggs. This was not exactly end-of-the-pier, knockabout stuff, and so it did not really surprise me when I learned later that he had passed his whole working life as a clerk in a legal firm.

Grandpa was my only surviving grandparent. My mum's mother had died many years before. Judging from photographs of her she was an elderly, rather ethereal version of Virginia Woolf. Her husband, Marwood Cross, on the other hand, was about as wraithlike as a warthog: a squat, short-tempered, assertive, graceless little man who in his time was, apparently, one of the most celebrated auctioneers in Weston-super-Mare. (Westonians habitually used inflated language to describe each other: doctors' names were spoken with a hushed reverence; surgeons and architects were invariably "eminent"; lawyers "distinguished"; businessmen "influential"; firms "prestigious"; schoolmasters "respected"; and tobacconists "renowned.") Well, there were half a dozen auctioneers in Weston, and they were all prominent, notable and self-impressed. When my parents chose my Christian names, they took John from Grandpa, and Marwood from this other oaf. Mother told me that in the future when people asked my name, and I said, "John Marwood Cleese," they would look surprised and say, "Oh! Are you by any chance related to Marwood Cross, the auctioneer?" Here's a multiple choice question for you, dear reader: how many times has this actually happened to me during my seven-plus decades on the planet? (a) 5,000 times, (b) Twice, (c) Never.

Marwood Cross was a celebrated, red-faced bully who ran a tight ship. When the table was laid for meals, a cane was placed by his cutlery, so that he could swat any of his children if their table manners faltered. He was also an eminent coward: when a burglar was once diagnosed in the basement, he appeared on the balcony outside his second-floor bedroom, ringing a handbell, and ordering his children and the maid to go and investigate. His main form of entertainment was writing poison-pen letters, which he would get my father to post from unlikely Somerset villages which he happened to pass through in the course of his quest to sell insurance policies. Marwood was also a past master of the art of auctioneering. If he fancied the look of anything he'd been asked to auction, he'd knock it down quickly to an imaginary buyer before the bidding got going, snaffling his prey at a cut-throat price while maintaining his reputation as a pillar of

Marwood Cross, eminent auctioneer.

the community. I'd like to apologise publicly for the fact that some of his genes are present in my body. They will be hunted down when the technology is available.

The final missing grandparent was my dad's mother. She had died in the early '20s, and I know almost nothing about her. This, I now realise, is because her death upset Dad so much that even many years later he never talked about her. I discovered this quite by chance. When I was about fourteen or so, I was rummaging through a tiny, ancient suitcase that contained all his old family papers, and I found a letter that she had written to him just before she died. When I showed it to Dad, a strange look flashed across his face, and he told

me he had not read it again since he had first received it. He opened
it and after a few seconds started to sob. It was the only time I saw
Dad cry. Later he told me that his tears were not just for her loss,
but because he had always felt a terrible guilt that he had been away

Strange assortment of Brent Knoll folk, with Grandpa Cheese at far right,
Mother (with squared shoulders), and me (with blunt implement).

in India and the Far East during the last four years of her life. Communication and travel were so slow in those days that he wasn't able
to get back in time to say goodbye. He believed that he had let her
down; that, in some strange way, she might have felt abandoned by
him. He showed me the last page of this, her final letter to him, and
how her signature trailed away towards the bottom of the page, a
long, thin straggly line, which he interpreted as her "giving up." I
was able, even at that young age, to realise that he had been carrying
this sorrow inside him for nearly thirty years, and that this was the
reason he and Mother never mentioned my grandmother's name.

Not only did I never see Dad cry again, I never heard him raise his voice in anger, nor utter the word "fuck." This is because he was a gentleman in the best sense of the word: not by breeding, of course, but by acquisition of a way of behaving that was based on a set of values he admired, those of the "English gentleman." During his time in the army, and after that in India and the Far East, he was able to watch some of the finest of this species, and was so impressed by their qualities of courtesy, kindliness, modesty, light-heartedness, courage, honesty, and a constant reluctance to burden others with their problems or difficulties, that he tried to model himself on what he observed.

But when he was born in Bristol, in 1893, all this lay in the future because his family was distinctly lower-middle-class. Young Reggie attended a Catholic school called St. Brendan's College, not because the Cheeses were Catholic, but because the headmaster was one of his father's best friends. He had a good, quick intelligence but no academic interests whatsoever, and so he left school early and took a job in an insurance office. One of his most endearing traits was his utter lack of ambition, which goes a long way to explain why he remained in insurance for the rest of his life. Another reason was that he was very good with figures, and could do quite complicated sums in his head. This came so naturally to him that he had fallen out with his St. Brendan's maths teacher, who insisted that he should "show his workings." Reggie didn't see the point.

I'm sure Dad was a useful clerk during the next few years. Given his facility with arithmetic, his excellent manners and his astute understanding of people, he was bound to have been. Moreover it was not in his nature to take pay without giving full value for it. But he was able to combine conscientiousness with light-heartedness. The life he led, full of the japes, pranks and put-ons that he and his pals perpetrated, sounded just like the one described in his favourite book, *Three Men in a Boat*. He and his friends even played tricks on visitors to the insurance office, coating a walking stick with treacle, for example, so that helpful people who picked it up to hand over to them would get sticky hands. Outside the office they were more boisterous, but never mean or the slightest bit violent. Weston, as the nearest seaside resort, was often the setting for their antics. They would take donkey rides, set off in different directions and then leave the donkeys in people's gardens to eat the flowers. Their most spectacular caper involved removing several small plucked chickens from a butcher's shop, smuggling them into the balcony at the Winter Gardens, and then, on a cue, launching them all high into the air so that they descended on to the orchestra that was playing while gentlefolk were taking afternoon tea.

Dad lived at home with his parents until he was twenty-two. With the outbreak of the First World War in the late summer of 1914, he tried to sign up, but failed the medical because he couldn't read the fourth line down on the optician's chart. Later in the war the army became less picky, but before that happened he volunteered again. This time he asked the man in front of him in the queue to memorise the line he couldn't read, and to tell him what it was on the way out. The subterfuge allowed him to join the carnage in France, albeit under an assumed name; he was fed up with being teased that he was a fermented curd, so he changed the "h" to an "l." I never understood what he was hoping to achieve; I was always called "Cheese" from the moment I arrived at a school. Perhaps his regiment, the Gloucesters, lacked the imagination to make the connection.

After he finished his training, he was made a second lieutenant, the lowest commissioned rank in the army hierarchy. He never knew why he was chosen to be an officer, but assumed it was because he spoke grammatical English. Arriving in France in 1915, he was, within weeks, wounded in the back and shoulders by shrapnel (the scars were still visible thirty-odd years later). So he wrote a letter of resignation to his commanding officer (the army was a very gentlemanly affair in those days), returned to England and convalesced. Once the wounds had healed, he enlisted again, this time as a private. A shout-

ing match ensued when the army discovered that he had previously
served as an officer, but they eventually calmed down and agreed to
let him return to France as a mere lance-corporal. I always thought
this was a loveably eccentric act on Dad's part, typical of his lack of
interest in career advancement, until I discovered years later that the
life expectancy of a junior officer on the Western Front at that time
was . . . *six weeks*. Because when an officer led his men over the top,
the Germans looked for the man with a revolver and a whistle, and
shot him first.

When, as a young boy immediately after the Second World
War, I used to accompany Dad in the car on some of his insurance
trips, he would tell me not only stories from his war years, but also
funny and fascinating tales of what happened to him next. Apparently when the Armistice was signed in 1918, his commanding officer asked him what he was going to do now that the war was over.
He said that he planned to return to Bristol and carry on selling
insurance. "No! No!" cried the colonel. "You must go and see the
Empire, young man!" and promptly wrote Dad a couple of letters of
introduction and recommendation. Just a few weeks later, therefore,
Dad found himself on a boat bound for Bombay where, thanks to
the colonel's contacts, he had secured a job selling marine insurance
with a big British company called the Union of Canton. And now
he began to live quite a posh life. He was no longer an insurance
salesman: he was a marine underwriter; and because he looked very
presentable and had the right accent and excellent manners and was
witty and amusing, he began mixing with middle-middle-class people from "good" public schools, and even occasionally with some
real toffs, many of whom proved to be friendly and good-natured
and cultivated. Mind you, these folk had a lot to be good-natured
about: they lived like micro-princes. When Dad found a house to
share, he discovered that there were fourteen servants attached to it;
when he suggested reducing this extraordinary number, the Indians
explained, with great charm and regret, that he was not allowed to

do this: it was his duty as an English gentleman to employ at least that number.

The fellow Dad found himself sharing with was called Wodehouse, and he turned out to be a brother of the great PG. Dad thought him immensely likeable: charming, wonderfully companionable and considerate, but, oddly, seemingly without any sense of humour. What was even odder, though, was the degree of Wodehouse's naivety. Like Dad he was in his mid-twenties, but it was only when visiting a doctor in Bombay that he discovered that his foreskin was retractable. It's hard to credit that a chap could get through a couple of decades without stumbling upon this fact (about a part of one's body of considerable interest to most males) but I think it throws light on PG's status as a great comic writer. If his brother was as naive as this, is it possible that PG himself lacked a certain degree of worldliness, of the everyday experience of the average man-about-town, of actual, ordinary *savoir faire*? And if so, is it possible that this very ingenuousness is connected with the rather simplified psychology of PG's characters, which forces me to regard him as a *very good* comic writer rather than a *great* one?

Not that I have anything against naivety itself: every single person I really like has a degree of it, and the people I detest the most are know-it-alls, but there is a point at the far end of the naivety continuum where it becomes indistinguishable from ordinary common-or-garden brainlessness. The question that must be faced is: is it more likely that a man would make a Nazi propaganda broadcast BY MISTAKE—as PG claimed he did—if he shared genes with someone who was unaware that his foreskin was retractable? To this, I believe that the answer is a resounding "Yes!"

All in all, Dad had a wonderful time in India (not least because he was not present when Wodehouse made his discovery), and he always talked of the Indians in tones of total affection. But there's no doubt that it was very much a colonial, master-servant relationship. Dad spoke some Hindi, but he once admitted that the only part of a Hindi verb that he ever knew was the imperative. He and his pals were a high-spirited lot—scarcely surprising given the horrendous war they had just endured. (To put this in perspective, it has been claimed that more damage was done to buildings in Cambridge on Guy Fawkes Night of 1945 by boisterous undergraduates recently returned from fighting in Europe, than was achieved by German bombers during the whole of the Second World War.) They had a tendency, therefore, to behave the way rugby teams traditionally do on Saturday nights. As a rule they were rowdy and naughty rather than nasty, but Dad did recall an occasion when things went a bit further. Apparently a Welsh friend called Davies invited him for a drive one Sunday afternoon in his open car, and Dad was surprised, as he climbed into the back seat behind the chauffeur, to find a small pile of bricks there. He pointed them out to Davies, who said he would explain what they were for in due course. Ten minutes later Davies picked one up and lobbed it through the front window of a shop they were passing. The Indian chauffeur found this as amusing as his employer. Dad was astonished, but reflected that at least it was a Sunday and the shop was shut.

Dad's misbehaviour was relatively low-key. He kept a letter, which he treasured, from a famous Bombay hotel, barring him from entering its precincts again, and listing at length his various pranks, involving butter dishes, and trays of that classic Anglo-Indian dish kedgeree, and the launching of other edible projectiles. But, once he became a member of the Royal Bombay Yacht Club, I suspect his conduct improved: he relished mixing with real live gentlemen, and I can see now that his admiration of them also involved studying their demeanour and habits, and mimicking them. And in due course, teaching some of it to me. "Never look startled, my boy. Move slowly. If somebody drops something, and you want to look, wait a few seconds, and then turn round in a leisurely way, and glance. Don't stare."

The only blight on Dad's sojourn in India was that he caught malaria, which was to afflict him for years to come. When an attack came, all he could do was to retreat to his bed for several days, trembling and sweating, teeth chattering, feeling so weak he could do nothing but stay there, patiently losing weight.

After three years in India the Union of Canton transferred him to their Hong Kong office, and shortly afterwards he was re-transferred to their main office in Canton. Outside the British Empire for the first time, he saw things that made Bombay look like Cheltenham. He visited an opium den; he got tattoos; and he ate a dog. (I'll rephrase that: he ate a delicious dish, which he subsequently discovered was "dog.") He also had a clerk working for him whom he much liked. A Chinese chap who spoke excellent English and was charming and highly competent. One day, however, he did not turn up at the office. Inquiries were made and it turned out he was in jail. Dad (typically) went straight to the prison and asked to see the governor, who greeted him most courteously and explained that his clerk had been found guilty of "illegal political activities." Dad asked how long he would be in prison. The governor said, "I am afraid we are executing him in the morning."

I used to think it was extraordinary that shortly after this, Dad was to be found back in Weston-super-Mare. Had he also been engaged in illegal political activities? Was he feeling bad about the dog? (Apparently it was truly scrumptious, so he could have been removing himself from further temptation.) Or was he just tired of excitement? Actually, the answer was simple: malaria. The attacks had weakened him and he was worried that unless he removed himself to cooler climes, he might kick the bucket. As it was, by the time he got back to Blighty, his weight was down to around eleven ounces, which is not much for a man of six feet: he was the standard "bag of bones." The attacks continued for several years before they started to peter out; meanwhile he was one of the few in Weston on quinine.

But first he went down to Bristol to visit his father, whom he'd not seen for five years, and stayed there to recuperate while his spinster sister, Dorothy, looked after him. They were very fond of each other and spent a lot of time together, engrossed in their common interest: smoking. Dad had formed a habit of forty a day (untipped) and Dorothy matched him, stub for stub. Despite this, he slowly regained his health, and started making excursions to the nearest seaside town, which happened to be dear old Weston-super-Mare. While visiting, he bumped into Mother, they started walking out together, despite Marwood demanding she should be home by ten o'clock (she was twenty-six), and fell in love. Within just a few months they decided to get married.

My parents, not planning to have a child.

And—here's the romantic bit—they eloped!

They had to. They came from families of different social class, and there was no way that Marwood Cross was going to give his blessing to a wedding between his daughter and a commoner. Well, not *a* commoner exactly, just someone commoner. The gap in status between Muriel Cross and this dubious tattooed proletarian lounge lizard was unbridgeable. You see, Dad came from, at best, the middle-lower-middle class; to be exact, he was middle-middle-lower-middle class. Whereas Muriel Cross came from the great auctioneering house of Marwood Cross, who were *almost* middle-middle class; their lowest possible social classification was upper-upper-lower-middle class. And so far as Marwood was concerned, a morganatic arrangement was out of the question.

So Dad and Mum eloped to London, to the far-off, urbane, cosmopolitan, liberal-minded heart of the British Empire, where nobody gave a solitary hoot for an inflated, half-witted provincial auctioneer with his head up his upper-upper-lower-middle-class arse.

Freedom! In Golders Green, where for two years they lived happily, and Dad acquired so many Jewish friends that he picked up a surprising amount of Yiddish. These fellows took great pleasure in introducing Dad to their unsuspecting friends, just to see the expression on their faces when this unmistakable goy launched into a volley of Central European demotic. I think Dad was secretly proud of his Jewish connections; in an age when there was so much prejudice, he did what he could to work against it, although he was prepared (with Mother) to make an exception of the Welsh. This is a well-established West Country trait, and rooting it out will take many generations, I fear.

But then . . . destiny moved against them. A reconciliation took place with Marwood Cross, and so, inevitably . . . they moved back to Weston-super-Mare, and lived there, reasonably happily at least, until I arrived (also in Weston) in October 1939, a mere thirteen years after their wedding. It seems that in the world of the Cleeses, all roads lead to Weston-fucking-super-fucking-Mare.

By the time Dad was regaling me with his memories of India, though, we had taken up residence in a small seaside town called Burnham-on-Sea, a few miles down the coast from Weston. (Burnham plays an important part in British history, because it was here that a bee killed Viscount Montgomery of El Alamein's first wife. Monty loved her very much, and had she survived the sting, he might have settled down to a happy retirement. As it was he went off to North Africa to defeat Rommel.) And the reason for the move to Burnham—assuming there was one—was to allow me, at the age of six, to start at a proper school.

The problem was that my parents picked a real stinker. My recollections of it seem to come straight out of Dickens: two large rather dark rooms illuminated by a fire, with fifteen or so children, all older than me, working in small groups, supervised by a solitary, curt, menacing old crone, who seemed to assume that I should know what I was supposed to be doing without actually bothering to tell me. After a couple of days of bewildered anxiety, things came to a head. The sour old cow gave me a sum much more difficult than any I had encountered before: say, a four-digit number divided by a three-digit number. I guessed how to do it, and got it wrong. Without offering help, she told me to do it again. I failed a second time; she warned me to try hard; I did; I failed again; and she told me to hold my hand out and, grasping it firmly, she caned the palm three times, hard. My first reaction was astonishment: none of my kindergartens had been Catholic establishments, so I was unprepared for this kind of assault. Then it hurt, a lot! My precious palm! When I first started having therapy twenty-five years later, this was one of the first traumas I recalled, and I was astonished at the power of the feelings that came flooding back: anger—no, fury; self-pity; humiliation; a deep, deep sense of hurt; and a pure indignation at not so much the unfairness, but the *insanity* of punishing someone *physically* for getting an answer wrong. It is terrifying how much of this deeply unkind, utterly pointless, in fact, mind-bogglingly COUNTERPRODUCTIVE kind of behaviour was meted out to children over the centuries by half-witted, power-crazed zombies like this heinous old bat—a large proportion of such psychopaths allegedly acting in the name of an all-loving God. (A friend of mine attended a school run by Carthu-

sian brothers. When one boy in class made a mistake, the priest produced a strap, asked the question again, and raised the strap to strike
him if he repeated his error. The boy remarked, "Well, that's not
going to help, is it?")

But I may have learned *something* from my brush with sadism.
The strongest feeling of all that re-emerged in this therapy session
of mine was the final one that bubbled up: an extraordinary, steely
determination that I WAS NOT GOING TO LET THIS HAPPEN
AGAIN! Somehow, something stirred somewhere in my precious,
six-year-old heart, which suggested that I might have a couple of ver-
tebrae knocking around somewhere, and that one day I might get to
use them.

So grim was this first experience of school that Dad took me away
from the nightmare establishment the next day, and enrolled me in
Miss Cresswell's Academy, a really nice, kind, happy and friendly
school, where I coloured pictures of mice in hats and then cut them
out very neatly with scissors. Thus I began to rebuild my academic
confidence and resume my wussy lifestyle.

Looking back I realise I was a fairly quiet and solitary child
(though not a lonely one). Mother said that as a baby I never cried—
I probably thought that if I did she might appear—and ever since
I read the psychologist Hans Eysenck's wonderfully clear account
of introverts and extroverts, I've known I am definitely one of the
former. Of course, there's a continuum between one extreme and
the other, with certain individuals, called ambiverts, falling in the
middle, with both tendencies in roughly equal proportions. For some
people the words only conjure up the caricatures at either end: the
tongue-tied, painfully shy Swedish archivist at one end, the loud,
insensitive Midwestern car salesman at the other. Such folk assume
actors must be extroverts, but a lot aren't; many performers are big
presences on stage, but quite shy off. There is, after all, a huge difference between pretending you're somebody else and being yourself.

Eysenck also said that introverts have a naturally high level of

mental activity, so they are seldom bored and in need of stimulation, because they have enough going on in their heads already. Extroverts, on the other hand, have a lower level of psychic activity:
they are prone to boredom, and so need a lot of external stimulation
to keep them alert. And that confirms my view that I'm an intro-
vert: I'm never bored, except when I am trapped at a dinner party
by people who are bent on impressing me; but I frequently feel overwhelmed, whether it's by the huge visual displays at Harrods, or by
too many emails and phone calls, or by hordes of people coming at
me on public occasions, each one determined to tell me that "We
have something in common!" ("My sister's husband was at Clifton
College about twenty years after you, and he used to go to the same
sports store where they said you had once bought a pair of batting
gloves." "No! Really?") But I've learned to function perfectly well
in extroverted situations and to enjoy them, although afterwards I
seem to need a bit of peace and quiet. On the other hand, if I spend
the day writing, then I really look forward to a social evening. It's not
black and white, it's more a question of balance.

Certainly as a six-, seven- and eight-year-old, I spent more time
on my own, and with my parents, than with my contemporaries.
I played happily alone, running a shop with the help of my stuffed
animals, making Meccano models, modelling Plasticine, collecting
postcards of British birds, and drawing and painting without revealing a shred of talent. I loved comics, reading them with great care,
as though I was trying to understand what motivated the characters. Thus I acquired the idea that kicking people's bottoms was very
funny, though in practice this didn't make them laugh as much as it
should have. I needed to spend more time with kids of my age.

So one evening my parents arranged for me to have supper with
two boys who lived in the same block of flats, and we listened to
a fifteen-minute radio serial called *Dick Barton, Special Agent*. The
adrenaline rush this caused flowed for several days and my parents
decided that the experience should not be repeated too often. An-

other time, I was left with some "nice" boys and girls for a few hours, and, with my eyes on the end of stalks, watched them playing Monopoly. I had simply never realised that life could be so thrilling. I could imagine myself actually joining in and playing a game like this when I was a few years older and it was safe to do so.

Two things about myself I am at a loss to explain. I suddenly became fascinated by cars, and would sit in the back of our little Austin 10, calling out the names of all the oncoming cars with great accuracy. "Lagonda! Humber! MGM! Wolseley! Hillman Minx! Jowett Javelin!" Then, one day, I completely lost interest in them. *Overnight!* From that moment on, they bored me rigid. Nowadays I assume that anyone reading a car magazine must be geeky. People comparing the advantages and disadvantages of competing models of *motor cars*, and showing off their detailed knowledge? Are they *insane*? One of my greatest fears is to be a key witness in a complicated car pile-up: the police interviewing me would think I was sending them up.

Even odder was my support for Australia at cricket. Where did *that* come from? Dad talked with real affection about the South Africans and Aussies and Canadians he'd met during the war, but why would I have suddenly decided to become an expert on Australian cricketers of the '20s and '30s? I knew them all: Woodfull and Ponsford, Bradman, Macartney, McCabe, Kippax, Richardson, Oldfield, Clarrie Grimmett (who was a Kiwi who played for Oz, and who could spin a ball so hard it would turn at right angles on a snooker table), Bill O'Reilly, Fleetwood-Smith (the worst batsman Test cricket has ever seen) and the awe-inspiringly fast bowling partnership McDonald and Gregory. Dad and I invented a form of living-room cricket to get us through the winter, which involved bowling a ping-pong ball at a tiny bat held in front of a wooden matchbox holder—and while he was always Hobbs or Sutcliffe or Harold Larwood, I was always the Australians. And this strange quasi-patriotic attachment lasted until the mid-'50s when I finally switched my allegiance to the England team. I have not the faintest, remotest, tiniest scintilla of an idea why I once cheered for the Aussies.

And, talking of rum behaviour, around that time something happened that puzzled me a *lot*. Mrs. Phillips, an old lady who lived in a flat upstairs, sent a message asking me to visit her, as she had something she wanted to give me. I can clearly remember climbing the stairs: they were rather steep, and she was sitting at the top, in an armchair, gripping something. She told me to hold my hand out, took my fingertips to steady it, and then stabbed my palm with a specially sharpened stick. (It was one of the thin wooden tapers which people used to help light fires, and she had trimmed the business end into a point.) A healthy, slightly more masculine boy would have taken the taper from her and put her eyes out with it, but, being me, I screamed like a stuck pig, and howled, and sobbed and . . . what? That was the whole memory, and what fascinates me is . . . what had I done to deserve it? Because clearly I *must have done something* for which Mrs. Phillips was punishing me. This palm-stabbing was not part of an established pattern of behaviour on her part; in Burnham-on-Sea gossip travelled fast—a good bowel movement could not have been hushed up for long—and Mrs. Phillips was classified as "highly respectable." Could she perhaps have gone berserk for these two brief minutes of her life, and then resumed normal service for the rest of her days (not, fortunately, to be reckoned in their hundreds)? Or had I *done* something sneaky and dark and woodsheddy—certainly nothing sexual, for at that age I had no idea what a girl's penis would look like, but something sordid like putting mustard on her birthday cake, or hiding a spider in her pencil box, or flaying her hamster? I have a strong suspicion I'd perpetrated something vaguely shoddy. What else could possibly explain Mrs. Phillips's premeditated behaviour, the careful planning, the ingenious choice of weapon, the meticulous sharpening, the crafty invitation, the sudden ambush . . . what was it revenge *for*?

Or was she just bored? I shall never know. And I shall never know whether or not to feel ashamed . . .

Not that I'm pretending that I led an entirely blameless life at the time. I did, for example, make a brief foray into the world of crime: I stole a submarine. Agreed, it wasn't a very sophisticated submarine, just a three-inch-long piece of grey lead shaped roughly like a submarine (worth about one penny at 2014 prices) which I'd come across at a party, but I did sneakily purloin it both KNOWING IT WAS NOT MINE and in full knowledge that I was DOING SOMETHING WRONG. Somehow I must have given myself away, because Dad worked out that I had thieved it and suggested I take it back and apologise. Which I did, although when I told my victims I'd taken something that belonged to them, I think they were a bit surprised when I produced this tiny lead submarine: they had assumed that the loot would be a bit more substantial. Dad, though, never harped on about what I had done: he simply explained that I shouldn't have taken it and then got me to return it. End of lesson. I was very lucky to have a dad like that.

Now a BIG thing happens. We have been visiting prep schools in the area, and they all seem rather large and severe and forbidding, but Dad explains that we will be moving to Weston-super-Mare, so I can go to a very nice school there, called St. Peter's, as a day boy. I've often been to Weston and it's huge—not as big as Bristol where Grandpa lives but *really big*, with a Grand Pier with a sign saying, "The Largest Covered Amusement Park in the World," and a Winter Gardens, and *three* miniature golf courses. More important, it so happens that in August the Somerset County Cricket team comes to Clarence Park to play *three* three-day matches in a row, Dad takes me to one of them (to show me how exciting it will be living in Weston), and I am immediately smitten. Just the one match, but it's a start. I've fallen in love for the first time—with cricket *and* with the Somerset team (especially Bertie Buse, whose moustache is like Dad's).

When I got back to Burnham, I organised a cricket match, and I made a century! There were only two other players (my Dick Barton friends) but I smashed the tennis ball all around our back garden and achieved a twenty-three-ball hundred! (It turned out to be the only century I ever made.)

So, at the beginning of September we moved to Weston, to the ground floor of a small house on a road called Clarence Park North, right next to the cricket ground, to enter a preparatory school called St. Peter's, where the teachers were mostly men, where there were grown-up boys of twelve and thirteen, and where the headmaster was bald and absolutely enormous.

3

Having managed to endure the relentless teasing of my horrid first day at St. Peter's Preparatory School, I lay quietly in my bedroom that night like a new arrival at Colditz, planning how I was going to survive. There was just one shaft of hope: my shadow. I was already very attached to my shadow. He was an older boy named John Reid, and under the St. Peter's system, he had been assigned to me, accompanying me wherever I went, guiding, explaining, warning, encouraging, and making sure that, wherever I was, I knew what I was supposed to be doing. He was very kind and supportive, and, all these years later, I still feel grateful to him, even though he left St. Peter's shortly afterwards, never to be seen again. (By me, that is: I don't mean that he was suddenly rendered invisible, or even transparent.) Without Reid's kindness, I think I would have slunk off and hidden in a dustbin, also never to be seen again, since all the other boys seemed to detest me. Certainly, my social skills were poor—for example, I still had the idea that kicking other boys' bottoms would eventually make me more popular—and I was irritatingly tall, and pathetic and wet, but Reid got me through the first two weeks. After that I had a chance.

I had one other survival technique: I sometimes said things that made the other boys laugh. When this happened I immediately experienced a moment of warmth, of acceptance, of feeling "Maybe I am all right, after all." Peter Cook always said that he quite deliberately staved off bullying by being funny. I think in my case it was less a conscious activity—more "Oh, that felt nice." And, as I relaxed, I became funnier, of course, because the spark was always there. So the bullying faded away, and I started, for the first time, to make friends.

So far as schoolwork was concerned, I was quite unexceptional. After a couple of terms of very gentle stuff—dictation, and making papier mâché puppets, and telling stamens from pistils—I moved up to Form II, where all the teachers were men. (Except the headmaster's wife, who was more than a match for any male at St. Peter's, including the headmaster.) Now I began Latin, which was taught by Captain Lancaster, a fine, military-looking man with an impeccable mane of white hair, a bushy but clipped white moustache, a very red face and a fearsome temper (according to tradition). Learning became a serious business because we were terrified of his getting into a "bate." A lot of our work with him involved rote learning, which I quite enjoyed: declining nouns and adjectives and conjugating verbs, and my God did he drum it into us, because even today I can still remember it all, without even pausing to think. Funnily enough, I never actually saw him lose his fearsome temper. But that was only because we made sure he didn't. (Later I discovered that despite his military bearing and title, and his reputation for fierceness, his tendency sometimes to seem a bit gruff was entirely due to his shyness: underneath it all, he was an extraordinarily gentle and sweet-natured man. He would tell us how to recognise birdsong, and read to us from *Three Men in a Boat*—*provided* we'd done the work. Somehow his terrifying reputation had obscured his essential kindness, and the fact that he taught PE and boxing and shooting and held the military title of captain all helped the deception.)

I was always quite good at Latin, and at maths. I'm not sure why. Perhaps it was because both had a certain simple logic to them that my mind could cope with: you learned rules and then applied them. When it came to English I was only OK, and I was rather bad at everything else, especially French, which left me bewildered: you had

to make strange noises I'd never heard before, which bore no relation whatsoever to the words on the page. Why didn't they? What
was the point? Then *history*! Why was I being told that King Alfred
burnt the cakes? If it was that they didn't want me to burn cakes, why
didn't they just say so? What had King Alfred got to do with it? And
anyway, if he was King, why on earth was he doing the cooking?
And what was King Canute up to, chatting away to the sea? Why did
they make him King if he was barking mad? Surely the courtiers on
the beach should have *hushed it all up*? None of it made any sense at
all, and that rattled me, as I was still at an age when I thought things
were meant to make sense, and I got quite anxious when they didn't.

Worst of all was scripture. Scripture actually frightened me. To
start with, it had all the random pointlessness of history. OK, there
was a man called Ahab who, the Bible says, "walked delicately," and
someone called John who "rode furiously," and probably someone
called Ezekiel who "drew badly." But . . . this was thousands of years
ago! Why was I expected to *memorise* this stuff? True, there was a
vague assumption that doing so would bring me closer to God, but
then who was God when he was at home? And why did he keep losing it with his chosen people, when he could easily have changed his
mind, and picked a more co-operative bunch?

Nothing was ever explained properly. Just as it was always taken
for granted that you knew why it was important to study Latin, or to
churn out papier mâché puppets, or to know where flax was grown,
so my teachers also unanimously assumed that I knew how Catholics
differed from Protestants, or that I understood what "eternal life"
was, as though I had seen it on a shelf in the grocery shops. But the
reason that scripture alarmed me the most was that it was clearly
supposed to be important, because it was read out by the headmaster
at prayers every single morning. Yet I could not grasp what any of it
was about, despite the fact that it appeared to be in English. If he'd
read it out in Flemish I would have relaxed, knowing it was not supposed to be comprehensible to me, but obviously I was expected to

take it in: "Let not thy left hand know what thy right hand doeth."
Come again? "Blessed are the meek." Oh, yeah? Well, it doesn't seem
to be getting me anywhere. "Thou shalt not covet thy neighbour's
ox." Are you joking? Any of this could have been interesting if the
teacher had chatted about it with us, and in terms of our experiences.
So why *didn't* they?

The neurologist and psychiatrist Maurice Nicoll told how he had
once asked his headmaster about a passage in the Bible, and after
he had listened to the answer for some time, he realised that the
man had no idea what he was talking about. What I admire about
Nicoll is that he made this discovery when he was only ten. It took
me another forty-five years before the penny dropped: very, very few
people have any idea what they are talking about. Imagine if just one
of St. Peter's schoolmasters had told me in 1949, "You must always
remember that ninety per cent of what you're told is purest bullshit."
Imagine what an intellectual kick-start that would have been! When
I went for my regular Sunday evening walk with Dad, during which
I would carefully discuss all my worries about the approaching week
and he would reassure me and give me the courage to go over the top
on Monday morning, a lot of my anxiety was about trying to understand just what the hell was going on, and what it meant.

However, the single most surprising (and indeed disorientating)
event in my early St. Peter's life took place one afternoon, during
"Rest" when we all sat at our own desks, reading *Biggles* and *Billy
Bunter* and digesting lunch. I glanced up from my book, and there,
about fifteen feet to my right, was one of my classmates. He had
stopped reading, and was carefully stroking something in his lap.
I was curious. What was it that he had there, that he was caress-
ing with such loving kindness? You, gentle reader, are some three
lines ahead of the nine-year-old Cleese, who was tossing out hypothesis after hypothesis in his search for understanding. Finally, it was
granted. Rather like those early Pacific islanders, who were unable to
see a big boat that had arrived on their shores, because it was entirely

beyond their experience that such a large boat could exist, I took a very long time to drink in the reality of what I was definitely observing. But then the scales fell from my eyes, and I consciously acknowledged that this classmate of mine was attending to his penis. In my own defence, I have to say, with the benefit of hindsight, that the calm, unruffled ease with which he did so, rather as though he was unhurriedly sharpening a favourite pencil, put me off the scent: it was not possible that a private part could be publicised in this matter-of-fact, quotidian manner. There must be some other explanation. As I sat there, frantically grasping for an alternative interpretation, a boy from my left, keeping low as he ran (so as not to be spotted by the master-on-duty, himself reading at the far end of the room) passed in front of me, over to the penis-boy, and crouched down beside him to obtain a ringside view of the proceedings. I could not have been more astonished at what I was spectating if the two of them had quietly levitated, morphed into pterodactyls, and flown out of the window.

From this moment my mind remains a blank. My next memory is sitting at home, telling all to Dad. Next day, he had a chat with Mr. Tolson; the following day I was allowed to stay home, while the headmaster addressed the entire school on the subject of private parts. It was typically decent of the headmaster Mr. Tolson to see that had I been there to hear his address, my facial colour would have identified the Fifth Columnist in the school's midst. (And I should explain that what I had beheld was not, for me, what adults would think of as sexual; it was simply that my understanding was that a penis was intended to be kept private.)

But in other areas I was becoming less diffident—or, in St. Peter's parlance, less "wet." Indeed, on one occasion, I actually got into a fight with a boy who was teasing me. There I was, lying on the floor, grappling with him, like a proper schoolboy; I even banged his head on the floor, at which point I thought, "Oh my God! If I start losing, he'll do this to *me*," and then, of course, started losing. Fortunately my form master, Mr. Howdle, arrived and broke the fight up. Funnily enough, it was about then that the bullying stopped. This first fight also proved to be my last. I had thought so, anyway, until I read in the *Sunday Times* recently that I had a fight with Terry Gilliam in the '80s. I think this unlikely: owing to the relatively rare occurrence of fisticuffs in the Cleese life it must be statistically probable that I would *remember* such uncommon events; they would tend to stand out sharply from the rather less pugilistic tone of the rest of my life. And I definitely *don't recall* having a fight with Terry Gilliam. May I also point out that if I had, I would almost certainly have killed him. I think the only possible explanation for the *Sunday Times* article—if it is true—was that Terry attacked me, but that I failed to notice he was doing so. Terry is very short, due to his bandy legs, so when he scuttles around, he stays so close to the floor that it can be difficult to see what he is up to down there.

But I digress . . .

Another reason for my decline in diffidence was that I was playing a lot of games with other boys which served to loosen me up a bit: not just those activities which required neither courage nor strength, like table tennis, chess and snooker, but also (because my hand-eye coordination was good) a few team games—except obviously for rugby, which was invented for large, nasty, rough boys. I never actually understood many of the rules of the games I was playing, but then that doesn't matter much to small boys; I once watched two boys playing a chess match and, noticing that one of the kings had actually been taken, pointed this fact out to them, only to be informed, "We know." Anyway, what happens is that every now and again you learn another rule until eventually you know enough to play properly. (Except for rugby, where even at international level only the referee understands all the rules, and has to explain them to the player—especially the very large ones—every time he makes a decision.)

It was about now that I encountered the teacher who made the greatest impression on me: Mr. Bartlett. He became my maths master, and during the first term he taught me, I have to confess that I understood next to nothing. But when he taught me the same things next term, I grasped them instantly: they had become self-evident. So I was moved up a form, where Mr. Bartlett introduced me to new mathematical ideas, all of them incomprehensible—until the following term when they became blindingly obvious, and I assimilated them effortlessly. Promotion, in other words, was followed by bewilderment, and the next term, by full comprehension. Mr. Bartlett was a very good teacher.

But Mr. Bartlett's ultimate significance—to every single one of us—lay in the psychological spell that he cast over us. It became astonishingly important to please him, not just individually, but as a form, too. So we attended to his every word, and when we had prep to do for him in the evening, we tried desperately hard to do good work. I can recall one evening, when we were all sitting in the Big Room, solving some geometry problems that Mr. Bartlett had set us, that a boy called David Rogers was experiencing technical problems with his pair of compasses—that gadget with a sharp metal point, which you stick in a sheet of paper while you revolve the rest of the apparatus around it to produce a perfectly drawn circle. I slowly became aware of Rogers' growing distress at the next desk: it seemed that every time he was on the verge of completing a nice, neat circle, the point of his compass slipped, and the pencil slid with it, producing a nasty blur on the page, and ruining his *almost* completed circle. At which moment Rogers would emit a tiny half-strangled cry of rage, seize his India rubber and savagely rub out his oh-so-near circle, then grab the compass and stab its point into the page—which after the first four or five attempts was beginning to resemble a lightly ploughed field—and start rotating the compass incredibly painstakingly until the pencil had described an arc of 350 degrees, at which moment the compass point would skid again, spoiling all his fine work up to that instant, and forcing from Rogers another muffled howl of despair, and sending him into a renewed frenzy of rubbing-out that began to resemble an act of pure revenge. But revenge on *what*? On life itself it seemed . . .

What was so funny, I decided later, was not the anger itself, but the fear that underlay it, the sheer terror of losing Bartlett's favour, of being cast into the outer darkness for the rest of term. That was the extraordinary power of the force with which he controlled us. It was not fear of his rage, it was fear of the *withdrawal of his approval*. Years later I realised it was just like a lover's sulk. And we all know the strangely powerful effect of that . . .

Now Rogers did something that was, up to that point in my life, the funniest thing I had ever seen. He went and borrowed a pen-knife, walked determinedly over to a waste-paper basket, and in a rigidly controlled, but slightly quivering mother of all cold furies, began savagely sharpening his compass point with it. The idea that the metal compass could be made pointier by whetting it with an or-dinary penknife, compounded by the icy, maniacally restrained way in which he was attempting it, while all the time just, *just* stifling the seething, roiling bloodlust motivating him; all of this masking the sickening dread of Bartlett's impending withdrawal of affection: such a perfect comic storm utterly wrecked me. The more I cried with laughter, though, the steelier became Rogers' determination to make the compass point more *efficient*!

Rogers' emotional state was, in fact, almost identical to the one Connie Booth and I tried to create for Basil as each episode of *Fawlty Towers* progressed. And since so much has been written about Basil's anger, and so much of it is simplistic or just plain wrong, it's perhaps worth trying to set the record straight. Though I suspect such an at-tempt is doomed to failure.

Basil's anger is almost always underpinned by fear: fear of a hotel inspector's bad report; fear of having poisoned a guest; fear of a health inspector seeing a rat; fear of upsetting important guests, like visiting psychiatrists or a lord; fear of offending German guests; fear of revealing that the chef is unfit to cook on Gourmet Night; fear of making a fool of himself in front of the friends invited to his wedding anniversary; fear of American guests discovering that the chef is not actually in the kitchen; fear of his wife catching him in compromising situations with an Australian blonde or an attractive French woman; fear of his wife discovering he's been betting on horses, or trying to save money by employing incompetent builders . . . need I go on?

Then, because of the stress caused by his fear he starts, at the beginning of each episode, by making small mistakes. As his efforts to correct the fearful situation misfire, he becomes increasingly panicky and desperate and consequently his decision-making becomes worse and worse, until he has dug a hole, or several holes, for himself from which there is no real escape.

It's just good, old-fashioned farce: (1) the protagonist has done something he has to cover up; (2) he makes increasingly poor choices due to his building panic; (3) he finishes up in ridiculous situations; (4) his sins are finally revealed (or he just escapes detection) and all's well that ends well.

(Incidentally, please forgive the "he" in the paragraph above, but I do not know of a classic farce where the protagonist is female.)

I should point out one other parallel between Basil Fawlty and David Rogers. It is *suppressed* anger that is funny. If Basil ever fully lost his temper, and started screaming at people, the audience wouldn't laugh. It's when he tries to control it, but shows tell-tale signs that he is failing (profitless sarcasm, smacking his own bottom, flogging a car, speaking in an exaggeratedly deliberate way, suddenly slamming down a phone), that he is funny, in the same way that David Rogers was when his measured compass-sharpening betrayed the dreadful fury underlying it. Another way of looking at this: real anger can work in real life; it won't work as comedy. Funny anger is ineffectual anger.

So, anyway . . .

Mr. Bartlett was impressive not just because of his teaching skills and the control that he exercised over us; he was also the first example I'd ever seen of a really impressive human being. This manifested itself in two ways. First, he seemed to know everything about everything. The slow realisation of this, along with my growing sense of awe, suggested to me that if only I could acquire enough information about all aspects of the world, I too could be in total control of my life, and invulnerable to the slings and arrows of outrageous fortune: specifically, put-downs and sarcasm and teasing. So I began to be obsessed with the feeling that I *ought* to know everything about everything. I may have lacked the brain and willpower to move this project forward, but that never shook my conviction that omniscience would solve all possible problems.

The second aspect of Mr. Bartlett's character that influenced me, and several generations of St. Peter's boys, was his fastidious demeanour: his life appeared to be a continuous one-gentleman crusade against all things vulgar. I'm not referring to what in Britain in 2014 would be called vulgar: crude talk about bottoms and breasts and genitalia, cursing, aggressive and insulting behaviour, body piercing, tacky clothing, drunkenness, bling, shaven heads, tattoos, reality television, marketing and all the other vibrant forms of conduct that make our great country what it is today. No, Mr. Bartlett was appalled (his favourite word) by much subtler stuff: for example, by the slightest hint of "showing off," or drawing attention to oneself—what he called "self-advertisement." What would he have made of our celebrity culture? This was the Edwardian gentleman's approach to life: courtesy, grace, restraint, the careful avoidance of embarrassing others, non-intrusiveness, considerateness, kindness, modesty—nay, more than modesty, self-effacement; the very things that would disqualify one forever from employment by the *Daily Mail*. But the charm of it all was that there was humour and, indeed, a hint of playfulness about his constant state of "being appalled"; and he was not often *deeply* appalled; sometimes he was only *slightly* appalled, for example at our stupidity, of which there was a lot about. There was a wonderful deadpan look of bemused astonishment to the way in which he greeted our latest imbecility; and if we pleased him, an almost coy twinkle. We craved that, and some boys—his favourites—received it now and again. He was our tall, long-faced, highbrow God, and we loved and feared him. If we'd handed in bad work, he would walk into the classroom looking as though his mother had just been fed into a mincer, and announce, "So . . . it's *war.*" Then he would stalk slowly over to the window and stare vacantly out of it, and we would all want to kill ourselves, and would pray for the moment when he would smile at one of us again. He didn't care for me at all, but I could always hope. Meanwhile I loved him for his jokes: when he called one boy "a waste of space" I thought it was the most brilliantly witty line that could ever have been said since the world began. (I still believe this, though I now know that it wasn't original.)

There was one master who quite liked me, no doubt in part because I quite liked him. Nobody else liked him, though—perhaps because he was physically unattractive. Actually that's not true. I was being polite. He was ugly. God, was he ugly. He could have won competitions without taking his teeth out. Rather surprisingly—and endearingly—he was also a bit vain: always fussing about his hair and glancing in the mirror. It was strangely touching to see him battle on in this way against insuperable odds—rather like Quasimodo using eyeliner, or the Elephant Man wearing a toupee.

His name was the Reverend A. H. Dolman and he was German. That's all we knew, although we had a pretty good idea what the A stood for. He was equally repellent in a variety of other ways, too. He was very fat (sorry! *Obese* . . .) and he waddled around, bumping people and blocking doorways, and his breath was *not* good, so we tried not to stand too close, and he told laboured pointless jokes which he then explained, and he had a rather guttural (surprise!) accent and spoke an unfamiliar dialect of English, peppered with certain pet phrases like "actually speaking" and "really speaking" and "generally speaking" and "normally speaking" and, especially, "in actual fact," which popped up every twenty seconds or so. So, naturally speaking, we started counting the number of times he said them all. He took over responsibility for teaching us Latin from Captain Lancaster; quite how I managed to learn from him is a mystery, but I did, because I liked Latin and that's the main reason, I think, why we finished up almost liking each other.

Which was just as well because when Mr. Tolson asked Mr. Bartlett if I should compete for a maths scholarship to Clifton College in 1953, and Bartlett killed the idea, dear Reverend Dolman insisted that I should be put up for a Latin scholarship. I failed to get that, but for some reason the enterprise yielded me the maths one (worth £35 a year). So put that in your pipe and smoke it, God.

As far as I can remember, I liked all the other teachers: Mr. Gilbert, Mr. Howdle, Mr. Sanger-Davies (called Sanger-Wagtail after the way he walked), Mr. Thom, who wore suede shoes with crêpe soles and seemed a bit racy compared with the others, and nice Mr. Hickley the music teacher, who eventually expelled me from singing classes because I was both tragically ungifted and also a bit subversive. (I had my revenge when, fifteen years later, I became the only one of his pupils ever to appear in a Broadway musical.) In fact, it was quite odd how fond I was of them all: when the boys played the staff in the annual cricket match (the latter using very narrow, shaved bats) I always wanted the masters to win, *even* when I was playing. I think because I trusted Dad so much and always believed he was acting in my best interests I somehow transferred my faith in him to the masters, who were a uniformly decent, kind crowd anyway. Whatever I felt about them, though, the only ones I suspect to have had a soft spot for me were the Reverend Dolman and the headmaster.

The first impression Mr. Tolson made was that he was BIG. Actually, he wasn't *that* big, but he seemed so to us. He was six feet tall, with broad shoulders and a barrel chest, and a large, round face, with a welcoming smile, and slightly unfocused eyes behind wide, rimless glasses; and on top of everything, a fine, expansive, completely bald,

surprisingly pink, dome. The second impression he made was that
he was sort of . . . important. You felt that he definitely owned the
school, and that what he said, went. More than that: the tone of the
school was an extension of himself. And thirdly—and most unusually, I was to learn—he was quite an emotionally open man, quite
unlike the exquisitely refined Mr. Bartlett, or the fearsomely gruff
and shy Captain Lancaster or the rebarbative Reverend Dolman. He
was basically optimistic, warm, encouraging and utterly decent, but
he was quite easily upset, especially if boys were wet, or disorder
threatened, or if our great rivals, St. Dunstan's of Burnham-on-Sea,
beat us at football. And he reserved his most ruffled (and pink) look
for occasions when he had tangled with the beautiful, elegant, and
almost imperial Jean Tolson, a dark, Latinate thoroughbred, who
could strike a man dead at thirty paces with one blow of her tongue.
For when I said that what Geoffrey Tolson said, went, this was not
true if he said it to Mrs. Tolson, because then it would not go at all: in
fact, it would probably back up a few paces and stay very still indeed.
Most of the time, though, he was cheerful, and he often had a humorous glint in his eye, and made well-intentioned jokes. I was hugely
fond of, and trusting of, him.

Oddly enough, the memory of him that stays with me the clearest was the occasion when he rebuked me for being "cocky." He took
me aside and explained he'd heard that the previous day my behaviour on the cricket field had been unseemly: not that I said anything
wrong, but that my body language had contained a hint of swagger,
of conceit, of what the Aussies used to call "putting on dog." And he
was right: recently I'd got the idea that I was rather good at cricket,
and yes, I had been showing off, I was "too pleased with myself,"
and "getting too big for my britches"! And Tolson explained, very
gently, that this kind of thing was not good form, and should not be
repeated. And I knew he was right, and I was rather ashamed, and
made sure it did not happen again.

What interests me about this incident was that this relatively small outburst of egotism (of "self-advertisement") had clearly been reported to the highest authority straight away, and that, within hours, the threat of such unmanly Mediterranean conduct spreading to other boys had been efficiently snuffed out. Here Tolson, Bartlett, Captain Lancaster and the others were as one: no swank, no flamboyance, no "putting on airs" . . . no bad manners . . . no ungentlemanly behaviour. Contrast this with my experience during a couples therapy session a few years ago in California, when I explained to the (very famous) therapist that "blowing one's own trumpet" was regarded in England as a bit unsophisticated, if not slightly common, only to be told that "tooting one's own horn" was perfectly mature conduct and entirely socially acceptable.

In an act that moulded my world view, Mr. Tolson once took the whole school to see *Scott of the Antarctic*. We were all deeply impressed by Scott's uncomplaining acceptance of suffering. But you couldn't help feeling that the message of the film was not just that the highest form of English heroism is stoicism in the face of failure, but that in Scott's case a whiff of success might have tarnished the gallantry of his silent endurance of misery. After all, he and his men all froze to death while losing the gold medal to the Norwegians, in the same way that the magnificence of the Charge of the Light Brigade was enhanced by its utter futility, and General Gordon's being calmly hacked to death was all the more impressive because it occurred during the course of the complete annihilation of his forces at Khartoum. On the other hand, Lord Nelson's and General Wolfe's heroism may have lost a little of its sparkle by the close association with two all-important victories, even if they did get extra marks for being killed at the moment of their triumph. I think Americans must suspect that General Custer may have been of English descent.

In fact, looking at the figures regarded as our national role models, it's hard to discern much joy or fun or optimism about any of them. There's almost a hint of depression around. It's interesting that the phrase *joie de vivre* is probably foreign.

Nevertheless, even while we were being shown edifying lessons about the value of failure, and Mr. Tolson was reminding me of the need to harness my ego, my confidence continued to grow, if not my self-esteem. I have to thank my friends for that. A few years ago an American psychologist, Judith Harris, scandalised the therapeutic establishment by suggesting that the influence of parents on a child's development had been overemphasised, while the impact of the peer group had been undervalued. Whatever the academic rights and wrongs of this viewpoint, there is no doubt that my wuss-rating was dropping and that my wetness was perceptibly evaporating, and that this was the result of playing with my pals.

It was definitely not to do with my achievements. They remained utterly mediocre, apart from in maths and Latin, and I gave no sign of creative ability. When the Reverend Dolman cast me as Malvolio in *Twelfth Night* I had absolutely no idea what I was supposed to be doing; or saying, for that matter. I can still remember declaiming "M, O, A, I; this simulation is not as the former. And yet to crush this a little, it would bow to me, for every one of these letters are in my name" without having a clue what it meant. Nobody explained anything (not even the significance of Malvolio appearing "cross-gartered"), but at least I went out there and said the lines in the right order, even if I don't remember getting a single laugh, and I didn't faint, and everyone seemed satisfied.

In my last year at St. Peter's, however, I really did seem to take a big leap forward. I once read a book entitled *Mastery* by a deeply impressive man called George Leonard, who helped Michael Murphy run the Esalen Institute at Big Sur, where some of the brightest people in America "went to talk about what was really on their minds." In it he pointed out that when we work at acquiring some skill, we do not improve gradually, like some ascending straight line on a graph; the improvements take place suddenly. After a period of not appearing to get better at all, *if* we just keep patiently practising, there will be an unexpected jump up to the next level. Plateau . . . jump! Plateau . . .

jump! Plateau . . . jump! It's a bit like saltation in evolutionary theory. That had been my experience of learning maths with Mr. Bartlett, and now I suddenly seemed to be good at a lot of things—and not just because I was now taller than any of the masters, including Mr. Tolson. (Although it did help in things like the high jump, boxing, hurdling, bowling, and making me feel a bit more important than I'd ever seemed before.)

Mr. and Mrs. Tolson, with Mr. Bartlett (far right) and me behind Mrs. Tolson.

I was now in a class of just six thirteen-year-olds. It didn't feel like school: it was more like an exclusive learning club. We were being individually taught, and I *loved* it. Every subject became exciting and fun, as never before (and, little did I know, as seldom again). I can remember thinking that in this atmosphere, I seemed to be getting cleverer, and I was even improving in areas of life that had previously been a closed book to me. Notably rugby. I was still too cowardly to be allowed in the first team, but as I was now about a yard taller than anyone else, when placed in the second team I proved unstoppable. In our first match against King's School Taunton I was passed the ball, saw the massed ranks of the King's second XV just melt away in front of me, ran through them and scored. There was another kick-off, St. Peter's got the ball, it was passed to me, and I scored again. Soon it became almost monotonous. In the old days when I had got the ball I would pass it quickly before I got hurt, but now I cantered gently forward, like a giraffe among pygmies, who each time fled before me like the Red Sea parting for Moses, allowing me to touch the ball down between the posts entirely unmolested. I estimate we won by about 430–0.

The return match was more interesting. King's School kicked off, St. Peter's got the ball, gave it to me, and I set off. But suddenly I saw a small King's jersey running towards me, instead of away. Naturally this attracted my attention. It was clear that there was a tiny creature inside the jersey, and as I slowed to get a better view, it suddenly lowered its head, accelerated right at me and butted me in the solar plexus. This produced a spectacular effect, akin to a slow-motion de-molition of the Eiffel Tower. I was carried off and had to lie at the edge of the pitch, unable to breathe for half an hour, while King's built up a hefty half-time lead. However, by the start of the second half, I was back on the pitch, and the moment I got the ball, I looked for the assassin. And there he was! Approaching at a good speed, too! So, timing my move carefully, I waited till he lowered his head, and then swivelled my hips . . . so that instead of his head embedding itself in my middle, the top of it was met by solid bone. That was the end of him. St. Peter's won by about 130–18, but it was still a much more even game.

I think that my last months at St. Peter's were, in a childish way, the happiest time of my life. I was doing well—I was even captain of the cricket team, although I can never remember making any runs or taking many wickets—learning was fun, I was feeling cheerful and confident, I liked everyone (and they seemed to like me, which was very important). Looking back it seems like a golden age, when all the slightly more grown-up distractions of wondering how you'd get everything done, and whether you were studying hard enough to pass your exams, and being disappointed that there were people who were better than you at things you really cared about, and worrying about your skin and feeling hopelessly uncomfortable around girls . . . were not even specks on the horizon yet.

In fact, I think the only speck around was . . . my mother. A speck? Let me explain.

The salient feature of the human perceptual apparatus—the five senses—is that they are designed to detect change. A movement, a new sound, a pinprick, a different taste or smell—we immediately register it. It's a survival mechanism. If nothing's changing, we're safe. So we block out anything that isn't changing: the drilling noise that irritates us this morning doesn't impinge on us in the afternoon unless we make a conscious effort to notice it. It's the same with "atmospheres." You habituate to them until they feel so familiar you cease to register them. Well, the following tale says a lot about the standard atmosphere in the Cleese household in Weston.

When I was twelve, we moved (again) to a second-floor flat right above St. Peter's (so that my parents could watch me walk down our drive, across the road, through a gate, and all the way to the school's back entrance, when I would turn and wave to them). It was in this house that my dad sat me down one evening and calmly explained to me that it was likely that Mother would be moving out in a few days and going to live somewhere else; and that his sister Dorothy would move in and look after us instead. Odd to recall, this did not feel particularly dramatic, or even surprising. I liked Dorothy very much, and I simply thought: "When Auntie comes here it will all be so calm and happy and everyone will be nice to everyone and everything will feel so easy."

But nothing ever happened. Dad didn't mention it again. Dorothy, who had been staying with us, went away, and I didn't see her again for a very long time. A year later we moved to Bristol, where I was soon to start as a day boy at Clifton College, and Mother, of course, came with us.

I rather liked the new home. It felt familiar because it had been Grandpa's for many years, and we used to visit him there; when he died in 1952 at the age of eighty-five he left it to Dad. It was the first time we'd had a whole house; it was semi-detached, with a tiny front garden and a small back one, at the end of which was Redland Police Station, which made us feel very safe.

It was my twelfth home in thirteen years. Partly because I have a poor visual memory, but also because I never spent very long anywhere, I have only fragmentary pictures in my mind of the first eleven—a bedroom where Mum pummelled Dad, the stairs up to Mrs. Phillips's, the back garden where I made a century, the living room from which our budgerigar escaped in Burnham. But I can recall every room in No. 2 East Shrubbery, Redland, Nr Clifton, Bristol, in some detail, because it was to be home for the next five years— practically a geological period by Cleese standards. And I spent a lot of time there, not just because I was a day boy but because even during the holidays we very seldom ventured far.

I remember it with real affection: it seemed a secure base from which to emerge into a rather more grown-up world.

4

The evening before my first day at Clifton College my parents took me to a posh Bristol restaurant to mark my rite of passage to fully fledged public school boy. I was mildly aware of the significance of what was being celebrated; but I think that for them it was a milestone. They were proud they were sending me to a "good school"; and they were also proud of the hint of upward social mobility this implied. Not that Clifton was *that* high in the rankings. Comfortably below Rugby and Marlborough, though slightly ahead of Sherborne, it was probably on a par with Malvern and Tonbridge and even Haileybury (these small gradations in the pecking order were a major preoccupation). Quite where Clifton stood in relation to Uppingham and Oundle I never fully worked out.

But the thrill of the evening for me was the food: it was the first really fine meal I had ever had, and the experience was comparable to the moment when I had first watched people playing Monopoly. A whole new world opened up: elegant, exotic, leisurely and intensely pleasurable. I had never known that food could taste this good. Even my mind seemed stimulated by it. That delight has never gone away; indeed I find, at the age of seventy-four, that food tastes better than ever. There are, in fact, only three comestibles that I do not allow to pass my lips: celery, sea-urchin and raw human flesh.

Strangely enough, my memory of the meal eclipses that of my first few weeks at Clifton, but I think that's because my life as a "new boy" was very ordinary. Now that I was growing up (I turned four-teen during my first month at Clifton), nothing seemed as impres-sive or daunting as it had in my early days at St. Peter's: the masters were people, not titans, and had no power of life or death over me. There was also something very undramatic about my new school life: it was calm and business-like and brisk—almost matter of fact—because Clifton was thoroughly middle-of-the-road in all things. It was a kind school in which there was no bullying; a well-mannered, unexceptional and decent place; and so . . . strangely unmemorable.

It was, however, big. There were about seven hundred boys, the vast majority of whom were boarders, split up into eight houses where they slept and spent their spare time. The day boys were divided be-tween two further houses, North Town and South Town, depending on what part of Bristol they inhabited. My house was North Town, dominated by a large central room lined with fair-sized lockers, and with a huge table in the middle surrounded by chairs. Each of us was allocated one of the lockers, which was expected to contain all our possessions and schoolbooks. Just off the Big Room there were two studies: one for the house prefects and the other for the housemas-ter. Upstairs were a library and an area where we could play chess or study. And right opposite North Town House, literally across the street, was the entrance to Bristol Zoo, from which throughout the day emanated sounds of gibbons and lions and elephants and wild dogs and parrots and American tourists. I liked these noises: they were reminders of an exciting world outside.

The great advantage of being in a house populated by day boys was that the people I came to like were always around: they did not disappear to various parts of the country for half-term and holidays. As a result, and also because I had become less wussy, and a little more fun to be with, I started to acquire plenty of friends, whose houses I would visit. Among this group were a couple of boys I was particularly close to, whose curious, playful and slightly mischievous mateyness brought out a corresponding "larky" part of me that had been dormant these past fourteen years (Adrian Upton is now Professor of Medicine [Neurology] at McMaster University in Canada, with a list of degrees as long as your leg; Michael Apter is a psychologist, who originated Reversal Theory: he has held visiting professorships all over the planet, and now works with Georgetown University in Washington, DC). They were brighter than me, but the three of us would use the Big Room to carry out "prank experiments" that we found both entertaining and revealing. One involved leaving a folded note on the huge table, with the name of someone in the house written on the outside: for example, "For Foster." The three of us would then lurk and observe just how compelled other boys felt to discover its contents: almost without fail they would hang around, glance to see if they were being observed, and then stealthily pick the note up and quickly look inside, to find a message like "Is your name Foster?" or "You are being watched"; at which point they would drop it and try to work out if anybody had seen them. Another prank was to swap the contents of two lockers: as each boy's entire life was in his locker, this gave us the opportunity to observe how people behaved when they were really panicked.

It strikes me that laughter was at the very heart of these closest relationships: the bonhomie and fun bonded us together, and allowed me to grow in confidence as I experienced acceptance and support and camaraderie. Of course, as young males we never talked about our feelings, but we discussed the insanity of the world, and at long last my personality was developing free of the influence of Dad and Mum, and indeed of any other grown-ups, including the teachers. In retrospect I can see I was on the way to being almost normal.

In my view, ordinary everyday sanity is harder for "only children" to achieve: they have nothing to moderate or dilute a parent's influence. It must be very liberating to be able to share your parents' attention, and indeed to have fellow offspring with whom you can actually *discuss* parental behaviour. I'm sure I could have dramatically cut the hours I spent in therapy if I had had a brother (or, better still, a sister) to whom I could have turned and asked, "What the hell has got into *her* today?"

Of course, I had gone to Clifton primarily to work, which meant to study for exams, and since O (or "ordinary") levels were coming up in two years, and it seemed undeniably important that I should pass them, I settled down to study the standard subjects: maths, Latin, English, French, history, chemistry, physics, and something else.

Now I found some of the work, like maths and Latin, moderately interesting: as involving, say, as a good crossword. In physics I found myself intrigued by optics and in chemistry by atomic theory; and I quite liked studying *Macbeth* and *Henry V.* But the rest of the time (in other words, ninety per cent of it) I was completely uninterested in anything I was being taught. This meant that I always had to make a conscious effort to concentrate. If I relaxed even for a few moments, I was away with the fairies.

My education, in other words, was a test of my willpower; and I accepted the challenge—to such an extent, indeed, that I think at some level of my teenage consciousness I truly believed that the whole point of going to school was to learn how to focus attention on subject matter that was of no consequence to me. The message I received at Clifton was: education is not primarily about understanding the world; its real purpose is character-building. As a corollary, I inferred that to study anything in which you had a real interest was, if not exactly *cheating,* certainly missing the point.

I probably had thirty teachers while I was at Clifton and I liked twenty-eight of them, although few made a real impression on me. One exception, though, was the diminutive "Jumper" Gee. He had fought in both world wars and was supposed to teach us English, but he would go off track a lot and tell us great stories, including one particular anecdote that was to assume a much later significance for me. Apparently in ancient Rome, he said, wrestling matches were sometimes held after dinner to entertain the guests, and on one occasion the two combatants fought so closely that they became completely enmeshed with one another. The sound of a loud crack followed, at which point one of the wrestlers revealed that his arm had been broken. The referee stepped in to disentangle the two men, told the other he had won—and discovered he was dead. The moral of the story, according to "Jumper," was "If you don't give up you can't be beaten." I was less than convinced but the tale stuck in my mind, and fourteen years later inspired me to write the scene in *Monty Python and the Holy Grail* where the Black Knight refuses to submit even when all his limbs have been severed.

There was also a very amusing history master called Whitmarsh, who was unable to pronounce the letter "r" if it came near the beginning of a word. Perhaps that wouldn't have mattered so much if he hadn't made a career decision to specialise in seventeenth-century English history. As it was, he spent all his time wrestling with Rrroundheads and Rrroyalists, Oliver Crrromwell and Rrrichard Crrromwell, Prrrince Rrrupert of the Rrrhine, the Rrrump Parliament and Prrride's Purrrge, and the Rrrestoration, the Rrrye House Plot and the Rrroyal Society. Each "r" required a strange sideways twist of the lips followed by a facial tic and a head twitch; we were therefore careful to construct questions that would give him a good workout. It seemed almost perverse he was not teaching us the eighteenth century: he would only have had to mention the Rrregency, and all the rest would have been plain sailing. Mr. Whitmarsh had my number, though. At the end of one term, he wrote in my history report the single sentence "Cleese indulges in subversive activities at the back of the room."

But perhaps the finest all-round entertainer we had was a tall, stooping old dotard with a mass of white hair called Sammy Beachcroft who, when he spoke, produced a strange buzzing noise, as though a bumblebee had become lodged at the back of his nose. Fortunately Sammy taught us about the Old Testament, a topic that involved no exams, so we were free to amuse ourselves to the limit; he must have been the oldest British teacher in captivity because when he talked about biblical events he seemed to have personal memories of them. Nobody could understand why at his age he was still on the staff: it was assumed he had something on the headmaster. He moved very carefully around the classroom like an arthritic gecko, but what was funniest about him was the slowness with which he responded to stimuli. It was as though his whole nervous system had been switched to "Proceed with care," so that his neurons moved very warily, eyeing each synapse for some time before daring to jump.

Sammy's reaction speed was best illustrated the time that a class-mate named Cleave decided to hide behind the blackboard. This was a large affair in one corner of the room, which could be slid upwards after the teacher had written on it, so that it could be more easily seen at the back of the classroom. Cleave squeezed behind it before Sammy arrived, and we pulled it down to writing height so that only his legs were visible. Now, Sammy came in and, failing to notice anything unusual, walked straight to the board, pulled out a piece of chalk and started to list prophets, his writing hand never moving more than a foot or so from Cleave's nose on the other side. This kept the class beguiled for about half an hour. Finally Sammy finished and slid the board smoothly upwards to find himself standing about eighteen inches away from the motionless Cleave. What was so funny now was not that he jumped a foot in the air (higher than he had been for several decades) but that THREE SECONDS elapsed between his first seeing Cleave and his jump. In comedic terms, it was the classic "single-take," the finest I've ever seen.

My own contributions to the "Let's surprise Sammy B" competition were comparatively low-key. At this time I had a pair of National Health glasses which were contained in a hard spectacle case that made a vaguely metallic ringing noise when it was closed. I would open it, hold it behind my back, open my mouth, and when Sammy looked at me I would shut my mouth and the spectacle case simultaneously, creating the impression that closing my mouth caused a weird clanging noise. He would stare each time, but never pursued the matter.

Early on I took to wearing my glasses upside down. The first time I did this, the effect was sufficiently remarkable to stop him in his tracks mid-sentence. He stared at me for a full five seconds, and then went on as though nothing had happened. Thereafter I wore my glasses upside down on a regular basis, twice a week, until near the end of term when he glanced at me and said quite casually, "Cleese, put your glasses on the right way up." It had taken him about ten weeks to react.

There were only two Clifton masters I did not care for: Billy Williams, the joyless dwarf who ran my house, and a physics teacher I had in my second year called Hazelton. He was a largeish, rather shaggy man, who spoke in a strange, very deliberate way, while whistling slightly through his lower teeth. After I'd been in his class a few weeks he looked at me thoughtfully and said:

"Ah . . . Cleeeese . . ."

"Sir?"

"Your housssemaster ssays you're intelligent."

"Oh!"

". . . I don't sssee it mysssself . . ."

I wasn't hurt or surprised. I took his remark as pure information. It was only when I recalled this many years later that I found myself thinking, "What was he intending to *achieve* with this remark?" And I came to the conclusion that it made him feel better about himself— the same reason people read snide gossip columns. Of course, the relief experienced when anyone (*anyone*) is put down is very transient, but for people like Hazelton it's probably better than nothing. His persona seemed very odd to me: it was as though he'd once seen an intellectual, and had spent the rest of his life impersonating him.

Since the tiny scholarship I had won to Clifton was in maths, it was assumed by the authorities from day one that I would specialise in science, so I assumed so, too (Dad had told me that the country was crying out for scientists). There was one subject that would have interested me, had I known it existed, but it wasn't on the Clifton syllabus, and that was psychology. After all, why waste good schooling time on studying the workings of the human mind, when there were crucial life skills to acquire like trigonometrical calculation or Old Testament history or how to ask a question in Latin if you expected the answer "No"? Let's keep a sense of proportion here. So my introduction to psychology had to come from other sources, notably the BBC, who during my time at Clifton showed a number of thoughtful programmes on the subject. One that I remember particularly vividly showed a volunteer being hypnotised to pour water from a vase of flowers on to the floor. The thing that intrigued me about this was not that he followed orders but that when the hypnotist asked him why he'd done it, he started "rationalising" his behaviour, claiming that he thought he'd seen smoke rising from an unextinguished cigarette stub and had therefore felt he had to take action to extinguish a possible fire. I was also interested by B. F. Skinner and his conditioning of the behaviour of rats and pigeons, and Solomon Asch's experiments about the need to conform, and later by Stanley Milgram's famous obedience tests.

Because the workings of the mind seemed to me to be associated with laboratories and experiments, I formed an almost subconscious plan to head towards biology, and once O levels were safely out of the way I asked the science school if I could move to the biology stream for my A levels. They said yes and proceeded to put me in the care of Dr. Davie, who allegedly taught botany, and Dr. Stubbs, who made the same claim about zoology. Both were believed to be largely nocturnal, but they had been known to appear in the classroom during the day, moving around a little and even making talking noises, though so quietly that you could never be sure that they weren't just breathing harder than usual. Whoever thought they could control a class should have asked for his money back: the two of them working in tandem couldn't have kept a class of teddy bears in order if they'd both been given revolvers. From the beginning my classmates and I were mystified about what we were supposed to *do*: ignore them, try to encourage them to greater efforts, or just to feed them now and again.

Our third main A levels teacher, who took the physics classes, was better—not a lot, but very slightly. He was called Lindsay-Jones (or Flimsy-Bones) and we liked him. No one, however, paid much attention to him, so when, after a few weeks, he gave us an exam, and I saw that I had come *fourth,* with only twenty-eight percent, in quite a large class, the writing was on the blackboard.

In a way, I'm quite proud of what I did next. I had enough self-knowledge to know around my sixteenth birthday that I had nowhere near the capacity to direct my own studies and that what I needed if I was to pass my A levels was good teachers. So I went to the authorities and asked to switch to the maths, physics and chemistry stream, and I was then safe, because I had three really good teachers, Mr. Liddell for maths, Peter "Stinker" Davies for chemistry and Freddie Mee for physics. The latter two were rather good fun as well, even if Freddie had a touch of the Dolmans about him. And the three of them got me through my A levels by making their subjects clear, and providing discipline and structure—everything that you need when you're not remotely interested. Bless them!

IF WORK is best defined as "What you have to do, but would rather not," there were two other Clifton activities that qualified: going to chapel and Officer Training Corps (i.e., soldiering for teenagers).

Chapel took up a lot of time. Just as at St. Peter's, there was a Church of England service every workday morning, a fifteen-minute affair which took place in Clifton's remarkably beautiful chapel.

Then, on Sunday, there was a full one-hour marathon, with a proper sermon, and hymn-singing, and crab racing, and fire-eating, and a trampoline act.

To look back on these religious practices from the peak of spiritual perfection that I have now achieved is to wonder, "What the fuck did we think we were doing?" We had all been taught how to behave: to walk more slowly than usual, looking downwards; to sit, fresh-faced and attentive and slightly awed, as we repeated well-known catchphrases of uncertain meaning ("Lord of hosts," "Son of God," "paschal lamb," "life everlasting"), none of which had ever been explained but which, if spoken with sufficient sincerity, would apparently keep the bogeyman away; then to stand and sing obscure lyrics about the hosts of Gilead creeping around after dark, or rousing military marches like "Onward Christian Soldiers" that were contrary to the idea "Blessed are the peacemakers"; and then to ask God to do us favours, even though the Lord's Prayer taught by Jesus specifically says, "Thy will be done on earth," which clearly indicates it *isn't*.

Yes, I know it's easy to make fun of the organised churches, but has it occurred to anyone to wonder *why* it's so easy?

What gets my goat is that "Religion" should be the most exciting topic of all. Is there an afterlife? Can we have a real purpose to our lives? How can we love our enemy, when it seems about as easy as levitating? To what extent is self-interest moral? Is there an experience of the divine that we can achieve? All the vital questions have been dumped in favour of half-baked, po-faced rituals which are basically a form of middle-class rain dance. Still, it did give me the chapel scene in *The Meaning of Life*.

The other "work" took place on Monday afternoons when we dressed up as soldiers and marched around, trying to look enthusiastic that we'd been given the opportunity to exhibit dog-like obedience. But it was useful to me because I realised after about thirty minutes of this that a military life is not an examined one, and so, according to Socrates, is not worth living, especially if you are a fraidy-cat. My sole aims in life have since become: not to fight in a war; not to have to give birth; and not to work in finance. So I deem my life a success (even allowing for *Fierce Creatures* and my third marriage).

After work there was play. Sports and the arts. God, I loved sports (except for rugby)! They were my *raison d'être*. If I could have played cricket for Somerset, football for Bristol City and squash for fun, I would have died a happy man at thirty-five. And, although Clifton was very much a rugby-playing school, in my last year, with the help of two friends, John Phillips and Robert Hill, we got soccer started at Clifton by persuading the head groundsman to give us a pitch, out at the playing fields beyond Clifton Suspension Bridge. I'm proud of this achievement.

And in the same year my cricket skills improved: I became quite a good off-spin bowler and got into the First XI team and played at Lord's in our annual two-day match against Tonbridge. I scored 13 not out in both innings. And . . . Clifton *won,* for the first time in umpteen years.

As for the arts, the best way to give you an idea of the Clifton College perspective is to present you with a single fact: the painting and drawing teacher was a former Scottish rugby football international. (For a Christmas present one year I bought him a painting-by-numbers set and delivered it by hand.) I missed out on music (too many games to be played), and so I have gone through life utterly ignorant of its grammar. When Sir Thomas Beecham said, "The English may not like music, but they absolutely love the noise it makes," I know exactly what he meant.

Not that all my life was a total cultural desert. Every Easter term, there was a house play competition, and in my third year, right out of the blue, I was asked to play a small role in the North Town production of a recent hit, *Seagulls Over Sorrento.* Quite why I was asked, I don't know: perhaps it was because my character was called "Lofty." I've always remembered the play as a comedy, but apparently it was about a research project concerning a high-explosive torpedo, so perhaps the audience were laughing for the wrong reasons. The following year, North Town put on a production of *Doctor Faustus*. Two of the boys were "interested in acting" so they got the big parts, Faustus and Mephistopheles. I was given the smaller but crucial role of Lucifer: the Prince of Darkness, the Embodiment of Evil, the Antichrist himself!

I realised, right from the start, that playing Satan gave me a chance to prove myself as a serious, straight actor, but I'm afraid it was a Devil too far. Part of the problem was my tights. Somebody had decided that in order to make my first entrance as terrifying as possible, I should be dressed in starkest black, with a scarlet cloak . . . and *tights*. Now you know how unmuscular I was, right? My legs were so thin I could have played a flamingo. And yet the director's vision involved putting me, of all people, in black tights. (It was clear to me, even at that young age, that this was a disastrous choice, but what did I know of the theatrical arts? I left it to the experts.)

On the day of the dress rehearsal, I stood in pitch darkness behind some black drapes, waiting for the cue for my entrance, accompanied by a junior boy whose job it was to show me where the gap in the drapes was to be found. Then I heard my cue, the boy parted the curtains, and I strode forward to announce:

"I am . . . Lu . . . cifer!"

Before I had time to open my mouth, however, I was hit by a wall of laughter that shook the building. It wasn't just the tights, of course: it was the *idea* that this spindly twerp could strike terror into people's hearts, when, instead of frightening the shit out of them, he was more likely to cause them to wet their pants. I'd created an alternative but unintended form of waste disposal.

Thinking quickly, and realising that the situation was lost, I ad-libbed:

"I . . . am . . . Lu . . . dicrous!"

Another big laugh.

Later that evening, at the actual performance, things began to go downhill early in the proceedings. I took up my position behind the black drapes, but this time a different boy was standing there, in the darkness. I peered at him.

"Who are you?"

"Tupman. Gould has a music lesson."

"So you're parting the drapes for me?"

"What?"

"You're parting the drapes? So I can get on stage."

"I don't know about that."

"What?! What are you doing here?!"

"I don't know, Cleese. He just asked me to stand in for him."

And now I can hear my cue coming up in about ten seconds, so I start groping the drapes in the dark, trying to find the gap myself, desperately grabbing at the pitch-black cloth in search of an opening, as the seconds tick away. And there's my cue! So . . . I just walk forward into the drapes and keep trudging onward against the weight of all the velvet cloth that is clinging to me, and the audience start to giggle at the sight of this strange, increasingly large bulge in the backcloth that is, ever more slowly, making its way towards them. The actors step back in alarm—at least I'm frightening someone— and I manage, just, to keep moving so that when I have reached a point about halfway to the front row of the stalls the drapes, at full extension, start sliding back over my head and finally fall back, revealing a strange creature, a lacquered stick-insect apparently in a fright wig, who announces:

"I am Lucifer!"

By which time most of the audience have lost contact with their chairs.

I didn't try straight acting again for another thirty-seven years, when I played Kenneth Branagh's tutor, Dr. Waldman, in his film of *Frankenstein*. But this time, I was a triumph! I didn't get a *single* laugh, not even when Robert De Niro stabbed me to death.

BRITISH JOURNALISTS tend to believe that people who become good at something do so because they seek fame and fortune. This is because these are the sole motives of people who become British journalists. But some people, operating at higher levels of mental health, pursue activities because they actually *love* them. Thus I was drawn to comedy in a way I can't quite explain but can definitely acknowledge. (And it was much more than loving to laugh, even if, as a teenager I was still capable of those helpless, glorious paroxysms, when you *really* want to *stop*, because it's actually hurting too much.)

For example, I sometimes saw a comedy film or a play that elated me, that excited me and made me feel that there was something going on that I wanted to be connected with: when Dad took me to my first Marx Brothers film, *A Night in Casablanca;* when we had a school visit to the Theatre Royal to see N. F. Simpson's *One Way Pendulum;* when I saw *Laughter in Paradise* with my favourite comedy actor Alastair Sim; when I watched comedy films produced by the Ealing Studios like *The Ladykillers* and *Kind Hearts and Coronets.* Of course, this feeling of being inspired faded away each time, but every now and again it was rekindled, like an itch I didn't know how to scratch.

Another more eccentric example: each term at Clifton we were given a Blue Book, a small, soft-covered notebook with masses of information about schedules, and lists of masters and boys and the big sports events and so on. We carried it everywhere; losing it was like mislaying your mobile phone. But I filled mine with humour: wherever there was a square centimetre of white paper, I wrote the latest good joke I had heard. Nobody else was doing this . . .

In addition, some Saturday nights the Clifton houses would organise "entertainments" and now and again I'd do a little sketch or spoof. I learned how to mime to records. On one parents' evening I did a silly orchestra skit with me as conductor. Afterwards I asked my mother how good it was. I very much hoped she would say, "Really good!" What she actually said was, "Quite good."

On top of all these indications of an unorthodox passion, every evening after I'd had supper and done my prep, I'd join my parents in the living room and watch television; and although Dad and I would sometimes look at thrillers or live sport, most of the time it was . . . comedy. The odd thing, in retrospect, is that so many of the best shows were American. We loved Jack Benny, and George Burns, and "Amos and Andy" (now Orwellian "non-persons," as they were played by white guys in "blackface"), and Joan Davis, and Ernie Kovacs, and our favourite, Phil Silvers as Sergeant Bilko. Well written, totally uncontroversial, funny . . . though not exactly *adventurous* . . .

The only sign of anything a bit quirky, or "wild," came in variety shows, when wonderful, original comics from the era of music hall (or "variety") would do unclassifiable routines: Max Wall, Tommy Cooper, Sid Millward and the Nitwits, Frankie Howerd, Wilson Keppel and Betty, Professor Jimmy Edwards, Norman Wisdom, Chic Murray . . . To me they were the funniest performers, but there were only occasional sightings of them. As a rule, British TV was devoid of zany, madcap, anarchic, crazy, wild, wacky, out-of-left-field, Pythonesque (sorry! I'm jumping ahead), off-the-wall comedy, of the Max Wall variety.

But not British *radio*. Because in the relative backwaters of BBC Radio lurked the Greatest Radio Comedy Show of All Time: *The Goon Show*.

If you know *The Goon Show*, fine. If you don't, I *envy* you. Because you are in the incredibly privileged position of being able to listen to it *for the very first time*! It made the best use of radio that has ever been achieved in comedy, mixing a huge variety of wonderfully silly voices and astonishingly creative sound effects to tell ridiculous stories with humour that was witty, insane, insanely logical, breathtakingly stupid and thoroughly subversive (all three performers had been in the armed forces and held the same views of the officer class).

I loved this show with an intensity that almost defies analysis. It was not just that it was wonderfully *funny* when I listened to it on the wireless in my bedroom, or two days later when I prepared myself to hear the repeat, by laying the radio on its side on my bed, putting my ear against it, and holding a cushion over my other ear, in an attempt to hear the five jokes I had missed (due to the audience laughter) on the original broadcast. It united me with my friends. We adored it, and discussed it, and swapped jokes from it, and it made us feel more alive. In some way, it was cathartic: it exhilarated us by lifting us up above our everyday frustrations and boredoms. It gave us a liberating perspective on this odd event unfolding around us, called "our life." And when, years later, I became bewildered by the reception of *Monty Python* by some of our looniest fans, I suddenly realised they were experiencing exactly the combination of emotions that had rendered me such a devotee of the Goons, and so I was able to forgive them.

So, let us raise a glass to the Goons: Peter Sellers, the greatest "voice-man" of all time; the adorable Harry Secombe, who played the raspberry-blowing nitwit around whom the stories always unfolded; and Spike Milligan, the genius who wrote the best radio comedy scripts of all time. *Salute!*

And if God had told me that, ten years later, I would be performing a *Goon Show* with these three titans . . . I would have ceased to believe in him (not that we were particularly close at that time).

MY LAST year at Clifton started on a sour note. On the first day back, I walked into North Town and strolled up to the noticeboard to confirm that Mr. Williams, my housemaster, had finally made me a house prefect. This was not an unreasonable assumption: in the summer, I'd been in the School XI, captained the House XI, passed three A levels, completely reorganised the house library, played the lead in the house play, and stolen more cricket equipment from the other houses than had ever been nicked before. Besides, all my other friends were not merely house prefects, but school *praepostors*, official Big Cheeses, and none of them seemed so vastly superior to me as the discrepancy in our social status would suggest; not to mention the fact that the position of house prefect was an almost automatic promotion in your last year, no matter how inept, malevolent and disgusting you were. It never occurred to me that "Billy" Williams would withhold this trivial act of recognition any longer.

But, as you have guessed, he had. I stood there, staring at the blank space where my name should have been, as I experienced first utter disbelief, then hurt, and then contempt. The hurt was not that I had wanted so much to *be* a house prefect; actually, that hardly mattered at all. What wounded me was the put-down, the undeserved insult. The dull ache of this stab in the ego began to throb, but was suddenly engulfed in an extraordinary upsurge of high-minded contempt, not just for Williams but for a system that could ignore merit and allow personal prejudice to produce such a ludicrous decision. It was not fair and therefore it was unworthy of my respect. It was as simple as that.

I believe that this moment changed my perspective on the world. Till then the example given by my father and the teachers at St. Peter's had fostered in me a belief that people in authority over me were basically fair. Williams's behaviour gave me a terrific jolt. I responded rather splendidly, throwing away my North Town cap that very day, and "borrowing" one from Wiseman's House, where many of my friends were located, and wearing it defiantly throughout my last year at Clifton, even inside the North Town House.

Up to that point I had tolerated Williams, but now I realised that

I really disliked him, and I knew exactly why: he didn't know the difference between being solemn and being serious. He was a dour, grim little gnome who could not understand that you can try to do your very best at something, and at the same time have *fun;* or that you can have a perfectly serious discussion, while making your points humorously. No, for him laughter was a sign of fecklessness. Pomposity and humour never go together.

To be fair, Williams was not a pompous man. He would like to have been, but he was so tiny he simply couldn't pull it off. It's tough being weighty when people can knee you in the head. So he had to make do with the kind of Cromwellian joylessness that banned Christmas puddings. Thus he wrote in my final school report: "I commend him for his dedication in practising his cricket." Dedication?! You might as well praise a boy for his dedication to strawberries and cream, or masturbation. I practised cricket whenever I could because I *enjoyed* it! Typically, that summer Williams awarded the house fielding prize to a boy who was noticeably bad at it, for no other reason than when he dropped a catch, as he usually did, he cursed so vehemently that it proved just how seriously committed he was to winning the game. Not surprisingly he had also been made head of house.

Much more significant than my disdain for Williams was the fact that I started to become sceptical of authority as a whole. I'd always been naughty in class (when I thought I could get away with it), but now I began to find my way around school rules, and to take the major authority figures less seriously. The school marshal was one victim of my new-found disrespect. Responsible for a wide range of disciplinary matters, he had always struck me as rather forbidding when he entered the classroom every morning to check on attendance. However, when he asked me, a few weeks after the beginning of my micro-revolt, why I had missed chapel that day, I told him that I had been walking along Lower Redland Road, and that as I'd passed the big block of police flats opposite the police station, someone had opened a window on the top floor and thrown a pan of hot fat all over me; and that, because of this, I had had to go back to shower and change my clothes. There was a stunned silence. The marshal stared at me, as did the class. I held my nerve and looked straight back at him. After about half an hour, he said, "Do you really expect me to believe that?" "Marshal, I swear that is *exactly* what happened," I replied. He gave me an odd look. I knew that he knew this was an outrageous fib. "All right," he said, and he ticked his clipboard and left. The class looked at me admiringly. But I think that he had enjoyed it too.

I was as surprised as anyone by what had happened. It was completely unplanned, and my sudden boldness startled me, but in a very positive way. It exemplified a growing confidence, or independence; instead of just fitting myself into the school schedules, I was acting more autonomously. And the timing could not have been better. My Cambridge and Oxford entrance exams were coming up and I needed to be able to wangle my way out of corps and games and Old Testament classes so that I could study harder than I had ever done before. Over the next weeks I crammed with a fierce discipline that I did not know I possessed, feeling that this was the first really important challenge I had ever faced.

I liked Cambridge very much when I arrived to take the Downing College exams, but found the college campus rather bleak. The exam papers were not particularly difficult, but then I had no way of knowing what standard was expected. A week later I was at University College, the oldest of the Oxford colleges, taking the science papers there. Halfway through the physics one, I realised I was not doing well. I'd given two rather sprawling and muddled answers, and had fallen badly behind on time. Looking for a calculation question to help me catch up on the clock, I started answering one about rocketry. This was not a good idea as I had never studied the subject. I had panicked. I finished the three hours in total disarray. I knew I had failed a key paper, and that there was no way back. I walked around

Oxford for the rest of the afternoon, feeling terrible and wondering if I should bother to sit the remaining exams. I got back to the room I was staying in, too gloomy to eat dinner. Then the phone rang and Dad told me I had been accepted by Downing.

But there was a twist to this. Because National Service had just been abolished, there was a bottleneck at all the universities, with people who had just completed two years' military duties immediately after their schooldays competing for entry with those who were about to finish their final year at school. So although I'd been offered a place at Cambridge, I was told I would have to wait two years after leaving Clifton before I could take it up, in October 1960.

Not that it concerned me at all. I never even speculated upon what I might do to fill this two-year gap. I still had some nine months of school left ahead of me, and that took considerations of the future over the horizon for a Cleese who'd only just turned eighteen. Moreover I was now encountering a new feeling of spaciousness, due to being free, for the first time in years, from the pressure of exams. I have always noticed that any kind of pressure narrows my awareness and stunts my curiosity, because once I apply my nose to the grindstone I find it difficult to stick it up in the air again to smell the flowers. Of course a degree of obsession often produces the best work; but it does not produce the best life.

But now, with my place at Cambridge secure, I didn't care whether or not I passed my S level exams. In fact, although I didn't register the significance at the time, I now paid very little attention to my scientific studies, and started to look around for other, more interesting matters.

My main criticism of my time at Clifton is that, at this point, when any master could easily have steered me in the direction of a new interest, I was left entirely to my own resources. And the truth is, I was not very resourceful. But then, in fairness to me, no teacher ever tried to stimulate my intellectual curiosity either. Nor, in five years, did any of them spot that I had *any* creative abilities whatsoever. I remember writing an essay on "Time," which I thought rather ingenious: I spent the entire essay explaining how I had failed to get down to writing the essay because I had prevaricated and procrastinated and wasted time, and the last line of the 1,500-word essay was an apology for not having written it. If I'd been a teacher reading this, I would have spotted talent. Unfortunately you have to have some creative ability before you can recognise it in others. At Clifton, I don't think any of the masters had this innovative talent and the institution itself seemed to limit its recognition of it to English essays that contained phrases like "carpet of snow" and "verdant foliage" (see earlier) and "autumnal hues," and to drawing and painting.

So in that last year, no teacher suggested that I should read a particular book or play, or try to acquire a new skill, or visit an exhibition, or anything that would have expanded my intellectual horizons; and these were very limited indeed, given that from 1955 to 1958, of the thirty-six lessons that I attended each week, thirty-one were in maths and science, and the remaining five in PE and Old Testament studies. I don't blame Clifton for this ludicrous imbalance, as it was dictated by the educational "authorities" of the time, via A levels. It was only thirty years later, when I read Howard Gardner's *Frames of Mind,* that I realised that there are many different intelligences (Gardner believes there are nine, which are almost unrelated to each other, which helps me to understand why I sometimes think I am quite bright, and sometimes feel like a complete dolt). Of these, the traditional English system of education developed only two: "logical-mathematical" and "linguistic," with two others—"musical" and "bodily-kinesthetic"— worked on outside the classroom. The other five were totally ignored. The staff couldn't have taught them anyway.

Consequently it was only in my mid-forties that I realised just how appallingly narrow this English "left brain" education was; and this enabled me finally to understand why so many people who had been academically distinguished did not seem to accomplish a great deal once they left university.[1]

So there I was, in December 1957, with a place at Cambridge, and time to broaden my horizons; but finding no stimulation from Clifton, and lacking the awareness or audacity to strike out on my own in any intellectual direction, I wasted my chance and enjoyed myself instead. I read adventure stories like Conan Doyle's *Exploits of Brigadier Gerard,* and detective stories like Agatha Christie's *The Murder of Roger Ackroyd* and the Father Brown tales of G. K. Chesterton. In the spring term I played soccer every day and pretended to be Tartuffe (we were rehearsing the play for that year's inter-house play competition). I began to realise that these two activities had a lot in common: I really liked being in teams—the collaboration, the "team spirit," the in-jokes, the sense of belonging, of support; all probably giving me a sense of family I'd never experienced before. And obviously I'm still at it. One of the happiest memories of the 2014 *Python* reunion was that the Python team took the curtain calls together.

In the summer, I played cricket, and even got the great England player Denis Compton out twice in one inning. He'd come to play because his son was at Clifton. The first time I got him out, nobody appealed because everybody in the team wanted to watch him bat; the second time, he hit a catch to a boy playing his first match in the First XI. Anyone else would have dropped it deliberately. The score: D. C. S. Compton, caught Whitty, bowled Cleese 27.

I also high-jumped 5′6″ and took part in a memorable sixth-form entertainment which took place in an open courtyard, right beneath the East Tower. I had decided nonsense-German was funny, so I dressed up as Hitler and harangued the audience. After a time, some-

---

[1] The final piece in this jigsaw was provided by Daniel Goleman's *Emotional Intelligence.* When I finished this, I tried to imagine what a traditional public-school emotional education curriculum would have looked like: thirty-one out of thirty-six lessons per week on "How to Tune Out Your Feelings," presumably.

one in the audience (a plant) objected, and two stormtroopers (the guys who were to become professors in America) arrested him, frog-marched him into the East Tower and disappeared. I continued my

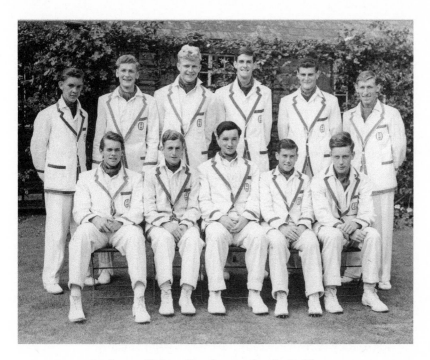

Cricket at Clifton. I'm the one that looks like me.

mock-Deutsch (my accent was quite good), and then suddenly the plant appeared at the parapet at the very top of the tower, scream-ing, "No! No!! For God's sake, *NO!!*" as the stormtroopers prepared to throw him off. A moment later, a life-size dummy, dressed *exactly* like the plant, was tossed over the parapet and sailed through the air five storeys down (while the plant screamed), landing with a huge, dull thump in the courtyard right next to the audience. There was a moment of utter, utter HORROR! I had achieved something that I signally failed to do as Lucifer: there were at least two brown-trouser jobs. Then, as they realised they'd been had, the biggest laugh that I'd get till I appeared at the Hollywood Bowl. (Incidentally, this is the only major jape I arranged at Clifton. Similar other pranks which are now attributed to me I'd heard about when I first arrived in 1953.)

AROUND ABOUT this time I got an unexpected call from Mr. Tolson at St. Peter's, inviting me to come down to Weston-super-Mare for a chat. He'd heard I had two years to kill before going to Cambridge. Was I interested in teaching at St. Peter's? Sitting in his study a few days later, I felt very tempted. There was, however, a problem.

"But, Mr. Tolson, what do you want me to teach?"

"I want you to teach the second and third forms English, history and geography."

My heart sank.

"But . . . I don't know anything about them, Mr. Tolson! For three years I've done nothing but *science.* . . ."

Mr. Tolson patted my arm.

"John, they're *ten*-year-olds. Just stay a page ahead."

Then he offered me £5 a week. It was a no-brainer.

Back at Clifton, it was the last day of term and, by tradition, "leavers" were allowed to walk out of the chapel first, even before the masters. When this had happened in the past, I had watched them walk down the aisle with a deep feeling of empathetic sadness. How awful they must feel, I thought, leaving their home, their life at Clifton, their very existence . . . for the last time. My heart would go out to them, in their bereavement. Really . . .

But now that it was my turn, I felt cheerful and optimistic. It was perfect! I'd got really bored with the place about six weeks before, and I was delighted to be out of there. And many times since I've thought, "What a really great frame of mind in which to die. I'm bored. I'm out of here!" Here's hoping. . . .

I wasn't exactly gone, though. A week later I was still a member of the Clifton College XI at Lord's, when I was out, first ball. It didn't matter though: the team won!

And after playing cricket through the whole summer holidays . . . I was going back to Weston-super-Mare.

5

And so in late September 1958 I arrived back at St. Peter's School, to take up my first job. It was immensely comforting to find that everything felt so familiar: the grounds, the main building, the trees, the school dogs, and above all the friendly, beaming face of Mr. Tolson. He still exuded an air of easy authority, even though he seemed a lot smaller than he had been when I was a boy. I had always liked and trusted him; and it was reassuring to realise that he was no longer allowed to cane me. I suddenly felt so much at home that my transition from pupil to teacher now seemed like a routine promotion.

In addition, I had a priceless advantage in my new role because a mere two months had elapsed since I had ceased to be a schoolboy and I therefore had an absolutely clear-sighted perception of the realpolitik of my situation. I did not need to consult Che Guevara, Ho Chi Minh or Lao Tzu to know that all new teachers are subjected to guerrilla warfare and that if they do not stamp their authority from the start, they are "goners," as they say in the teaching trade. I vividly recall, sixty years after the event, what one particular Clifton class perpetrated on a sweet-natured but naive chemistry teacher called Baynes. The poor creature lasted only three weeks before a nervous collapse saved him from further punishment. I can still visualise him being driven away in an unmarked van to the sound of cheers . . .

So I knew that the next few days were not for the squeamish. I expected no quarter. But I was up for the fight, and I had chosen my weapon. The black mark!

The St. Peter's black mark was purely metaphorical. It could be awarded to any boy who was guilty of a breach of discipline. To impose it the teacher need only inform the boy, listen for a few seconds to his complaint ("Oh, sir! That's not fair, sir. I thought I saw a warthog, sir!"), confirm his crime, and then go to the staff common room and write down the boy's name, plus a brief description of his offence—talking when "on silence," fighting, impertinence, arson and so forth.

Now to those of you who might scoff at the potential effectiveness of "black marks" in, for example, checking the surge in the number of armed robberies in South London, I have this to say: it was very effective at St. Peter's in 1958.

Every Saturday morning, at school assembly, after prayers, Mr. Tolson would announce the names of all the boys who had received black marks that week, and, believe it or not, those boys were definitely discomfited. So I ask you to imagine the effect on the whole school when, on the first Saturday of term, Mr. Tolson began reading out the details of sixteen black marks, and twelve of them turned out to have been awarded by this parvenu apprentice called Cleese. The boys, who had started assembly by eyeing me as their legitimate prey, now registered first surprise, then disbelief, and finally a growing, watchful apprehension, as they had it brought home to them that this particular newcomer was not going to be taken alive.

I sat there, pretending this sort of thing happened to me every Saturday morning, and trying to conceal the wave of smug satisfaction that was passing through me, very similar to the one Himmler must have experienced just after the successful completion of the Night of the Long Knives. Even some of the other teachers seemed rather impressed.

Now I know that some of my readers will suspect that I am exaggerating the warlike nature of the relationship between schoolmaster and pupils. I accept that there are two major differences. The first, of course, is in armaments. The second is that in most wars both sides want to win. In schoolroom wars, however, both sides want the teacher to win, because when he or she has, life can settle into a predictable pattern, allowing everyone to relax.

I came to this realisation because I was puzzled by the blatant unpopularity of one of the other young masters, who seemed to me rather an amiable fellow. He left after a single term, and so I was able to seek guidance from one of the forms that he used to take. They were unexpectedly clear about their reason for detesting him. "You never knew where you were with him, sir," they told me. "One day he was really strict, and the next we could do what we liked, and suddenly he'd get really angry."

To my surprise, they were telling me exactly what they wanted from me: consistency. It was fine to be strict like Captain Lancaster, because he was always strict; nevertheless all the boys were fond of him. It was also fine to be easy-going if you were always like that. But if a teacher imposed one set of rules one day, and another set the next, the boys hated it. And him.

There was only one drawback to my "black mark" strategy: I had to wait until Saturday for the full force of the headmaster's authority to be stamped on my decisions. Meanwhile I learned that the first lesson in "How to keep order" is: learn the pupils' names. Otherwise:

JOHN CLEESE: So basically the king had to keep order
    without either having police . . . stop talking!
BOY 1: Me, sir?
JC: No, not you. You!
BOY 2: I wasn't talking, sir.
JC: I'm not talking to you.
BOY 3: I wasn't talking, sir!
JC: I'm not talking to you either, I'm talking to *you*!
BOY 4: . . . What, sir?

JC: ... What do you mean, "What, sir?"?

BOY 4: Sorry, sir, but what's the question?

JC: Er ... the question is ... er ... why are you talking?

BOY 1: I'm not, sir.

JC: Not you, him!

And so your control of the class seeps away, like guava juice through a semi-permeable membrane.

No, the first thing you do is to get a piece of paper, do a rough sketch of where the desks are, and then ask each boy for his name, writing it down in the right place.

The St. Peter's sixth-form room. Note the waste-paper basket.

The second thing is: never tell a boy, "Stop talking," because he will always claim he wasn't. You must say, "Don't talk." Then, when he denies that he was talking, you can say, "I didn't say you were, I said, 'Don't!'" This leaves him with nowhere to go.

The third thing is: when you ask a question, always formulate it in full before you give the name of the boy who is to answer it, because if you start with his name, everyone else will immediately stop paying attention (except for the swots and toadies).

The fourth thing is: if you catch a whiff of impending insurrection, use sarcasm. They just can't handle it. It's wonderful. It's like shooting fish in a barrel, or making fun of Donald Trump. It's so easy, it's embarrassing. But don't overuse it: keep it for . . . that special occasion.

I began my career as a schoolmaster with one considerable disadvantage: as I had confessed to Mr. Tolson, I knew nothing about the subjects I was supposed to teach. This is no exaggeration. I had once passed a history exam, but God knows how—I still got confused about how dates with 16 on the front could occur in the *seventeenth* century. That's about as basic as history gets . . . So far as geography was concerned, I had to look the word up, to see what it comprised other than looking at maps. I was less clueless about the basics of English, though I didn't realise at the time that I was assuming that English grammar was the same as the Latin grammar I had been taught so well. (I remember that the first week I was there, a boy asked me during prep whether *ager* was second or third declension and I was able to tell him *without pausing for thought* that *ager*—a field—was second declension, so it went like *annus*, but that it dropped the "e," as opposed to *agger*—a rampart—which was third declension, and retained the "e." "My God," I thought as he walked away, "Captain Lancaster did a good job." My next thought was, "Lucky the boy didn't ask me what a rampart was. . . .")

But given that I was teaching ten-year-olds, Geoffrey Tolson's advice to "stay a page ahead" seemed perfectly sound. So I had no reason to believe, as I strode purposefully into the classroom to teach Form III their first history lesson, that I was walking into an ambush.

After getting all their names down on a floor plan, I started "teaching" them some stuff about William the Conqueror which I had carefully memorised the previous evening. Things were going uneventfully when a small boy with very white hair in the second row put up his hand and asked, "Sir, what are the dates of Henry the Eighth?" I immediately countered that we were not discussing Henry VIII, and that the date of the Battle of Hastings was 1066, but that I was prepared to talk to him about Henry VIII at the end of the lesson (by which time I would have had a chance to pay a quick visit to the masters' common room to look up the dates in question).

So at the end of the lesson he comes up to me, and I pretend I've just noticed him and say, very casually, "1509 to 1547," and he says, "I know, sir, but what are the dates of Charles the First?" and I feel a flash of panic and nearly say, "That's not fair," and then think twice about saying, "I'll tell you in a moment but first I have to get another piece of chalk from the masters' common room," and in the end settle for "Well, what do *you* think they are?" and when he replies, without batting an eyelid, "1625 to 1649," I smile inscrutably and say, "The most interesting thing about Charles the First is that he was a foot shorter at the end of his reign than he was at the beginning," thinking this might get a laugh and take the pressure off, but the little bastard now tells me he has memorised *all* the dates of the kings and queens of England, and he challenges me to ask him one, and I venture, "Richard the Fourth?," and he blurts out, "There wasn't one!," thinking that I am trying to catch him out, and then he says he knows all the capitals of all the countries in the world as well, and of course I have to teach him geography the next day.

I can't recall how the conversation ended but the next thing I can remember is hiding up in my garret and cramming the dates of all the kings and queens of England (carefully excluding Anne II, William V and Darren I), and then all the world's capital cities (or hamlets).

I would like to take this chance to thank the little white-haired bastard, because knowing those dates enabled me for the first time to enjoy learning about history. Before then I never seemed to be able to "get into" the subject, but now I had a framework on which I could hang odd bits of information, and slowly the whole thing began to make sense in a *post hoc, ergo propter hoc* sort of way.

I am not striking a rhetorical attitude when I say that I genuinely don't understand why the skill of memorising ("learning by rote" as its detractors always refer to it) has got itself such a bad name. True, it was overdone in the past; but that doesn't make it bad in itself. I'm grateful that one of the compensations of acting is discovering how to learn lines. I enjoy it when friends more literate than I can quote an apt passage of prose or poetry, and I enjoy it even more when I can remember a snippet myself. It can be fun to learn a short poem:

> I really rather care for fish,
> In fact they are my favourite dish.
>> I love the sole,
>> I value dabs,
>> I prize all carp,
>> I lust for crabs,
> I like to take small bits of dace
> And put them right into my face.

This didn't take me more than a couple of weeks to learn, yet I enjoy knowing it. When I can persuade a real actor like Kevin Kline to do a bit of *Hamlet* over dinner it can be quite thrilling.

Once I had negotiated my first few days, and learned all the boys' names, I was able to settle into a very comfortable routine. There had been very few changes since 1953: the Reverend Dolman had taken a parish in the Midlands, so Mr. Bartlett had resumed teaching senior Classics; competitive boxing had been abolished, much to everyone's relief; and one of Mrs. Tolson's corgis had died, also much to everyone's relief; but otherwise things were much as they had been when I was a schoolboy.

There are great advantages to being in an institution. Everything

(Above) Me *(left)* aged nearly one, and *(below)* a bit more than one.

(*Above*) Me at a different age, and (*below*)
with Mother and best friend.

Dad had a kind face.

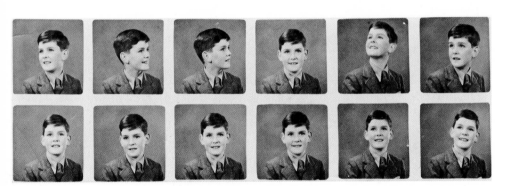

I had lots.

Details from the 1949 St. Peter's school photograph showing *(anti-clockwise from left):* me, Captain Lancaster, Mr. and Mrs. Tolson, Mr. Bartlett, and Rev. Dolman.

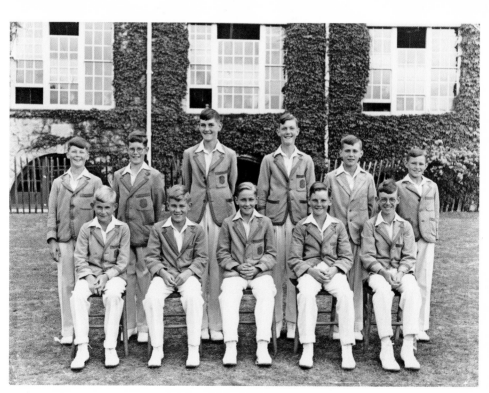

The St. Peter's cricket XI, 1952.

(Above) Emerging from Clifton after the scholarship exam, summer 1953;
(below) a pretty picture of Clifton College.

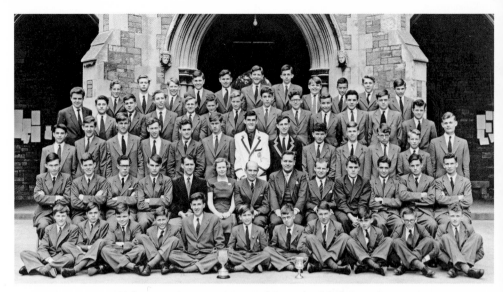

Clifton, with me in First XI blazer highlighting the
humourless gnome below me.

Me as Lucifer, terrifying Faustus.

Return to St. Peter's as a teacher. Happy days.

St. Peter's teacher (with beard).

(Above) I was late for this Downing College photograph, taken in the summer of 1961. I had forgotten my gown, too.

(Left) An uninspired photograph for the 1962 Footlights revue; *(below)* the programme for the 1963 revue.

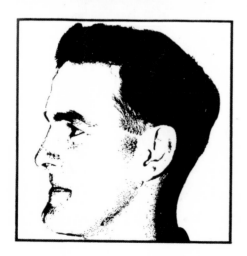

John Otto Cleese : Intelligent, charming, ex Public School (23), smattering French, driver, requires interesting remunerative employment july onwards Do anything, go anywhere. (A non-lollard, and utterly trend-less, he was converted from Luddism by watches, and cannot ride a bicycle.—Ed.).

is predictable: you know exactly what you have to do; everything else is done for you. I woke up at 7:30, and made myself presentable before joining the school at breakfast; then I sat in the masters' common room, where Mr. Bartlett was masterminding the *Times* crossword; trooped (last in line) into assembly for prayers, where all the masters were seated, facing the boys, while Mr. Tolson read out some prayers and an extract from the New Testament; stood to join in the hymn, a high-pitched cacophony which to the ears of a neutral observer must have sounded like a deliberate attempt to annoy the Almighty; seated myself to receive Mr. Tolson's blessing, followed by a few words about what was on his mind that particular morning; and then taught form lessons roughly resembling English, history and geography before retiring to the common room half an hour before lunch, to get my breath back, exchange the morning's howlers with my colleagues and watch Mr. Bartlett continue with the crossword.

Then off to lunch where, in accordance with my status, I sat at the end of a long table of nine- and ten-year-olds. It took a little time to learn how to converse with them. I once sponsored some research into the intelligence of cats, as I had been irritated by my vet's derogatory assessment of one of mine. After a few months I received back from the Sussex University professor whose palm I had greased, "Cats are very intelligent at all the things that cats need to be intelligent about," which was only slightly less irksome than the original veterinary put-down. Be that as it may . . . a nine-year-old schoolboy is as intelligent as he needs to be. But not more. For example, at my first meal I asked one of the boys how old he was, and he asked me the same question. I suggested he should try and guess. "Forty?" he ventured (this was before I grew a beard). Another time I showed some boys the old optical illusion by which you look as though you have removed the top joint of your thumb. When they tried, some of them became rather upset that they couldn't do it. They hadn't realised it was a trick . . .

So provided I avoided irony, conversation flowed quite easily, even if it was a little limited. What they liked best were stories of pranks I had played on my teachers. What they were keenest to tell me were statistics about dinosaurs and cricket and how people were tortured to death in China.

After lunch came the splendid St. Peter's custom called "Rest." The boys went into the Big Room and sat at their desk and read something they enjoyed; except for the very youngest, who lay on the beds in an upstairs dormitory and were read to by Miss Lovell. The staff claimed their armchairs, and smoked and dozed and finished the *Times* crossword.

In the afternoons there were lessons and games. I was put in charge of the youngest boys' soccer and since I'd loved the game for as long as I could remember, it came as a complete surprise that they had absolutely no idea how it was played. I had spaced them out at the start, explaining to each one what his position was as I placed him in it—centre forward, left half, right wing, goalkeeper—but the moment I blew the whistle the boy nearest the ball kicked it as hard as he could, in no particular direction, and then they all ran after the ball in a pack until one of them caught up with it, and then he kicked it and they all hared after it again, without taking any account of the whereabouts of the goalposts. It was all so wonderfully random and mindless that I stood there crying with laughter and unable for some time to summon up the breath to blow the whistle. By the time I did, they had disappeared into a field of cabbages, where they continued to play, apparently quite unaware of the change in the terrain. A few blasts and some shouting brought them back to me, so that I could calm them down and explain that some of them should try to kick the ball towards *this* goal, while the others should aim at *that* one, and that they should try to spread out a bit. They nodded, I blew the whistle and they continued exactly as before. I blew again. Same explanation. Same result. They were not being disobedient; my authority was not being defied; it was just that they could not understand, so the moment the whistle blew, instinct took over. Eventually I just let the "match" continue. They were getting plenty of exercise and we had at least achieved stage one: they were kicking the ball, not trying to eat it.

Once games and afternoon lessons were over, my official duties for the day were done, so I could mark tests or prepare lessons for the next day, or just play chess or snooker with the boys till they went to dinner. Or teach myself some history, geography and English.

In the early evening I would join the Tolsons for dinner in a corner of the dining hall. Mr. Bartlett was always present, as were a couple of the younger masters. I have no recollection of the kind of conversations that took place, but I think this was where I learned that the main purpose of such a social occasion was to avoid any embarrassment. Everyone was polite and well mannered, and there was even restrained laughter on occasion, and some evenings a glass or two of Bulmers Woodpecker Cider. In two years, I never heard a disagreement, or a belch, or a moment's tactlessness, or a risqué joke, or a political or religious opinion, or a rude interruption, or even an embarrassing silence. A fart would have been physically impossible.

On Sundays we were all invited after dinner to the Tolsons' drawing room, where we would sip coffee and listen to the radio. In retrospect I wish I could have taken everyone to watch an evening's cage fighting. I can't imagine what they might have made of such a display of bad manners. I know a woman who was in Paris once with her father, and because the rain was so bad they took refuge in a cinema that was showing a recently released movie called *Last Tango in Paris*, with Marlon Brando. Her father sat through the whole film (including the infamous butter scene) and didn't speak until they emerged back into the daylight, at which point he announced, "Well, I thought that was all rather unnecessary." I think Mr. Bartlett might have found the cage fighting rather unnecessary.

Now that I was an adult (or nearly one) I found that the impressions I had formed as a child of Geoffrey Tolson and his colleagues required a certain degree of modification. Mr. Tolson, for example, still came across as the good-hearted, straightforward, decent chap I recalled from a few years before; but now I began to notice odd moments that suggested he was not the brightest lighthouse on the coastline. For instance, he once got very cross during assembly because he felt the boys had become lazy, and so he demanded that every single boy in the school should improve his ranking in class in the course of the next fortnight. It was not only the maths teachers who thought this too much of a stretch.

It was just as well that his instincts for running the school were so pitch-perfect because if he had to hold more than a certain amount of information in his head at any given time he could easily become confused. At the end of lunch one Saturday he made an announcement in the course of which he stipulated that boys who were going out with their parents that weekend should get their hair cut *after* they had been down to the changing room to move all their sports clothing on to the lower peg, *if* their peg number was between 1 and 37, to allow the visiting school's teams to use the upper pegs, *unless* they were going out as the *guest* of a boy's parents that weekend, in which case they should first collect their fortnightly reports so that they could include them with their letter home, *provided* they were not "off games," in which case they should *first* collect their chit from matron, but *not* until they had moved their clothes down to the lower peg, and then present the chit to the master on duty and *then* . . . Here he went silent for some time, his brain having decided to go on strike. The entire school waited with bated breath in the hope of clarification of what the hell everybody was supposed to do next. Slowly Mr. Tolson's face took on a peaceful, if slightly sad expression, as scenes from his past life flashed before him; and then he inhaled deeply and announced impressively, ". . . should all get their hair cut!" At which point he sat down. A bewildered silence followed, as the entire school sat there examining their nails and pretending they had not noticed that the person who was in charge of the place had just gone mad.

Twenty-three years later I had huge fun trying to recapture this moment on paper, for the start of the sex lesson in *The Meaning of Life*. I found I could not come up with anything better, so Mr. Tolson's real-life words became the introduction to the demonstration.

One aspect of Mr. Tolson was that he could be charmingly old-fashioned. He was, for example, the only man I've ever met who literally put his tongue in his cheek when he made a facetious remark. He also adored great English sporting traditions, like cricket. If England had done well he would interrupt prep, beaming, to announce the scores; and he never missed attending the Varsity rugby match at Twickenham—as a good Cambridge man he was slightly crestfallen if Oxford won.

When it came to the world of emotions, I suspect he would have found something rather discreditable about a man discussing his innermost feelings (except, perhaps, in exceptional cases, with his wife). And yet he abolished the boxing competition, because he was touched by the boys' complaints that they didn't like punching their friends; and on another occasion, when a boy who specialised in pushing masters over the edge so infuriated me that I pulled his hair, which shameful act he naturally reported, Mr. Tolson took me aside and told me gently about the boy's background and how he had been adopted by parents who never ceased to remind him how lucky he had been and how much he owed them, and explained that was why he compulsively goaded authority figures, all of which enabled me to make a proper apology and, to my delight, develop a much better relationship with the boy. I can still recall the tone of the conversation with Mr. Tolson and my surprise at finding someone, apparently so bluff and hearty, also able to show such concern and understanding for a boy generally regarded as a complete pest.

Despite his compassion, our headmaster did have a bit of a temper. Fortunately, though, bystanders could always see the explosion coming. This was because as he got angrier he got pinker. He was already quite pink to start with, with his fine, bald, domed head dominant, but as his ire built, he passed through a remarkable range of shades of the colour on his way to puce, enabling an expert to calibrate accurately the right moment to depart. The reasons for his anger were never hard to discern: they always boiled down to a lack of moral fibre on the part of someone (or something). Such feckless behaviour was inevitably described as being "wet."

What was unusual about Mr. Tolson's temper was that he always lost it. Once "wetness" (in any form at all) was sighted, and the first sign of extra pinkness displayed, there was no way to abort the process—it took on a life of its own and could only be resolved with a good deal of noise. I think he literally did not know that anger could be directed into any other outcome.

This led to difficulties when the explosion had to be delayed. One Saturday, our great rivals from Burnham-on-Sea, St. Dunstan's, beat all five of our teams at soccer. In the aftermath Mr. Tolson apparently decided that this shameful thrashing was due to serial acts of cowardice by members of our teams, to do with turning their backs on St. Dunstan's players who were about to kick the ball hard. (This was an eccentric analysis of the reason for the defeats, which was clearly to do with St. Dunstan's being much, much better at football than we were.)

The staff had no wind of what was brewing when the next day we assembled in the common room a few minutes before the Sunday morning prayers service was due to begin. We intuited that our headmaster would be feeling a bit snippy about the previous afternoon's debacle, but when he knocked on the door, to lead us into the service, we were alarmed to note that he was a shade of pink hitherto unreported, one the other side of shocking pink, but none the less shocking for that. As we solemnly marched behind him into the Big Room to take our seats facing the congregation, I found myself wondering whether he might dispense with divine service altogether and get to his point straight away. But no, formalities had to be observed, and so prayers began.

There is something quite disorientating about hearing the teaching of our Lord Jesus Christ delivered as a murderous rant, but Geoffrey Tolson was in the grip of a pink mist which temporarily obscured from him the beauty of the Gospel of Love, so that his delivery of the Lord's Prayer made it sound more like an ultimatum, and the final blessing, as he tore through it at record speed, more like a war cry, as he grew nearer to the moment when, beetroot-pink, he revealed the cause of his fury . . .

". . . and now in the name of God the Father, God the Son and God the Holy Ghost, may all good things be with you evermore, life without end, and now I want to talk about our dreadful performance and especially St. Peter's boys turning their backs on St. Dunstan's boys as they were about to kick the ball . . ."

At last! With no noticeable transition whatsoever from the sacred to the profane, Tolson stormed away at the sheer moral turpitude of St. Peter's boys turning their backs just because someone was going to kick a big, wet, heavy football right into their private parts. Slowly he went from extra-shocking pink, to beetroot-pink, to puce, to carnation, to flamingo, to amaranth, to geranium, to coral, to incarnadine, and then . . . slowly . . . back down again to normal, everyday, common-or-garden . . . pink.

And so calm was restored and the St. Peter's boys looked suitably less moist.

The only other manifestation of Tolsonian wrath was bilateral. Sometimes, in the later evening, a few of us would be correcting homework or reading in the common room, just a few feet from the Tolsons' living room, when we would hear bursts of shouting and door-banging, which left us frozen in our chairs. We were all terrified at the thought of the embarrassment that we would experience if any of us bumped into one of the Tolsons immediately after they had concluded a shouting match. Since the avoidance of embarrassment had become the main purpose of our lives, and since knock-down-and-drag-out quarrels were major infractions of genteel middle-class values, being caught as a witness of such a fracas would be rated only slightly better than accidentally observing them copulating. I think we all shared a nasty if unspoken suspicion that if such a situation arose, the teacher in question might be obliged, out of a sense of honour, to shoot himself.

So, for some time after the noise of battle had subsided, we would sit very still, until one of us felt bold enough to creep towards the door and put his ear to it, and then, after opening it a crack, judge if the coast was clear enough for us to risk scuttling to our bedrooms. Had Mr. Tolson seen his teaching staff behaving in this truly pathetic way, he would have promptly labelled us wet and fired us anyway, but then the whole reason for our mouse-like behaviour was to avoid being spotted. I feel our discretion cancelled out our cowardice.

Being caught red-eared by Mrs. Tolson would actually have been worse, as she was deadlier than the male, if not as noisy. The key to her personality was that she could be charming. But then, so could Stalin, and, like her, Joe knew how to throw his weight about. In Jean Tolson's case this was not a lot of weight physically, but what she had she threw about very stylishly, and with considerable effect. This was not a woman you wanted to get on the wrong side of.

But she was charming (and almost friendly) most of the time, *provided that you played your cards right.* Most noticeable of all, she was attractive, and in a town like Weston-super-Mare, she stood out like a matador at a Quaker meeting. Tall, elegant, and slim (very slim by Westonian standards), she had immaculate dark hair and a striking, almost sharp-featured face that was handsome rather than pretty. Owing to my stunted sexual development I was not, at that age, able to discern whether she was sexy, though in retrospect I think she must have been. That said, anyone harbouring carnal thoughts about her would have been taking his life in his hands, because she exuded an air of designer barbed wire. But what was most intriguing of all was her slightly exotic, or perhaps just un-English, appearance: her complexion was somewhat Portuguese, her lipstick rather bright, and she conveyed the impression of a pent-up Latin temperament, albeit one that, in Weston, had to be expressed by slamming doors rather than through smoking Gauloises, or flamenco, or honour-killings.

Looking back fifty-odd years later, I can now see that Mrs. T was really much too stylish and sophisticated to be married to a prep-school headmaster in a backwater like Weston. I think she would much rather have been the wife of, say, the president of France, using her excellent grasp of French to entertain visiting statesmen, and to host soirées of debonair *nouvelle vague* film directors and *soignés enfants terribles* and moody relatives of Jean-Paul Sartre, instead of being forced to hobnob with a bunch of moth-eaten teachers whose conversational staple was county cricket.

In a moment of unusual self-revelation, Mr. Tolson once told me that at the end of their first year running St. Peter's, he and his wife had gone up to London, planning to spend a few weeks there taking in some shows and generally enjoying nights out on the town. After viewing the bill at the end of the first week, however, they were forced to beat a retreat back to Weston-super-Mare with their tails between their legs. I was rather touched that he had confided this to me, and felt a little sad that the lifestyle bubble that they must have imagined for themselves had been burst in this way, but I couldn't help feeling that Mrs. Tolson must have been the more disillusioned.

All things considered, I think Jean Tolson had accepted the diminution of her hopes with considerable grace, and that the easy condescension with which she treated the teaching staff was not only understandable, but indeed justified.

The only member of staff immune from her *de haut en bas* attitude was Geoffrey Bartlett. He was too obviously an Edwardian gentleman (and a scholar) to be treated as just another dowdy non-entity, and if not exactly an equal, he would certainly have found a place in the same lifeboat. When I met him again on rejoining St. Peter's, I was rather apprehensive, as I was still a little in awe of him, and I knew that he had not really liked me as a boy. Not that he'd ever

been unkind, but there was something about the young Cleese that
he had clearly found slightly distasteful—an incipient crassness, perhaps, that his refined, indeed, fastidious nature could not warm to.
But now he greeted me with a courtesy that approached warmth (the
boys told me that their punning nickname for me—Themistocles—
came from him), and we settled into a surprisingly comfortable relationship, based on my real respect for him. I began to notice that
he was somewhat quieter than I remembered, but it was hard to tell
whether this was shyness, or his cultivated Edwardian gentleman
manner, for he took moderation and restraint to extremes: to have
done anything with gusto would have been inconceivable to him.
When he bowled in the practice cricket nets, he did so in his sports
jacket, and without removing his pipe from his mouth. He was the
epitome of the Oxonian code of "effortless superiority," whereby to
be seen trying really hard to achieve something was in many ways
worse than actually failing at it. I'm sure that many of us boys who
had been in such awe of him mimicked his attitude, not least because
it came across as a distinct moral requirement, rather than just a matter of temperament. If we had hero-worshipped Mr. Tolson instead,
we would have left St. Peter's believing that the most important thing
in life was to try jolly hard to do one's best.[1]

Bartlett's air of effortless superiority imprinted itself so strongly
upon me because it chimed in with what I'd absorbed from my father's stories of the upper class's way of behaving, some aspects of
which seemed (and still seem) to me admirable. Genuinely good
manners are, after all, essentially a way of moderating one's own

---

[1] Recent research shows that children respond much better to the Tolson approach, where effort and determination are praised, than to one where parents
and teachers applaud them for their intelligence, or creativity, or other apparently permanent talent (which often leads to a fear of failing to live up to expectations, and to an unwillingness to slog on when difficulties arise). Of course, as
I've already said, Mr. Tolson went to Cambridge.

egotism, often in the service of considering the egos of others. Even if it's done mainly for show, it's still a start.

It would have been unimaginable for Bartlett or me to have suggested a meal together—not improper, just beyond the bounds of possibility—but sometimes when we were in the common room alone, he would tell me a little about himself. He was obviously considered very promising as a boy at Uppingham, and when he left for Oxford to read Classics, I think he felt he might become a real scholar. But he had an experience at the hand of R. G. Collingwood, the famous philosopher and historian, from which he never recovered. Collingwood's obituary in *The Times* just a few years later pronounced him "one of the six finest minds in Europe," so Bartlett was thrilled to discover on his first day at Oxford that Collingwood was to be one of his tutors. He was assigned some reading before their first meeting, and, studying as he never had before, he prepared what he thought was a very insightful and original question, which he posed to Collingwood as soon as they had made their introductions. Without pausing, Collingwood told him that if he, Bartlett, would care to go to the bookcase behind him (he did not bother to look round) and, from the second shelf up, take the sixth book from the left, the one with a red cover, and then turn to page 134, the fourth paragraph would answer Bartlett's question better than Collingwood could ever hope to himself. Poor Bartlett got up and found the book so described, and there, in the fourth paragraph of page 134, was a perfect complete answer to his question. At which he sadly thought to himself, "What is the point? Why devote one's life to something like philosophy when there are people as outrageously brilliant as Collingwood, with whom one could never hope to compete?" Not that Bartlett was ever hoping to get so far as the quarter-finals of the All England Metaphysics Championships, but if one can't participate on roughly equal terms with the best, why bother? And at that moment, as far as I could tell, a shadow fell across Bartlett's life which never entirely faded.

Then he told me another Collingwood story that was even more alarming. Bartlett had spent his entire life in one of the posher parts of Cheshire, and he knew the terrain like the back of his own hand, as they used to say but don't any more. He discovered that Collingwood had once spent a holiday there and, during a short spell in a hospital when he had nothing better to do, had written a small guidebook to the area . . . *from memory!*

So Bartlett raced out and bought a copy, and went through it with a fine-toothed comb (as it were) until he found a mistake. Collingwood had described a stile by a country lane, which Bartlett had walked along all his life, a stile which he knew did not exist. Triumphantly he raced, guidebook in hand, from his house until he came to the spot where the alleged stile was supposed to have been . . . and *there* it was! With the extinguishment of his ray of hope that Collingwood had finally made a mistake, Bartlett turned, trudged home and shot himself. (Metaphorically, of course.)

I suppose one could argue, though, that Collingwood *had* made a mistake. If a good tutor's job is to nurture pupils intellectually, to stimulate their curiosity and above all to encourage their love of learning, the Waynflete Professor of Metaphysical Philosophy rather blew it, didn't he? Instead of engaging Bartlett and drawing out his abilities, the professor pulled what might be described as a cheap music-hall "Mr. Memory Man" trick which instead had the effect of discouraging his student for good. One might have hoped that Collingwood's love of wisdom would have discouraged such a faux-casual showing-off. But great "intellects," ironically, are often allied to stunted emotional development.

When Bartlett left Oxford, his academic hopes unfulfilled, he decided like many of his friends that war with Germany was coming, so he took a job teaching Classics at St. Peter's as a temporary measure. Not long after, he joined the army as an artillery officer, was made a major, and commanded a battery of guns during the Allied advance up Italy. What he was very proud of was not his bravery (to have been proud of that would have smacked of self-advertisement) but that the final position of his guns, after several months' advance, was less than fifteen yards from the position he had calculated on his map, using his trigonometry skills.

At the end of the war, he returned to St. Peter's to find that his position as senior Classics master had been filled by the Reverend A. H. Dolman. This did not surprise him: he expected Tolson to find a replacement; what rather irked him was that Dolman was a German. Since Bartlett was quite practised at killing them, I think he was tempted to add just one more to an already impressive total. Who would notice? But his good manners got the better of him, inevitably, so he took over the teaching of mathematics instead.

Many years later, when Python was performing the stage show in Liverpool, I lunched with Mr. Bartlett. He was, of course, retired by then. He told me that he had left St. Peter's after a disagreement with Mr. Tolson, and had spent short periods at a couple of other schools, before giving up teaching. There was an air about him that suggested disappointment—that he felt he had not been fairly treated. At the end of the meal, I plucked up the courage to ask about the "disagreement," and he told me that he had discovered inadvertently that Mr. Tolson had been paying him, as senior Classics and mathematics master, less than Mr. Jones, the school odd-job man.

In retrospect, it seems strange that despite the general air of affability, the St. Peter's staff seldom socialised except when sometimes, after the evening meal with the Tolsons, two or three of us would wander down to the saloon bar of one of the local pubs, where I slowly worked my way through the brightly coloured bottles containing international liqueurs. My usual sipping companion was a chap who taught history, named Anthony Viney, whose life by his own description abounded with a certain kind of comedy scene, where a well-meaning innocent accidentally creates chaos and destruction. For example, when Tony took on a Christmas job as a postman, he was given an enormous, extravagantly wrapped box of goodies to deliver to a particular house. As he struggled to carry the huge crate up the drive, the children inside saw him coming and raced out to greet him, jumping up and down in excitement and thronging round him—so much so that as he reached the doorstep, he failed to see several milk bottles there and tripped, breaking a couple, losing his balance and, in the process, dropping the box on the head of the smallest child and treading on the family dog. The screaming and yelping brought the parents to the door, and they proved understandably angered by this gratuitous assault on their family life. Tony picked himself up, apologised, attempted to comfort the damaged child—and then suddenly realised that he had brought the magnificent Christmas offering to the wrong address. Embarrassed beyond endurance, he tried to stammer out an apology, but the father was now shouting so loudly that Tony gave up, grabbed the crate and ran back down the drive as the children sobbed and howled at this sudden and incomprehensible turn of events.

What I found so funny about this tale was the enormous gap between Tony's intention and the outcome. To start with, the story would immediately cease to be amusing if Tony had caused any of this chaos on purpose. (Similarly, in *Fawlty Towers* Manuel regularly wrecks Basil's plans out of a fervent desire to help him—again, if there were any intent to hinder, the joke wouldn't work.) Next, Tony was a particularly kind and considerate man, and to have inflicted the emotional distress that he did on this unsuspecting family was agonising for him. The story is, in my view, funnier for this awareness on his part than it would be if he hadn't realised what he'd done, or if he had realised, but simply hadn't cared.

In the case of Tony the Postman, we can see the whole picture: the purity of his motives; the inconsequentiality of broken milk bottles; the fact that the hijacked goodies were not intended for the family anyway; and, *above all,* that the emotions suffered by the family (and the dog) were ultimately transient and so harmless.

When James Thurber described humour (or humor) as "emotional chaos remembered in tranquility" he was only pointing out that things that seem very important at the time usually aren't, and that it's not unkind to laugh at temporary upsets, especially when they're our own. In fact, it's rightly considered healthy to be able to laugh at oneself, and we all much prefer people who do not take themselves "too seriously." A good sense of humour is the sign of a healthy perspective, which is why people who are uncomfortable around humour are either pompous (inflated) or neurotic (oversensitive).

Pompous people mistrust humour because at some level they know their self-importance cannot survive very long in such an atmosphere, so they criticise it as "negative" or "subversive." Neurotics, sensing that humour is always ultimately critical, view it as therefore unkind and destructive, a *reductio ad absurdum* which leads to political correctness.

Not that laughter can't be unkind and destructive. Like most manifestations of human behaviour it ranges from the loving to the hateful. The latter produces nasty racial jokes and savage teasing; the former, warm and affectionate banter, and the kind of inclusive humour that says, "Isn't the human condition absurd, but we're all in the same boat."

Which brings me to another story that Tony Viney told me, which is very cruel. And quite hilarious, I hope . . .

Once upon a time, a very kind and gentle history teacher called Tony was driving home at the end of a summer bank holiday. The traffic was even worse than he had feared, and by the time he reached Salisbury Plain the cars were bumper to bumper and moving forward at a rate of about one car's-length every other Thursday. Tony was very hot, as well as bored and sleepy, when all of a sudden he saw a rabbit. And it was not a happy bunny. In fact it was a sad and miserable little bunny, because it was in the last stages of myxomatosis (this was in the '50s, when the virus was devastating Britain's rabbit population), and it lay there, hardly breathing, its face disfigured by swelling, its eyes so puffed up it was no longer able to see, sores and tumours clearly visible all over its body, and with just hours, if not minutes, to live. And Tony, being a kind and gentle man, and an ardent animal lover to boot, was appalled to see such awful suffering, and his heart went out to the pitiable animal; so he left his car and crossed a few yards of grass until he stood by the dying creature. And seeing its nasal discharge and its swollen ears and its strangely enlarged genitals, he choked back his tears, swallowed, and vowed that very moment to put the poor, dear thing out of its misery. He reached down and picked it up by its ears, held it well away from himself, took a deep breath and karate-chopped the back of its neck—giving it the deadly "rabbit punch" which he had read about somewhere.

Unfortunately, however, the poor creature had not read the same piece, and so the blow caused it to spring to life and start leaping about (inasmuch as a rabbit can leap about when it is being held up by its ears) with a suddenness that scared its would-be assassin out of his wits. In the normal course of events, Tony would now have dropped the rabbit and run for his life, but his determination to do the right thing by the rabbit was so great that his nerve held, and, realising that his first karate chop had failed simply because he had not struck the dying creature firmly enough, (out of kindness) he held it up again, grasped its ears even more tightly, and let fly at it once more.

Alas! In his haste to do God's work, he had neglected to take aim properly, and so he caught the rabbit (which was, to be fair, now a moving target) with a glancing blow on the side of its head, thus spurring it to further exertions, while at the same time releasing a surprising quantity of nasal discharge on to his suit. However, the latter event was a matter of very little importance to Tony at this juncture: the question of how to terminate this remarkably resilient rabbit was now occupying his mind so totally that feelings of shame and inadequacy and self-hatred could hardly be sensed through his all-consuming panic.

How, in God's name, was he going to kill it?

Various options flashed through his mind: shooting, hanging, drowning, electrocution, impalement, crucifixion, a guillotine . . . something *sharp*! A knife? A saw? A dagger? An axe? . . . A penknife! I've got one in the car! I'll cut its throat! Perfect!

He turned towards his car, and froze. Up to this moment Tony had been so focused on the poor rabbit that he had completely failed to notice the crescendoing sound of car horns and angry shouting that now suddenly enveloped him. As far as the eye could see (Salisbury Plain is famous for its flatness) motorists and their passengers, all still stuck in the traffic jam, were shouting and shaking their fists and cursing him and screaming threats. A number were opening their car doors and getting out.

For a few seconds Tony was astonished. Could all these people really believe that he was beating up this rabbit for fun? That he had left his car and pounced on the poor, unsuspecting bunny as a form of blood sport? And that he had then started using it as a punchbag, just to pass the time till the traffic started moving again? That he, kind and gentle Tony, was in fact a sadistic, vile murderous brute destined for the front page of the *Daily Mail*?

Well, I'm afraid that's exactly what they thought. Unfair, wasn't it?

So . . . what was Tony to do, in the light of this latest development? Plan A, which was to take the rabbit back to the car where he could quietly stab it to death with his Swiss Army knife, seemed too lengthy a procedure, given that people were now actually heading in his direction. He needed something a bit quicker. To his credit, he never even considered following his natural inclination, which was to throw the rabbit away and run. The creature had suffered enough already, he could not let it down. To be dying of myxomatosis, and then, in the middle of that, to be attacked so gratuitously and, after that, to be abandoned to myxomatosis again was a fate no one deserved. So Plan B was . . .

"Wait a moment!" thought Tony. "If it's called a 'rabbit punch,' since rabbits can't punch, it must *actually* kill rabbits. Eventually. So if at first you don't succeed . . ."

And he started hitting it again, with greater determination. The approaching mob stopped in astonishment. Was he deliberately *baiting* them? A howl of fury arose from them that froze Tony's blood. They moved forward again.

And now he panicked.

He threw the rabbit to the ground, and jumped up and down on it.

Then he checked it was dead, shrugged, and waited to be lynched.

And at this very moment, God intervened.

He caused the traffic to begin to move.

And the mob, hearing engines starting up behind them, paused. They were faced with a stark choice. Either they could exterminate this fiend from the face of the planet, or they could regain their place in the queue. A moment of indecision, and then good sense prevailed. They hurried back to their cars, still shouting curses over their shoulders, jumped inside and drove off, in a huff.

Tony pretended to faint, and fell into a position where he could keep his eye on the traffic. He lay there motionless until all the cars that had been in sight during the murder had passed on, at which point he pretended to wake up, and then casually strolled back to his car, got in, and fainted for real.

And it was not as though this kind of thing happened to Tony now and again; such occurrences were a regular part of his day. It was as though God's Department of Practical Jokes had singled him out for special attention, along with Job. I should have become his Boswell.

WHEN I look back at my two years teaching at St. Peter's, the phrase "halcyon days" pops into my mind and the *Oxford English Dictionary*

tells me it refers to "a past time regarded as idyllically happy and peaceful."

Why was it so happy? Well, for a start, it was so free of stress. There were no public appearances, very few deadlines of any importance, a contented and relaxed atmosphere, congenial colleagues, plenty of fresh air and exercise, and . . . I really enjoyed teaching.

Of course, it was in ideal circumstances. The classes were small, the ten-year-olds well mannered and cheerful and respectful and unarmed, and, by and large, they wanted to learn. Discipline was no problem, once you had gained the ascendancy, provided only that you were "fair." The boys were very keen on "fairness." I won a lot of brownie points once when I wrote the non-word "wooly" on the blackboard. They remonstrated with me and pointed out that when they misspelled a word, they had to write it out several times. So I took the chalk and wrote "woolly" one hundred times, all over the board. They approved. Honour was satisfied, and I never spelled "woolly" wrong again. And, maybe, it gave me an idea for *Life of Brian*.

Best of all, I discovered when I walked out of a class at the end of a lesson, leaving behind some ten-year-olds who could now tell the difference between an adjectival and adverbial phrase (a distinction that had been beyond them forty minutes earlier), that I experienced an inexplicable satisfaction. Partly, perhaps, because I could now tell the difference, too. My job, after all, allowed me to fill in some of the many gaps in my education left by the Clifton science curriculum.

However, during the two years, there were a couple of occasions when something happened which I found quite disturbing.

The first time, I was teaching Form III about Africa. We were looking at our atlases, and I was pointing out the big countries and giving them snippets of information. Then we moved on to the big rivers, and found the Nile and the Zambezi, and the Niger and the Congo. Except that one boy I'll call Smith couldn't find the last two. I told him that he would find the Niger in Nigeria, and the Congo in the Belgian Congo. He looked very confused, so I gave the class something to occupy them, sat down next to Smith and asked him what the problem was.

"I can't find them, sir."

"OK. Let's look for the Niger. It runs through Nigeria. Do you remember where Nigeria is?"

Smith suddenly gave a big smile and pointed to Nigeria.

"Good. Now can you see where the river Niger is marked?"

"Oh! Yes, sir."

"Good. Now the Congo river flows through the Belgian Congo [remember, this is 1959]. Where's the Belgian Congo?"

"Here, sir!"

"Good. Now can you see the blue line? That's the river Congo. OK?"

"Yes, sir."

Now it began . . .

"Well done. So . . . where's the river Congo?"

And Smith pointed to Nigeria. I shook my head.

"Er . . . no . . . it's there in the Belgian Congo, see?"

Smith looked puzzled again, as though I had asked him to do the square root of 567,917 in his head. I pointed to the Belgian Congo, and waited for his agreement. But Smith was still uneasy. I waited. I wasn't going to rush him, because then he would be anxious, and when little boys get anxious, they cannot take anything in *at all*. So I smiled, and nodded encouragingly. After a time, I felt I should offer a little more help.

". . . So . . . the river Congo is in the Belgian Congo . . . isn't it?"

Smith wasn't sure.

"They've both got the word 'Congo,' haven't they?"

Smith was cudgelling his brains but there was still something not right about this.

"See? *River* Congo . . . *Belgian* Congo? . . . ? . . . ? . . . ?"

What was I getting wrong? Was I not being *clear* enough? Had I not articulated properly? So . . . very slowly . . .

"River . . . *Congo* . . . Belgian . . . *Congo*! You see, they both have 'Congo' in them!"

But no, the penny wouldn't drop. Smith gave me a brave smile. He was game to go on.

"Smith," I said. "Let's start again. We are talking about two different rivers in two different countries in Africa. One river is called the Niger, and it flows through the country called Nigeria. Niger . . . ia? OK, now we move to the second of the two rivers, which is not called Niger, but instead is called the Congo, and the river called the river Congo . . . is found . . . in the Belgian . . . CONGO! Now . . . which river, the Congo or the Niger, is found in . . . Niger . . . ia?"

Smith looked at me and made the "I am really thinking this one out" face, which involves screwing up your eyes and puckering the mouth and staring intently about a foot above the teacher's head, and which means that you don't even know what the question means.

My heart sank.

"Smith," I said, "I promise you this is not a trick question."

"The Congo!" he announced.

At this moment, I was paralysed by the realisation that I was never, *never* going to find a way of transferring this piece of information from my mind into his. I would have been more gainfully employed explaining the concept of antimatter to a hamster. Never before had I comprehended that no matter however obvious a thought may be, to understand . . . that always requires a tiny little jump of the intellect, a minute hop that connects one thing to another, and that there exist humans who cannot achieve this transit no matter how microscopically small it is made for them.

To "get" a joke requires a similar mental skip, and the tricky part of constructing one is judging the width of the jump needed for the joke to be "got." If you spoonfeed an intelligent audience and make the joke too obvious, they will not find it very funny. But the opposite danger is to make the jump too long, so that the connection is not made, and they don't laugh at all.

So, anyway . . . there was one other puzzling experience, also involving a geography class. To make the lessons fun, all the boys were expected to have their atlases open in front of them when I entered the classroom, and I would shout "China!" or "Poland!" and they had to point to it, and I would run round the class, pretending to rough them up if they had their finger on the wrong country, and they would laugh and shriek, and a good time was had by all for about five minutes, during which they learned some basic geography. At the end of term I gave them an outline map of the world with the frontiers of the countries marked on it, but no names, and then I gave them a list of thirty countries and they had to write the countries' names on the map in the right places. Ten were easy, like Australia and China; ten harder, like Switzerland and Chile; and ten difficult, like Laos and Bolivia.

At the beginning of one term a new boy joined us. He was a little introverted, so out of fellow feeling I let him settle in very gently. He became quite comfortable in class, and seemed rather thoughtful. At the end of term he took the world-map-outline test and I was surprised, and pleased, to find that he had written the name "Bolivia" in exactly the right space.

However, that was the only one he got correct. He marked the continent of Australia as France, Sweden *and* Norway as Brazil, and he placed the British Isles right in the middle of the South Pacific. I was drawn inexorably to the saddening conclusion . . . that Bolivia was almost certainly a fluke.

But what perplexed me was this: what had been going on between his ears during the twenty-odd lessons when the rest of the form had been learning Basic World Geography? He had looked passably interested; he had manifested no anxiety; he had never asked for help, even though I encouraged it, and always praised boys when they did.

So, if he felt he did not need help, what did he think he was trying to accomplish? For what purpose did he imagine he was sitting there? To practise circulating his blood?

I should have asked him, because it was keeping me awake at night. At last I found consolation in the thought that he had succeeded in writing the names of the thirty countries on the right planet. And I pinned up his exam paper on the noticeboard in the masters' common room along with the comment "Abandon hope, all ye who enter here."

When Mr. Bartlett saw it, he stared for some time and then, with real feeling, remarked, "The sad thing about true stupidity is that you can do absolutely nothing about it."

6

I left St. Peter's in the July of 1960. I was quite sad, though I also knew it was time for me to move on . . .

In August my parents and I had our normal summer holiday: ten days at a hotel in Bournemouth called the Devon Towers—and yes, that is definitely where I got the "Towers" for my fictional hotel. I loved the Devon Towers because there was a fine, full-sized snooker table downstairs which no one seemed to know about, and which I could therefore monopolise for hours at a time. I never yearned for an opponent, content with my own company, enjoying playing all the shots myself. That said, I was happy enough when Dad popped down to give me a game.

The other main sporting entertainment in Bournemouth was the Cleese family outing to the huge ice rink in the middle of town to laugh at the beginners.

Now there is something fascinating about the nameless panic that grabs people when they are trying, and failing, to keep their balance, even if they only have a short distance to fall. I accept that it was mean-spirited to take such pleasure in watching the antics of these terrified creatures, but we did at least have the good manners to sit some distance from them, and we tried to keep our volume down. Anyway, it wasn't our fault that they were so funny. Falling over is always entertaining, but these proto-skaters were very special. Mother laughed more at them than at anything else I ever saw, and afterwards Dad and I would have to take her out to tea, to calm her down.

Back in Weston, I spent the rest of the holiday reading my way through various books that were alleged to prepare me for my legal studies. Cambridge had originally given me a place to read physics and chemistry, but I had very swiftly realised that I simply wasn't interested enough to be able to compete with proper scientists. However, given my lack of other A levels, I had been left with a simple and stark choice between two subjects I could start from scratch: economics and law. I decided to opt for the latter. (My father had once told me there was a tradition of law in our family; I subsequently discovered he was referring to his father's position as a solicitor's clerk.) So I now sat down to pore over the reading list provided by the Cambridge Law School. Why Grant and Temperley's *Europe in the Nineteenth Century: 1789–1905* was considered useful preparation for the study of trusts and settlements or Roman law I don't know, but I dutifully ploughed through it without getting any real grasp of the reality behind the words. This is a good example of one of my worst characteristics, which is, when faced by something unfamiliar, to do exactly what I am told without applying my common sense.

SO HERE I was, about to enter one of the world's finest universities, and these were the sum of my academic accomplishments:

- An ability to speak and write grammatical English, and to spell well; some knowledge of maths and science, rapidly fading.
- An acquaintance with the dates of the kings and queens of England; a little Latin; a thin patina of geographical facts;

a working knowledge of *Henry V* and *Macbeth* and some
twenty poems.
- No biology, psychology, economics, philosophy, political
  science, statistics, music, electronics, world history, art,
  engineering, geology, archaeology, architecture, Greek,
  etc., etc., etc.

In a way, I was too unsophisticated to realise just how unsophisticated I was, which is why I was not consciously very anxious about
leaving my life in Weston and setting off into the unknown. Nevertheless, the day I was due to take the train to Cambridge, I suffered a
dreadful stomach upset and was unable to travel. What a strange coincidence! Of course, the idea of psychosomatic illness was unknown
in the lower-middle-class culture I inhabited (if it was known at all in
the England of that time). Cartesianism ruled, on moral grounds. It
was quite acceptable to have a physical illness; what was not allowed
was any form of mental abnormality. This would have been seen as
a sign of weakness, lack of moral fibre, and degeneracy. Ailments
needed to be kept physical.

The next day I felt better, and so dear old Dad drove me all the
way to Cambridge, with Mum helping from the back seat. I have a
clear memory of kissing them both goodbye outside Downing College, and then of turning away and walking through the gates. I knew
it meant we were finally separating, and while I was apprehensive I
also felt a sense of relief, of having finally escaped from a mould.

Writing this now, though, I feel a deep sadness for Dad. I had been
the focus of his life for so long—perhaps the main source of meaning for him—that it must have been a very painful moment for him
to watch me disappear like that. Much less painful for my mother,
who, after all, still had herself to think of. But then, if Dad suffered
from my absence, Mum had suffered from my presence. I think their
relationship had been quite a close one until I came along, but that as
the rapport and warmth between Dad and me began to develop, she

may have felt increasingly excluded from our intimacy, and therefore from her own relationship with him.

So, anyway ... once inside the gates, my first impressions of Downing College were very positive. It was a friendly place, and as a first-year student I was fortunate enough to have a room in college—a large ground-floor one near the Porter's Lodge. It also seemed easy to find out what one was supposed to do. The only shock came when I arrived rather late for dinner in Hall that first evening. Grace was about to be said, and so I slipped into the only vacant space I could see along the many long benches. A few words of Latin, and I sat down to find myself surrounded by chemists.

"So I tried chlorobenzylacetate!"

"No!"

Hoots of laughter from everyone around me.

"What about sodium pentathalamide!" Giggles.

"You're not serious?"

"If I wanted a precipitate, I would have used zinc polychlosterate!"

Howls of mirth, slapping of thighs, wiping of eyes, and a couple of sly glances at the tall bearded guy in their midst who clearly had no sense of humour. At that moment I felt very alone. I knew Downing was *the* science college, but I certainly hadn't expected anything like this. I mimed that I had a hearing problem, and ate my dinner quickly.

The next evening proved to be momentous. Setting out early for Hall, to give myself a better chance of spotting chemists before it was too late, I half-recognised someone who turned out to have been a fellow pupil at Clifton. Martin Davies-Jones was two years younger than me, so at school we had only a nodding acquaintance (more than that and the police would have intervened) but we were soon chatting away and he in turn introduced me to his new friends, Alan Hutchison and Tony Robinson, and we sat down to dinner together: four "nice" public school boys (they were more middle-middle class than me) in sports jackets, speaking standard middle-class English—

and none of us chemists. We got on so well that the four of us finished up sharing digs for our last two years. And this transformation
in my social fortunes occurred on my second day!

In the interests of historical balance I feel I should mention that
Alan remembers this quite differently. He is sure that the first time
he set eyes on me was when Martin brought him over to my room
to introduce us, and that as they looked in through my ground-floor
window, they saw me trying to wriggle under my bed. They thought
this weird as they had no idea that I had a pet hamster. Since I had
been at Cambridge at least two weeks before I purchased the hamster in the street market, and I had *certainly* met Alan by then, I dis-
count his version.

Now I settled down to study the five subjects that made up my
law degree. Two of them concerned Roman law, the idea being that
we would broaden our understanding if we gained a bird's eye view
of an entire legal system. And I have to say that some of what I discovered about the Romans reflected impressively on them: it struck me,
for example, that putting people guilty of parricide into a sack with a
viper, a cockerel and a dog, and then throwing them into the Tiber,
seemed very likely to deter others, and was certainly less expensive
than imprisonment. English constitutional law I found fascinating.
I was intrigued to learn how the rules for running the country had
developed over the centuries, and it occurs to me now that earlier
parliamentarians understood conflict of interest, and the concept of
checks and balances, better than they do these days. International law
seemed to promise a glamorous jet-set existence, especially to someone who had not yet been outside England. And finally, there was
English criminal law, which was great fun, even without the vipers.
Altogether there were about ten lectures each week and a tutorial
every fortnight in each subject when we had to hand in an essay—so
maybe twenty essays a term in all, just over a couple a week.

This was quite manageable. The trouble was . . . I was conscientious. I could have arranged, around my studies, an interesting and

even slightly adventurous life, but I didn't. I kick myself now when I think how other undergraduates took their Cambridge life by the scruff of its neck and spent their time doing what really mattered to them. (Stephen Fry, for example, never went to a lecture; he just read, and appeared in thirty-six plays.) But I trudged off every day to attend every required lecture, at least half of which were deeply uninspiring. And I sat there dutifully taking notes, trying not to miss anything.

One of our professors described a lecture as "a mystical process by which the notes on the pad of the lecturer pass on to the pad of the student, without passing through the mind of either." It would certainly have been so much more efficient and absorbing if our lecturers had provided full notes for us, and had then discussed them. There could have been real interaction, question and answer, even argument, instead of dictation. But this never happened, and my ingrained meekness meant that it took me two terms before I dared to drop even the ghastly Whalley-Tooker, whose ramblings reminded me of King Lear on Valium. I also took essays far too seriously, and wasted a lot of time on polishing them, though they didn't teach me much. All in all, my diligence gave me a false sense of not having much spare time to explore Cambridge life.

But before I fell into this pattern of thinking I did at least go to the Societies Fair, which was held at the Corn Market on the first weekend of term. I was astonished at the variety of activities on offer: there was a multitude of stands manned by keen young undergraduates all trying to persuade you to sign up for potholing, bridge, bell ringing, drama, the Young Christians, sky diving, brass rubbing, water sports, paranormal studies, martial arts, the Union, photography, the Marxists-Leninists, taxidermy . . .

As I drifted around, feeling slightly overwhelmed and not at all bold, I had at the back of my mind (and really quite a long way back) the word "Footlights." Not that I had any real idea of what that meant. It was just that when I had done various entertainments at Clifton, a couple of masters had said, "So, when you get to Cambridge, you will be joining the Footlights, then." I knew therefore that it must all be something to do with humour.

Nevertheless, when I spotted the Footlights stand and a couple of friendly fellows sitting there, smiling invitingly, it took me some time to wrestle down a strong sense of impending embarrassment. That done, I pretended I had suddenly seen the stand, strolled over, smiled as best I could, and said, "Ah! Hello! The Footlights! I was wondering if I . . . might . . . possibly be . . . interested in . . ."

"Of course!" one of them cried, handing me a leaflet. "Do you sing?"

"*Sing?*" I thought. "What are they talking about? Sing? No, I don't sing. I am the worst singer in the world. Mr. Hickley had me removed from singing classes at school because I was so bloody terrible. There is *nothing* that I do worse. Why, in the bowels of Christ, are they asking me if I sing? What on earth has that got to do with being funny?"

"Not *really*," I responded.

"Never mind," said the other Footlights representative. "Do you dance?"

"*Dance?*" My head began to swim.

"Yes, dance," he repeated.

"No," I said. "If I wanted to dance, I would probably be standing at the Classical Ballet stand, or the Modern Dance stand, or the Ballroom Dancing stand, or the Tap Dancing stand, or the Morris Dancing stand, or the Dancing for Chemists stand."

Well, all right, I didn't say this. What I actually said was, "No, I am not very good at dancing. Sorry!"

They nodded kindly. "So . . . what do you do?"

Embarrassment, confusion, humiliation, indignation, all welled up.

"I try to make people laugh!" I blurted out, and I ran for it.

And that was the end of my show-business career.

As far as I knew. Or cared! It may seem odd, but the whole grisly episode soon faded from my memory. I had no sense that I had missed out on something important, that some talent lurking within me was yearning for expression.

After all, I was going to be a lawyer—apparently, though I couldn't remember exactly how the decision had been taken. Law, then, had to come first. And law seemed to be a lot about arguing, about putting your case or dismantling somebody else's, so maybe learning to debate would help me. Accordingly I went along to the Cambridge Union to see a debate from the balcony, and watched as a series of very young men, aged between nineteen and twenty-two, stood up and pretended to be fifty-five. They all wore suits with waistcoats, they all tucked their thumbs into their waistcoat pockets, and they all spoke a weird, oratorical bombastic language that was utterly unlike normal speech. Clearly, they were trying to create the impression of being promising politicians, yet they had no idea how ridiculous they seemed, all behaving in the same manner when, to the rest of us, they were so obviously inflated, self-satisfied, slow-witted duds. The gap between the impression they were trying to create and the way their fellow students actually viewed them was truly extraordinary. It would have been even more astounding had I known that several of these fat-heads would finish up in John Major's Cabinet. I'll say it again. The very group that was most disliked and belittled at Cambridge in the early '60s was running the country thirty years later. Or sort of running it.

So, since the Cambridge Union was rubbish, what else was there? Well, the one activity that my consciousness had been shaped to accept was sport. So I signed up to play college soccer, took part in a trial game, and made a small impression. As it happens, I wasn't bad at soccer—I had good control, I could trick an opponent and sometimes thread a nice pass. Playing inside left, I even created the occasional goal. The trouble was that I was far too tall, embarrassingly skinny, a bit slow on the turn, physically quite weak, nowhere near fit enough—and I couldn't shoot.

Despite these handicaps, though, I was *just* good enough to get a place in the team and so became one of two "Southerners" in the Downing XI. A "Southerner" was defined as someone born south of the river Trent, and I was regarded by the rest of the team—with tolerant affection—as "posh." This was a surprise to an insurance salesman's son, and I wasn't quite sure how to react.

You see, in the early 1960s Britain was so ridden with class distinction that it coloured every aspect of life, though generally in an unspoken way. (Ten years later, when we were making *Monty Python*, we assumed that the whole system was on its way out, that it was fading away, but the fact that it is still alive and well today suggests we were quite deluded.) Take money, for example. In the '60s, money was . . . well, vulgar. At least to talk about it was vulgar, and any blatant attempt to acquire large quantities of it was crude and aesthetically offensive. My friend Tony Jay once summed it up: it was all right to *have* money; it was just *getting* it that was vulgar.

It's also almost impossible to convey the attitude then to the world of business. Businessmen (there weren't many women) were regarded as peripheral, half-educated creatures whose academic failures had forced them to earn a living in the dull, second-rate world of commerce. Interestingly, nobody resented their making piles of money, because it was felt that this was the one compensation the world offered them for undertaking such stultifying activities. In my entire three years at Cambridge, I met only one undergraduate who intended to enter the world of business: he was going into soap powder so that he could retire at forty. It was fascinating to see how the aristocratic attitude to "trade" had infected the public schools, and even brainwashed little plebeian gits like me.

What did matter at Cambridge was professional reputation. There were the grand jobs—like being a surgeon, or a barrister, or a professor—and there were the more mundane occupations, like being a solicitor or an accountant or a general practitioner. The aim in life was to become very good at whichever category of job you went for, and to earn the respect of your colleagues, and enough money to lead a very comfortable life. It was also vital to have a few cultural interests outside your work. The aim was to be "well rounded," educated, accomplished, well informed and comfortably off.

My position in all this was a delicately poised one. I knew that the real toffs would never accept me as a kosher English gentleman, but because my parents had spent their savings on sending me to Clifton, I was at least able to pass myself off as middle-middle class if I wanted to, which I eventually did all the time in the roles I was acting. Casting agents never thought of me as Mexican bandit-chief material; nor did cheerful cockney or Slovenian hit man roles come my way. No, only the respectable and even slightly grand professionals. If I wanted to play anything else, I had to write it myself. And I could see no harm in trying to turn myself into a fake English gentleman, because I had incorporated my father's view of gentlemanly behaviour. I recalled being told stories about guests at royal banquets who had picked up the "wrong" fork, whereupon the king had done likewise to avoid embarrassing them, and all the other guests had followed suit. And I was touched by this. It was nothing to do with snobbery. I read once that the journalist Auberon Waugh reproached a guest who had taken off his jacket and put it on the back of his chair, telling him it was "not gentlemanly." I thought it was not gentlemanly to have pointed this out.

I saw little friction between the classes at Cambridge. I met very few of the upper classes, but when I did, I realised how different their lives were. They genuinely liked chasing things and shooting them and hooking them out of the water and asphyxiating them. Death seemed the inevitable result of all their entertainments, despite their excellent manners. The working-class students—they were more students than undergraduates—seemed, by contrast, a little less outgoing and took work much more seriously than my upper-middle-class friends. Few if any of them regarded university as any kind of finishing school. The scientists were especially formidable in this regard, preferring their chemistry labs to ordinary habitations. And if the average public school boy was not a natural dancer, the chemists were unnatural dancers. They looked as though they had borrowed their bodies for the weekend and had not yet figured out how to work them. One tall, red-haired chemist with half-mast trousers moved like a Bournemouth proto-skater even when he was just crossing the quad. Alan, Martin and I would watch out for him, and were once treated to the sight of him completely losing the knack of walking, and falling in a heap on the ground.

The only slight awkwardness that existed between the classes seemed to be between the public school boys and the grammar school boys. The latter were just as bright, but the fact that their parents had not had to pay school fees drew attention to the fact that they came from less affluent homes, and they could seem a little ill at ease socially. As I got to know them, they all told me the same thing: that most public school boys had a confidence that they felt they lacked, and so, in social situations, they often felt ill at ease. They wondered how the public school chaps had acquired their sense of self-assurance, and I certainly couldn't tell them. I guessed that some people took their position in the social hierarchy so seriously it made them feel superior and act accordingly. Since most of the really confident people I met were actually rather stupid, it was very easy for them to think that it was class rather than intelligence that mattered. Self-confidence seemed to me more mimicry than anything else and I suggested visiting Clifton Zoo to watch the leaders in a group of baboons, and learn from them: make your gestures slow and deliberate; cultivate a deeper voice; appear casual at all times; eschew all rapid movements. That was all you had to do to look confident. I also knew that I could "do" confident, and it helped enormously socially that I appeared to be able to fake it no matter how insecure, anxious, or inferior I actually felt. And I did feel insecure. It was the Bartlett effect: the sense that I should be formidably well informed about everything, when in reality I was quite ignorant. Since I believed that knowing lots of facts was a sign of superior intelligence, my life was one long struggle to suggest (subtly) that I knew a lot.

And then, after just a few weeks, I had an epiphany. I was talking to a very well-informed fellow called Peregrine something-or-other, and nodding knowledgeably, and smiling wryly at I knew not what, when on an impulse I suddenly said, "I don't know about that. Will you tell me about it?"

There was a moment of silence, but the ceiling did not fall in. Peregrine something-or-other did not slap me contemptuously with the back of his hand, or spit in my face. Instead, he visibly brightened and proceeded to give me a thoroughly good explanation of what he had been talking about. He enjoyed explaining it, and I enjoyed understanding it, and he clearly liked me better for having given him the opportunity to display his learning. Instead of humiliation, then, I had initiated a profitable transaction. It was a revelation, and I found it such a liberation, and a relief, to be able to abandon that phoney omniscient posturing.

The other main cause of my social insecurity, my painful inability to talk to women as though they were from the same planet, lay a little ahead, since I was seldom within earshot of anything female in my law lectures. There were, in fact, just three women in amongst 200 men and, overall, eighteen all-male colleges to set alongside the all-female Girton and Newnham.

So my social life was very uneventful: the odd curry, the occasional film, regular coffee with a few friends, and now and again, a party.

At one of these I got drunk for the first time. My old Clifton friend Adrian Upton asked me over to his birthday party and met me with a challenge—to down a glass of Yugoslavian Riesling in one go. Which I did, thinking myself dead cool. Some fifteen minutes later, he repeated the challenge. Down the hatch! Soon I was feeling unaccountably happy, then a little dizzy but even happier, for Adrian had spiked my drinks. Two-thirds of each glass of Riesling had been gin.

God now provided some cabaret. The son of the Secretary General of the United Nations started quarrelling with Adrian, and blows began to fly. But not to land, because Adrian and he were standing so far apart that contact was made only when, in the course of frantically windmilling at each other, their knuckles occasionally brushed. It was wonderful.

The sight of such frantic aggression producing such tiny results struck me as epoch-shatteringly funny. Add to this the fact that one combatant was the son of the man who, above all others, was trying to reduce the amount of fighting in the world and the punch-up seemed to have all the appearance of a divinely scripted farce. I laughed so much that I made a spectacle of myself. This annoyed the combatants, and the speed of their windmilling became even more frantic—and *funnier*. At which point the room began to revolve, nausea, panic and regret took over, and I was forced to focus on survival.

I have never got really drunk since.

My Cambridge life now settled into a routine, and I became a rather dull fellow. Martin Davies-Jones says he always thought of me as "odd." Well, I was six feet four inches tall, extremely thin and bearded, so I certainly looked odd. And I had a hamster, which was unusual, and a strange wheezing laugh, and I spent quite a lot of time in my own company (and the hamster's). But odd? No. *Dull.*

And then in an attempt to liven me up, fate intervened. Alan Hutchison happened to bump into an old friend from Radley College who was on the Footlights committee. He asked Alan if he was interested in such things, and Alan said he wasn't particularly but he had a friend who had done shows at school, and somehow Alan and I finished up in the Footlights clubroom, chatting with this guy. This time, there was no mention of singing and dancing.

From our point of view, the main attraction of the Footlights was the clubroom itself. It was relaxed and comfortable, with a tiny bar and some lunch tables and sofas, and at one end a small permanent stage with curtains and lights. But what really excited us was that it was plumb in the middle of Cambridge—the perfect place to pass time between lectures or to grab a quick and incredibly cheap lunch.

To gain membership, one had to do an audition piece at one of the "Smoking Concerts" that were produced every month by a couple of the senior members. These were very friendly events, for the simple reason that because every member of the audience was expected to do a turn at some point in the evening, it was in everyone's interest to keep the atmosphere jolly and encouraging.

So Alan and I trudged back to Downing and sat down to figure out an audition piece. After discarding several ideas, we hit on the notion idea of doing a mock television news broadcast. Fifty years later a more hackneyed and overdone format could not be imagined, but in early 1961 it was quite unusual.

To understand how this could conceivably be the case, you have to grasp just how deferential, stuffy, compulsively super-polite and excruciatingly cautious British culture was at that time. I can recall a brief TV interview from the late '50s where a journalist, asking the Chancellor of the Exchequer about the budget he was about to present, came up with the following convolutedly polite question: "I wonder, sir, if you would be prepared to say a few words about what you are about to reveal to the House of Commons?" It was like a head boy at a major public school doing a pretend-spontaneous interview with his headmaster. And this reverential attitude towards authority extended to the BBC itself, where seriousness of purpose easily toppled into pomposity. So for us to send up the evening news was ever so slightly *daring*.

Drawing on the fact that the newsreaders at the time read the news from sheets of paper, rather than any form of prompter, the first thing Alan and I wrote went as follows:

> Good evening. Here is the news. (*Newsreader stops and peers at sheet of paper.*) I'm sorry, here *are* the news. The Queen . . .

The newsreader smiles beatifically, lays that sheet of paper reverentially aside and turns to the next sheet.

   . . . and Prince Philip (*another ethereal smile*) together visited
     Balmoral . . .

I remember we included a few topical items, one of them inspired by the news that General de Gaulle had just blocked Britain's entry into the Common Market:

> At a moving mid-Channel ceremony, the traditional
> Anglo-French *entente cordiale* was rekindled when President de Gaulle and Prime Minister Harold Macmillan
> opened the escalators connecting the French Channel
> Bridge to the English Channel Tunnel.

Transplants were also in the news:

> Mr. Gerald Dawkins, who in a major transplant operation last year received the heart, liver, lungs and spleen
> of a pig, is now completely recovered. He is back to his
> former weight of eleven stone, he takes two brisk walks a
> day and costs eight shillings a pound.

Then there was a long final item about a Cornish mine disaster, sending up the serious tone that the BBC adopted when tragedy was in the air.

> This evening, prospects of a successful rescue are rapidly diminishing. Nevertheless, whilst any hope remains,
> operations are being continued by floodlight. Betsy, the
> eight-year-old collie belonging to the Clark family of
> Mabshurst in Cornwall, who has been trapped on a ledge
> a hundred and twenty feet down a disused tin mine, is

weakening, despite quantities of brandy and rabbit lowered to her. Earlier, Mr. Clark and his son Ronald tragically fell to their deaths during the descent, when within
barking distance of the dog. Julia, Mr. Clark's teenage
daughter, then descended, and actually reached the ledge;
but fell to her death when bitten by the dog. Mrs. Clark
(thirty-nine), the one surviving member of the family,
said before attempting the perilous descent this evening:
"Inhuman people will say this is madness, but I know it is
what my husband would have wished."

This was about as far as satire went in early 1961.

Alan was to play the newsreader, so I needed my own piece to
perform, and I decided to use a monologue I had written when I was
still at school. I had stolen the idea for it from a television performer
called Professor Stanley Unwin, who managed to talk complete nonsense that somehow sounded just like English. The first time I heard
him I became so hysterical with mirth that I frightened my parents;
further exposure to Unwin's jibberish had the same alarming impact. (I had a similar reaction when I first heard Charlie Chaplin's
fake German in *The Great Dictator*.) I didn't understand why this kind
of nonsense so convulsed me, but I watched Unwin obsessively and
slowly figured out how he did it—which was to take certain syllables from very ordinary words and mix them up with syllables from
other equally common words, so that the sounds were totally familiar English ones, but the overall effect quite meaningless. His version of "Goldilocks and the Three Bears," for example, began: "Once
apollytito and Goldiloppers set out in the deep dark of the forry. She
was carry a basket with buttere-flabe and cheesy flavour."

I have at times suspected that what I seem to laugh at most are the
things that frighten me. I find anger, like Basil Fawlty's, hilarious—
provided it is ineffectual, as real anger might be too disturbing.
I'm terrified of violence, yet I shout with laughter at great slapstick

comedy that threatens people's physical safety (think of Harold Lloyd or Chaplin, or of Eddie Murphy crossing the freeway in Steve Martin's *Bowfinger*). My sense of humour has been described as cruel (mainly by BBC executives), yet I am almost obsessively appalled by torture. And I howl at absurdity and nonsense when my deepest psychic fear is a sense of meaninglessness. Am I trying to diminish a fear by laughing at it, and thereby belittling it, reducing its threat?

So, anyway . . . once I had worked out how Stanley Unwin produced his strangely convincing gobbledegook, it was easy to scribble out another example for the Footlights audition. Of course, it was an absolute bugger to learn, but I decided to present the piece as a scientific lecture, which allowed me to glance at my notes whenever I thought I was about to panic.

The show we were auditioning for was being produced by two experienced third-year Footlighters and they encouraged me to do another idea, which I had stolen from a BBC radio show. It was a parody of the last two minutes of a typical BBC detective thriller, when all the suspects gather together and the detective explains the whole plot. The idea that I pinched was that in order to make the plot exposition less boring, the detective delivered it during a final hand-to-hand combat with the villain, who himself added plot clarifications at appropriate moments between punches. The dialogue was easy to reproduce:

> INSPECTOR: So when Henderson went to the antique shop,
>   to get the map from Colonel Harding (*whack! Aaagh!*),
>   he happened to see Lady Pendleton emerging from the
>   Chinese laundry. Take that! (*splat!*)
> VILLAIN: Exactly, Inspector, so Henderson thought . . .
>   etc., etc.

I managed to persuade Adrian Upton, fresh from his recent combat with the son of the Secretary General of the United Nations, to perform the fight with me, which involved much enjoyable rehearsal, and on the night of the performance all three sketches went well and the three of us were elected members of the Footlights.

If it seems that I have taken an age to relate to you some trivial auditionings for a mere Footlights Smoker, it's because all three sketches turned out to have an unexpected afterlife. The newsreading sketch was performed later that year in the annual Footlights revue, and then again on *That Was The Week That Was*, when David Frost read it as the final item in the last show of the first series. The Stanley Unwin rip-off has become a standard part of my cabaret routine, last performed on my one-man show's UK tour in 2011, fifty years after its first appearance at the Footlights clubroom. And the plot-explication fight appeared in the 1962 Footlights revue (the first in which I performed), then on *That Was The Week That Was,* and then again, rewritten and expanded, in the 1963 Footlights revue, which played in the West End for five months and finished up on Broadway in 1964.

However, if you think my first Smoker appearances seemed to bode well, they didn't. My next few suggestions were so feeble they were turned down, and the couple that were accepted for performance only just avoided being embarrassing. This was probably because I was trying to think up funny ideas of my own, instead of stealing a good one from writers who knew what they were doing.

The fact is that it is exceedingly difficult to write really good comedy. Those who can do it possess a very rare talent. Of course, there are a few writers who can think up decent jokes. A few more can do parody well. But the number who can invent an original comedy situation, and build that situation in a convincing but unpredictable way, and, above all, get the emotional development of the characters right . . . is infinitesimally small.

On the other hand, there exist vast hordes who can write bad comedy, and they do so in immense quantities, entirely uninhibited by any awareness of just how atrocious it is. At the beginning of my career, I often used to read scripts that I had been sent by unknown writers, and it seemed to take me about twenty years before I realised that they were all, always, awful.

So if I may give a word of advice to any young writer who, despite the odds, wants to take a shot at being funny, it is this:

Steal.

Steal an idea that you know is good, and try to reproduce it in a setting that you know and understand. It will become sufficiently different from the original because *you* are writing it, and by basing it on something good, you will be learning some of the rules of good writing as you go along. Great artists may merely be "influenced by" other artists, but comics "steal" and then conceal their loot.

Still, even if I couldn't come up with any decent ideas in these early days, I could at least use the Footlights clubroom. What a delight that was! I found there the nicest bunch of fellows I had come across. Friendly, funny, good-natured, from a wide mix of subjects, bright without being show-offs—a complete contrast to the occasional group of actors who would from time to time infiltrate the club. Invariably dressed in black leather jackets and jeans, the actors would gather around a table and sit, leaning forward, carrying on intense soul-searching discussions about "motivation" or "alienation," which made me anxious because I didn't know what those words meant, and felt rather rattled by the sheer intensity of it all.

Looking back, I now see why the actors were so different. It was because they all intended to become professionals. The Footlights chaps, by contrast, had no intention at all of making careers in the chancy world of show business: they were all headed for the law, medicine, teaching, advertising, and they took part in Footlights activities for the sheer fun of it.[1]

---

[1] Well, in 1961, anyway. Within five years all that had changed. Because the 1963 revue *Cambridge Circus* was so successful and every member of the London cast became part of "The Profession," students started coming to Cambridge with

So, I was far more concerned about the exams I was to take in June. This was no doubt in part because I had no sense of what level of knowledge was expected by the examiners and this gave rise to a lurking sense of panic. My worry about whether I was doing enough work was neatly summed up by a cartoon in a Cambridge magazine showing two undergraduates sunbathing by the Cam. One is saying, "If only we had done some work in the winter, there wouldn't be this mad panic now." In my case the anxiety increased, but my hours of study didn't.

As I panicked a letter arrived, inviting me to audition for the 1961 Footlights revue. I was initially quite excited, until I realised that this was a mere formality extended to every member. I turned up at the Arts Theatre nevertheless, only to be asked to *sing* "Mama's Little Baby Loves Shortnin' Bread" and to *dance* the cha-cha-cha. A sickening sense of déjà vu descended on me. I felt like those poor French infantrymen in the First World War, who went over the top and ran towards the German guns, bleating like sheep.

Fortunately it was all over in a few seconds.

But there was an unexpected award for my humiliation, because as I stood after coming off stage in a state of shock, a tall chap waiting in the queue for his punishment offered a few words of consolation, and then minutes later I was having coffee with my main writing partner for the next twenty years.

My first impression of Graham Chapman was of physical strength. He was slightly shorter than me, but much tougher, in the lean, angular way of a sportsman. He did not surprise me when he said he was a medical student who climbed mountains and played rugby football. He was wearing a rather hairy tweed jacket and heavy brogues, and he soon lit up a pipe. He seemed dead butch, and slightly taciturn. We chatted for a time, had a couple of laughs, and then drifted on our

---

the specific intent of using the Footlights as a gateway to the Wonderful World of Light Entertainment.

way. The only clear memory I have is that I didn't really connect with him, and consequently didn't feel I particularly liked him.

Exam panic now peaked. One evening I was looking so depressed that Martin Davies-Jones picked up the old-fashioned gas ring on which we could boil a saucepan, and offered it to me. I didn't even smile. In the event, though, my fears turned out to have been misplaced. The exam papers were not bad, and all the worrying proved to have been a waste of time. The problem was that I carried around with me a tendency to feel that other people's respect for me would vanish if what I did was second rate. And while I accept that this "perfectionism" is likely to stimulate the production of better work, it doesn't, unfortunately, go hand in hand with a relaxed and happy attitude to life. This is especially the case in comedy, because if you are trying to make people laugh, and failing, it is so intensely embarrassing. There is no escape. As my daughter Camilla once said, "Being a comedian has a lot in common with being a matador. The feedback is so instant you can't argue about it."

After the exams I went to see the Footlights revue that I had auditioned for. I was impressed by the professional sheen to its presentation, and I liked the individual performers. David Frost in particular stood out, and I felt a thrill when he read out some of our news items, the "Cornish Mining Disaster" going particularly well. I had occasionally seen David in the clubroom. He was obviously a big star in university circles, and I had been very impressed by his friendliness towards us small fry. It's strange to think that he would become the single strongest force shaping my career.

AND NOW I headed back to St. Peter's to help Mr. Tolson out with a medium-sized teaching emergency. Apparently, a teacher had resigned rather suddenly and the school needed someone to fill in for the last six weeks of term. From my point of view, the timing was perfect.

When I arrived back at St. Peter's, I was touched by the warmth of my reception by the Tolsons and the staff with whom I had been teaching just a year before. After dinner Mr. Tolson took me into his study and invited me to sit down. Then he slumped in his chair and revealed the circumstances of the emergency that had necessitated my recall. Apparently, he explained, before the summer term had started he had needed to find a new teacher, and, having interviewed several applicants, had opted for one with particularly good qualifications. After a few days, though, it became clear that this new teacher was a bit odd: he wore strange, almost inexplicable pieces of clothing; he revealed startling areas of ignorance; he occasionally let out disagreeing sounds during church service; and, what seemed to worry Mr. Tolson most, he insisted on holding a six-foot piece of bamboo while umpiring cricket matches. Everyone had tried to be tolerant, but there had been unease.

Then, one night, Mr. Tolson was woken by shouting. Two men had gained entrance to the school grounds—two very angry men—who alleged that the teacher had been getting up to no good in the local town and that their sons had been involved. There was a public fuss, and the name of St. Peter's School was mentioned. Mr. Tolson felt that he had been guilty of grave professional misconduct.

I liked Mr. Tolson so much—he was such a decent man—that I tried to defend him. "But, sir," I said, "you said he had excellent qualifications."

Mr. Tolson looked at me. "I never bothered to check them, John. You see, when he came for his interview he was wearing an MCC tie." I nearly laughed out loud, but then I felt sad for him: that his deference to a much-hallowed institution—the home of English cricket—had let him down so badly. He was devastated. The rest of the term, though, passed off pleasantly, and a few weeks later I left St. Peter's for the third and last time.

I used to think that the world was basically sane with patches of madness here and there which would recede as rationality and good jokes pushed their boundaries ever inwards. Now I have the opposite view entirely. But one of the patches of sanity that I treasure is my memory of St. Peter's, where people seemed to be doing a useful job in a conscientious way, where money seemed quite secondary, and learning, good manners and good sportsmanship were the values that guided its inhabitants. It was, as Mr. Bartlett would have said, highly civilised.

7

I spent the rest of that summer living with my parents (who had now moved to Totnes in Devon), loafing around, reading and playing cricket like some 1920s aristocrat, before returning to Cambridge in September. (It never occurred to me to take a job: my "work" was at university.) But before I talk about my second year I need to backtrack a little to mention something that had happened the previous term. A very boring something, but, for me, enormously significant.

Towards the end of my first year, I had suddenly remembered that in a few months' time Downing would cease to provide me with a room in college, and that I had better start looking for digs for the rest of my undergraduate studies at Cambridge. I strolled off to the relevant university office and asked what advice they could give me. And the advice was that I should have started looking about three months earlier, when everyone else had been, because there was now nothing left less than about thirty minutes' bike ride from the centre of town. The moment of horror that hit me then was truly unforgettable: a vision of endless Sisyphean cycling through the Fens—and I couldn't even ride a bike.

And then: "Oh!" said a nice friendly lady in the office. "What was that call we got this morning?" She checked her notes and told me that a Mrs. Risely, who offered digs in the middle of town, had phoned to say that she had just had a row with Queens' College, had told them that their undergraduates would never be allowed to stay in her rooms again, and wanted the university office to know that they were therefore vacant and available once more.

Ten minutes later, I was shaking Mrs. Risely by the hand. Not only were her rooms in the middle of town, but they were *right smack* in the middle of town, in the old part, about five minutes' walk from the Law School. What's more—and here is the spooky, coinciden-tal, fateful, omen-packed bit—just two minutes from the Footlights clubroom! It was a gift from God! And even better—how could it be better?—the rooms were for four students, so I was able to take my three great Downing pals Alan, Martin and Tony into the centre of town with me.

With all that sorted, I was able to return to Cambridge that au-tumn and settle into the easiest and most convenient of routines: a couple of law lectures, a stroll back to digs, a bit of study, round the corner to the Footlights clubroom for a cheap lunch, a cheerful chat with other members, back to digs, write an essay, take a break, din-ner, wander back to digs, a couple of hours' study and over to the clubroom again for two packets of cheese and onion crisps, and a couple of pineapple juices with the most relaxed, good-natured and funny guys in the whole university.

On my first visit of the term to the Footlights I saw a few faces I knew, and several I didn't. Spotting a group huddled around a no-ticeboard, I strolled over and discovered that they were looking at a list of that year's Footlights committee. To my amazement, my name was on it. To several other people's amazement, so were theirs. We hardly recognised each other from the previous year and yet we had all been selected. I'd been made registrar: nobody knew what it meant so I assumed it was not onerous.

The reason for our sudden promotions was that every single se-nior Footlighter had left in June, and before the last one departed he had written down any names he could remember from the years below and assigned them jobs on the committee. So the October 1961 Footlights committee were, in effect, all new boys. I vaguely remem-

bered the new president, Robert Atkins, who had done a couple of
funny sketches in Smokers, and I recognised Humphrey Barclay, who
had actually been in the show with David Frost (Humphrey was the
only one from our first-year intake to get into the cast). But otherwise
we had to get to know each other virtually from scratch. This actually
had a very positive effect. Because there was no hierarchy there was
also a very informal and democratic atmosphere. So I began to spend
time with Graham Chapman (I must have forgotten that I didn't like
him), Tony Hendra (a flamboyant Catholic, rather intellectual but
wonderfully disrespectful), Tim Brooke-Taylor, David Hatch, Humphrey, and a cluster of others, most of whom seemed to be at Pembroke College, just down the road from Downing. The Pembroke
contingent started inviting me to have dinner there, and after a couple
of months I realised that the Pembroke dinner staff assumed I was a
member of the college. I therefore dined there scot-free most evenings
for the next two years. In fact, I saw so little of Downing that when I
did go in for a meal during my last year, I was challenged by the bur-
sar on the grounds that I was not a member of the college.

I grew to adore Pembroke: it was a very pretty college, not too
big and with exquisite lawns. It also had a warm, welcoming atmosphere. And it was at the Pembroke Smokers that I first came across
Graeme Garden and Bill Oddie, with whom I was later to do over a
hundred radio shows. I was also introduced to Eric Idle, who proved
to be extremely funny and who treated me with remarkable respect.
Well, I am four years older . . .

Life settled back into a routine, but a far more enjoyable one than
I had experienced in my first year, partly because of the companion-
ship at my digs and at the Footlights, and partly because I now got
down to work properly, managing my work schedule better and so
finding everything—contract law, torts, constitutional law—easier
to handle, and therefore more interesting and enjoyable. I was also
becoming more confident, for all my naivety, especially as there were
no women to feel awkward and clueless around.

I started trying to write more sketches for the Smokers, and found myself collaborating with Graham Chapman. Our first meeting hadn't been particularly auspicious, but this time around I increasingly felt myself drawn to someone with the same sense of humour. When you begin to write comedy, the biggest worry is simply: is this *funny*? Writing with a partner ensures you get priceless feedback, and Graham and I worked together well: we found each other funny and when we did laugh, we really laughed, Graham screeching and me wheezing. We did not have a lot in common otherwise: his dad was a policeman, and he had been to a grammar school where he had been head boy, but we had similarly uneasy relationships with our mothers, which later on provided us with a lot of material. At this early stage we didn't produce anything very good, except perhaps one parody of a sermon. Graham, like me, carried a grudge against the nonsense we had been fed at school in the name of religion and we had huge enjoyment writing a ponderous homily in which a vicar who begins by reading out the text about Lot's wife being turned into a pillar of salt suddenly *realises* what an extraordinary thing this was to happen, and then speculates about God's choice of condiment. When Graham performed it, it worked well, especially the punchline, delivered after a very long and puzzled pause—"Hymn 42!" Graham later worked with the author of *The Hitchhiker's Guide to the Galaxy*, Douglas Adams: did our sermon inspire him when he pondered the answer to life, the universe and everything?

I wrote some stuff on my own, including one sketch that made fun of the way broadcasters tried to enliven astronomical statistics. Talking about a star called Regella, I wrote: "It is a very bright star, over 360 billion times brighter than an ordinary 40-watt bulb. It is also very large. If you imagine this orange [at this point I held one up and showed it around] is the size of the dome of St. Paul's Cathedral, then Regella is 3.2 trillion times the size of the Isle of Wight. And to give you some idea how large 3.2 trillion is . . ." etc., etc., etc. Two Smokers were produced each term. They were perfectly enjoyable, but I think I was aware that there was nothing in them of outstanding quality.

Which is why what happened next was of such startling importance.

On Saturday, April 26, Alan Hutchison came back to our digs, waving a couple of tickets for that afternoon's matinee at the Arts Theatre, which he had heard was "really good." And three hours later I found myself watching the funniest, most brilliant and utterly joyful performance I have ever seen in my life. *Beyond the Fringe,* with Peter Cook, Jonathan Miller, Dudley Moore and Alan Bennett, featured four comic geniuses so hilarious that I experienced a reaction I have never had since: as each sketch ended, I felt a pang of disappointment, immediately replaced by exhilaration as the lights came back up to reveal a different combination of the four about to start a new sketch.

The material itself was so astonishingly fresh, not least because it made fun of major authority figures in a way we simply hadn't seen before. Peter Cook's impersonation of a doddering old Harold Macmillan ("I went to Germany to see the Chancellor, Herr . . . Herr . . . herr and there") was hilarious in any case, but it was also so rude, so contemptuous, that the sheer shock of it forced laughter of a phenomenal volume. When they played Civil Defence officials explaining the steps the government was going to take to defend the British people against nuclear attack, and Dudley, from the audience, remarked that the four-minute warning did not give people much time, and Peter Cook retorted that he "would remind doubters that some people in this great country of ours can run a mile in four minutes," not only was there a side-splitting howl, but the government's defence policy seemed to collapse at the same time. And Alan Bennett's mock sermon brought a kind of screaming laughter I had never heard before: there was hysteria in it, the hysteria of liberation as the audience realised they would never, ever, have to listen respectfully again to the kind of bone-headed rubbish we were all so familiar with. "Life," his clergyman said, "is rather like opening a tin of sardines. We all of us are looking for the key. And I wonder how many of you here tonight have wasted years of your lives looking behind the kitchen dressers of this life for that key. I know I have."

There was pure absurdity, too: Dudley's one-legged man auditioning for the role of Tarzan; Peter Cook's astonishing monologues, which had a kind of insane logic (Jonathan called it "schizophrenic") that totally unhinged audiences despite its thoughtful pedantic energy; and for me the funniest scene of all, where the cast played four bland, half-witted, overconfident public school boys in a restaurant unable to locate their wallets—a sketch almost without words, just consisting of the waffling noises such people make—during which I discovered I had my scarf in my mouth and was chewing on it: ordinary laughter could not on its own release the joyous energy that had taken over my body.

I have one final memory from two hours of utter comedy bliss—a moment of the most exquisite embarrassment, as Jonathan and Peter told the audience that while they came from good families and had public school educations, Alan and Dudley were from the working class. Nevertheless, they said, it was proving to be an enjoyable and stimulating experience to be working with them and treating them as equals. Alan now pointed out that while Dudley and he were indeed working class, some of the audience might not realise that Jonathan Miller was a Jew, and that Alan himself would rather be working class than a Jew. Dudley mused how awful it would be to be working class and a Jew, at which point, Jonathan interrupted to say that he wasn't really a Jew, "Just Jew-ish. I don't go the whole hog, you know." I'd never seen an audience reaction like the one this produced: half of them howled at such prejudices being discussed in this casual, factual manner; the other half froze with gut-wrenching horror, thereby providing the first half of the audience with more to laugh at, albeit in a slightly sneaky way.

What a show! Off they went to London to launch the "Official

Opening of the Satirical Sixties," as Michael Frayn calls it, and to earn phenomenal success.

MEANWHILE, BACK at the Footlights, we were in the first stages of producing our annual revue, *Double Take*. Our director had, by some mysterious process, been chosen: a friendly, shaggy chap called Trevor Nunn, who had apparently produced several successful plays for the university drama society. After a few anxious hours, he announced the cast of the 1962 revue: Humphrey Barclay, Robert Atkins, Graham Chapman, Tim Brooke-Taylor, Tony Hendra, Alan George, me, and two non-Footlights people, Miriam Margolyes and Nigel Brown, both of whom came from the world of Cambridge drama.

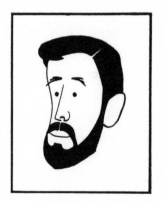

JOHN CLEESE

Bluff, slate-faced, 22-year-old Registrar, he reads Law and plays soccer for Downing. He grew his beard to avoid being mistaken for Pete Murray : an enthusiast for verbal humour, he is nevertheless always prepared to stoop to slapstick, where he rates the custard pie above the banana skin. He has a laugh which is coarse and ingenuous to boot: he says he cannot sing, and keeps a locked piano in his room to prove it.

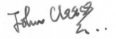

From the 1962 revue. I did not write the accompanying text.

In view of what I am about to write, I want to make it clear that being in the 1960s Footlights revue was a very happy, enjoyable and interesting experience.

That being said, why does the prospect of actually telling you about it not fill me with excitement? Whatever the reason, it must be a sign that I should not linger on details, as I can scarcely expect you to be more interested in it than I am.

The first thing to say about the show is that it was as though *Beyond the Fringe* had never happened. Perhaps because so much of the material had already been written during the year for the Smokers; perhaps because unconsciously we knew better than to draw comparisons. So it was very predictable, the sort of thing the Footlights usually did. I thought it was terrific, of course, but I was wrong.

Nevertheless, the moment we met Trevor we realized this was someone who knew what he was doing. His right-hand man was Humphrey, the only one of us to have been in a Footlights revue before. First, they gathered the best sketches from the year's six Smokers, and Trevor cast them. Then, writing with Humphrey, he created opening and closing numbers and wrote some material for Miriam (the rest of us were hopeless at this, as we had literally never written for a woman).

Next, we started rehearsing. It really excited me to work with a director who would let us play and experiment, but who was also in control in a way that made us feel safe that we were moving in the right direction and at the right speed to produce a proper show. But what I liked most was being part of a team, and working with a common aim in a co-operative spirit. The in-jokes, the friendly teasing and the mutual helpfulness created a confidence, a feeling of being emotionally supported, that was the most motivating force that I had ever experienced. I'd had a taste of it playing in Clifton sports teams, but nothing like this.

So far as the actual show was concerned, there were ten of us in the cast, and we all had about the same amount to do. I had one monologue about the astronomical statistics; a sketch with Tim and Graham about mountaineering, based on a hair-raising climb we had actually done; another sketch with Tim and Graham, where I refereed a karate contest between them in which a moment's pressure on the right nerve would produce phenomenal convulsions; a full-cast number about a board of directors presenting a retiring employee with a loaf of bread; two other full-cast numbers; and finally, a couple of musical numbers about which the less said the better.

I was, without doubt, not one of the stronger performers in the show (garnering one passing mention in the four reviews we received). Several of the others had much stronger material which showed off their greater talents: Chapman's mime; Hendra's splendid operatic take-offs; Brooke-Taylor's talent for funny, precise physical comedy; Barclay's bland authority figures; and Margolyes' magnificently overblown monologues.

Yet despite the fact I made a minimal impact on the show, I was proud to be in it. I thoroughly enjoyed the whole experience. I believed it was a very good show, and so did the critics, the audiences were warm and enthusiastic, the whole thing was just fine.

So why does it not seem interesting to me in retrospect? Because it was conventional? Because there was no overall style or shape to the show? Because the best performers were in the 1963 show, too, and I shall be going on about them at inordinate length?

No, I think it's simply because there was nothing in the whole damn show that was really funny. And I think that, deep down, that's what has always really motivated me. When I've had enough artistic control, I've always aimed at being as funny as I can possibly be—not at being clever or witty or amusing or charming or whimsical or quite funny—all the things that our revue could claim to be. And being really funny is much harder than being clever or witty or etc., etc. And we weren't quite up to that yet.

But there were four priceless things that I learned. Firstly, the incomparable comic education you get from performing the same piece night after night. It means you can carry out a series of little experiments, discovering what works and what doesn't, and if it doesn't, trying a little cut here, a rephrasing there, then trying different performance variations until you hit on the one that fixes the problem.

Every single night you learn something more about the psychology of audiences. And so few non-professionals are lucky enough to get sufficient performances to experience this.

Secondly, *Double Take* brought home to me that I really only had one talent—timing. People think of me now as quite a physical comedian but in my early days I didn't move well—I was tentative and awkward. When I was on form, however, my verbal timing could be really good, partly because I listened to audiences very carefully and was able to adjust to their reaction very fast. There is a split second after you do a joke when you have to decide whether to go on, or to wait for the laugh. If you go on, and then they laugh, you tread on that laugh and suppress it, and then have to repeat the line again, which is inelegant and loses you pace; but if you wait and there isn't a laugh, the audience may pick up that something's misfired.

Thirdly, I realised I was much more afflicted by nerves than the rest of the cast. Some people love to perform, and I envy them, but I was often scared that I would make a mistake, get a rhythm wrong, not get the laugh. It was a mixture of lack of confidence and setting myself high standards. Comedians are always talking about how they see the audience as a potentially hostile force that has to be won over. For my first few years that's exactly how I felt. And my only strength—my timing—depends on confidence; you cannot do great comedy if you are not relaxed. I think there is an exact parallel between timing in comedy and timing in sport: when you time an off-drive in cricket, or a forehand in tennis, the ball flies away effortlessly. But that only happens when you are playing with confidence and nothing tightens up as you make the shot. It is the same with comedy: any anxiety, any tension, and the flow goes wrong, you snatch at the joke, you force too hard, you lose the rhythm. But when the confidence is there, it is such a great feeling when the audience gets on a roll, and you play them as you would play a fish, keeping the line slightly taut but not tight—now letting them have a little slack, then reeling them in a touch—as you bathe

in their laughter and their enjoyment. Work doesn't get much better than that.

Fourthly, I began to notice after about fifteen performances that
the greatest cure for anxiety is familiarity. The better you know the
sketch (not just the words, but the moves and the props and the sets
and the feel of the theatre), the more effortlessly it starts to flow,
and the less opportunity there is for distraction, which is always the
cause of a lapse.

And in addition to all those lessons, *Double Take* gave me my first
taste of fame!

One night as I was walking back past the Arts Theatre after the
show had ended, I was recognised by a family who said, "Look! He
was in the show," and they pointed and waved. I can still remember the sudden feeling of warmth around my heart that swelled and
swelled and lifted my spirits. It was as though I had been accepted
into a new family, and acknowledged as having brought them something special that they really appreciated. It was only a moment,
but it was wonderful, and they didn't even know my name. It was a
long time before something like this happened again, and in today's
celebrity culture it must be hard to imagine that a tiny moment of
recognition like that could feel so uncomplicated and positive, quite
uncontaminated by feelings of self-importance and competitiveness.

So my second year at Cambridge ended happily. The exams
proved to be a doddle, and I had a visit to the Edinburgh Festival in
August to look forward to: fifty of us drawn from the Footlights, the
Cambridge Mummers and the Amateur Dramatic Club, and called
collectively the Cambridge Theatre Company, were set to stage two
"serious plays," a late-night revue and a nightclub with cabaret.

Meanwhile there were a few weeks to kill and Alan asked me if I
wanted to earn some pocket money by digging holes on a building
site for the offices of *Which?* magazine. We'd be paid three shillings
and sixpence an hour. This turned out to be one of the most enjoyable tasks I have ever undertaken—hours and hours digging away in

great weather, listening to the England–Australia Test matches, chatting with Alan, and every six hours racking up yet another pound. Not much to do in the evenings except read.

In the middle of August, staggering under the weight of my pound notes, I hitchhiked to London, jumped on a coach with the other members of the Cambridge Theatre Company, and spent twelve hours travelling to Edinburgh while trying to do the *Times* crossword with Graham. Looking back now, I find it odd to think that the pair of us had never performed a sketch together in *Double Take,* and that we had only co-written two pieces for it (though we penned two others with Tim Brooke-Taylor). Yet people recall thinking of us as a team. Graham had graduated that summer, and after Edinburgh would be heading off to St. Bartholomew's Hospital to become a doctor, while, in a year's time, I would be set to become a solicitor. Ah, well . . . we still had time for some good laughs in Edinburgh before we said au revoir.

Our first laugh came when we arrived (with twenty-two clues uncompleted) and saw the magnificent house Edinburgh University had lent us for our stay. Unfortunately that's all it was—a magnificent house. It was completely empty. Not a stick of furniture to be seen, though we found marks showing where chairs and tables and sideboards had once been. We were each handed a pillow, an inflatable lilo and a sheet, and given the news that there were three bathrooms between the fifty of us. I have never seen such queues. Then we were given ration cards, one for each meal. It was like the Blitz, with great comradeship but less noise. Graham encouraged us to sing patriotic songs, to keep our spirits up.

Next we took what might easily have passed as a van, and rode over to see where we would be performing. We had been lent a Presbyterian hall, where a group of carpenters, all to our surprise from Cambridge, were busy erecting a stage. Then to our even greater surprise, Trevor Nunn, who was putting on a production of *Brand,* informed us that he needed some extra villagers, and summoned us to a rehearsal room, where we were coached in how to crawl along a floor, shouting the word "fish," while giving the impression we were ascending a mountain. *Brand* is one of Ibsen's heavier comedies and the whole miserable experience soon had us fuming. We all liked Trevor but we had not signed up for this, so I'm afraid that we misbehaved, laughing in the wrong places and pretending we had hurt our knees.

Fortunately, we were rescued by the nightclub organisers, who decided they needed a cabaret act from us—a twenty-minute show on the hour every hour—to start the following evening.

On our first night, Graham, Alan George, and I were still huddled off-stage agreeing on the running order of the first show when one of the nightclub student impresarios appeared and said, "It's completely deserted. Relax. We'll do the first show at seven." "OK," we said. Graham lit his pipe, while Alan and I started running our lines. Then the guy raced back. "You're on! The audience has arrived." So we rushed up the stairs singing our opening number, and accustoming our eyes to the spotlight. And after a few moments we located the audience. There were two of them, a nice young couple in their twenties, who had made the mistake of looking into the club, had been pounced on, given a glass of wine each, and rushed to the best seats in the house—the two right in the middle of the front row. The young woman, realising that she and her boyfriend were only about ten feet from a cast that outnumbered them, registered shock, then fear, and then put her head in her hands and began to cry. Her boyfriend put his arm around her, gestured to us "She'll be all right in a moment," and started trying to laugh to encourage us. The sight of his poor girlfriend sobbing at our antics was heart-rending, but there was also something horribly comic about it. We made the decision to bring the show to an early end, allowing the young woman to run wailing into the street, pursued by her boyfriend, who clapped our performance over his shoulder as he disappeared into the distance.

A couple of days later, the Footlights cast started rehearsing for the late-night show—when we were allowed to. By which I mean that it had become clear that the "serious" actors were the ones whose rehearsal requirements had to be catered to, while we had to fit in and use the stage and rehearsal room when the important artists didn't need them. To say this got up our noses was an understatement.

However, when the play started, we saw vengeance done. The dramatic actors faced audiences of two or three dozen, who at the end of each performance had to fight their way through the excited crowds waiting to rush in to grab their seats for the Footlights show. We were packed every single night. Lawrence Durrell and Henry Miller came. Twice! But I expect it all seemed a bit vulgar to the drama crowd.

Our show had definitely got better since its Cambridge incarnation. It was now only sixty minutes long, teaching us that if you have an average show, and you can dump half of it, it doesn't get a bit better—it gets a lot better. In fact, there seems to be a basic, rather brutal rule of comedy: "The shorter the funnier." I began to discover that whenever you could cut a speech, a sentence, a phrase or even a couple of words, it makes a greater difference than you would ever expect.

I also soon found that late performances are easier than matinees. Audiences get more relaxed as the day goes on, and by the time our audience arrived they were so loose and responsive that the shows became a joy to do. When you play to a great audience, they lift you up, and the laughter hanging in the air makes you funnier—you're in the moment, free of inhibition and so able to try little things that you have never done before—and they work! The only drawback is that the next night is invariably never quite so good.

There's also no doubt that the tremendous reception we were getting was partly due to the context. An audience's response is absurdly dependent on their expectations. If you throng into a grubby little church hall and are surprised to discover something good, you feel a kinship with it, a delight that you helped descry it. If you later see the same show in a West End theatre you tend to be less impressed because you now judge it by standards that have changed, but have done so unconsciously. Thus when delightful little Edinburgh Festival shows transfer to the West End, critics often write something meaningless, like "The production has failed to make the necessary transition to the West End stage." What's actually happened is that the production is being judged by higher standards.

When we finally boarded the coach back to London I knew I was soon going to be saying goodbye to many people I had become fond of. We all therefore avoided the subject and made the usual promises about staying in touch. In Graham's case the promise was genuine on both our parts, though we had no idea how easily fate would facilitate this. At least, though, we had nearly completed the *Times* crossword—only three blank clues left after twelve hours. Chapman hung on to it.

Then God made a little joke. I got on the London Underground and immediately spotted a copy of the *Times,* with the crossword untouched. I idly picked it up, glanced at the corner that had been defying our efforts to solve it and immediately worked out one of the answers. I filled it in, and with the new letters was able to deal with the other two clues. I looked around and noticed that several passengers were casually watching. So I then filled out the entire crossword from memory in two minutes, tossed it aside, and looked around for something more challenging. I felt really intelligent for the first time in my life.

MY MIDDLE year at Cambridge had been pleasant and reasonably productive. But if I was expecting the same when I went back for my last year I was in for a shock.

It started with the weather. In November, winter set in and produced a record-breaking cold spell: a bitter, arctic, numbing, glacial deep-freeze so brutal that even the two-minute run from my digs to the Footlights never failed to remind me of Captain Oates (along with his friend Captain Scott, another of England's glorious failures). Soon the ground was so frozen that all sports had to be called off. I found ice in my wash basin, and for the next four months had to abandon my bedroom, sleeping instead on the sofa in front of my gas fire, swaddled in every layer I could find: bedclothes, overcoats, jackets, newspapers, shopping bags, face flannels, anything . . .

Almost as chilling was the discovery that I now had to study the two dullest subjects known even to law students: real property, and trusts and settlements. How was it possible to spark even the tiniest glimmer of curiosity in these dismal, vast accumulations of details concerning how people could give things (with exceptions, and exceptions to the exceptions, and exceptions to the exceptions to the exceptions)? The *willpower* it took to plough through this detritus.

However, at least I had international law and jurisprudence to stimulate my mind. There was also the law of evidence. But although I embarked upon this readily enough, I then turned my back on it, hoping it would go away. And the reason for this was that now I went a little bit mad.

And the cause of my madness, which began to disrupt my work, my sleep, my Footlights life, indeed every corner of my daily routine, was this: I fell in love.

When I say I fell in love, I didn't actually have much to do with it. I simply became engulfed in a storm of emotions, so unfamiliar, bewildering and overwhelming, that I basically came apart. Inside, anyway.

Because I had spent so little time around women, I had not previously experienced even the mildest of romantic twinges. I had no idea what this "falling in love" business might actually *feel* like. So the sensations I experienced when I developed a crush on one of the tiny handful of women who attended the law lectures were actually frightening, because they had no connection with anything that I knew. The pair of us had never had so much as a proper conversation, and yet here I was developing obsessional romantic thoughts, even though she had an attractive boyfriend with whom she was obviously very involved.

You may wonder why, given the strength of my feelings, I didn't attempt to make them known, but you have to remember that the middle-class culture I inhabited found any public suggestion of romantic attraction problematic. And as for hints of anything more physical, these would have been viewed as a vulgar lapse. In the society in which I had grown up, the most trivial remark or moment of bodily contact could be construed as embarrassingly sexual: touching became foreplay, and a cheeky remark an invitation to risk pregnancy, while everyone sensed that the words "I love you" landed you at the altar. In the Victorian era, the sight of a well-turned ankle would arouse men, and some upholders of Christian virtue covered the legs of furniture, lest the sight of the naked lower half of a dining table led to Bacchanalian festivity. Thus, from my point of view, even holding a girl's arm to guide her across the street could become carnally significant if contact was maintained for more than two seconds after the pavement was reached. So, if I ever summoned up the courage actually to make a pass at a girl, she was very unlikely to notice what I was attempting to be up to.

And because I was convinced that even a negligible advance on my part implied something much more momentous, I found myself acutely unwilling to put my foot, however gently, on the first step of the romantic process; I was fearful that I would embarrass the object of my affections by suggesting a course of action which she might experience as alarming, distasteful or downright repellent. This punctilious concern not to offend or distress was, I'm sure, the camouflage that my unconscious employed to hide from myself my deep fear of rejection. I didn't think of myself as remotely physically attractive, and I found it extremely improbable that anyone sane would want to get close to me. Unless, that is, they could, over the course of time, come to see that I was polite, amusing and obedient enough to allow them to overcome their initial, very understandable, distaste.

For some time, therefore, I wandered around in a mooncalf dream, falling further and further behind in my work, scared, frozen and wonderfully unhappy. Then Alan wandered into my room one day and said, "Come on, what's going on?" And for the first time in my life, at the age of twenty-three, I found myself talking about "feelings." I made a huge discovery: by being able to talk about them I could alleviate my sense of bewilderment. As Alan and I chatted, I began to realise that I wasn't losing my mind, I was just experiencing one of the world's most clichéd situations; that the romantic agony was ridiculous; and that the best short-term tactic was to see a lot of my friends. Thank God they were just around the corner. So off to the Footlights I went every day, and slowly began to feel ever so slightly more normal. I had a lot of good friends there now and getting involved in the next Smoker helped to distract me from the pangs of unrequited (or, rather, unnoticed) love.

One Saturday evening, someone insisted that we gather round our television set to watch the first episode of a new satirical series called *That Was The Week That Was*. We were astounded by it. It was unlike any television programme we had ever seen before: funny, raucous, and deliberately rough in style. But what took our breath away was its impudence and its brashness, and above all its complete disrespect for all the traditional figures of authority. It was a huge and irreversible cultural tidal wave. What *Beyond the Fringe* had done for London, *TW3* (as it was popularly known) now did for the whole of Britain. Retired colonels throughout the land bewailed the End of Civilisation as they knew it, and the programme made David Frost, who presented it, an overnight star. Suddenly, he was everywhere.

Most astonishingly . . . he was in our clubroom, getting permission to use some of our best material for *TW3*. We were startled how little impressed he seemed by what had happened to him. It was as though he thought it the most natural thing in the world. In a rather endearing way I don't think David was ever at all surprised by his success.

From then on we had the thrill of sitting in the clubroom every Saturday night, clustered round the set in the hope of seeing one of our sketches being performed in *the* hit show on national television.

That winter of 1962–63 proved to be one of the coldest on record, and the arctic weather continued into the New Year. So, to an extent, did my romantic agonies. I was, however, coping slightly better now in that I felt miserable rather than insane. This was definitely a step up. I started writing more, and my ideas seemed to be getting quirkier. For example, I wrote a sketch about a recruit being interviewed by the head of the Secret Service (played by me) which started to release a vein of comic insanity that I must previously have been holding in check. I also did a parody of one of those tight-lipped Somerset Maugham scenes where a colonial officer and his wife are having dramatic realisations about the state of their marriage. What I liked about my version was that neither of them actually ever finished a sentence. It was all dramatic pauses and "You don't mean . . . ?" and "Oh God . . ." and "But I thought . . ." But more ambitious still was a long, ten-minute court sketch involving a series of witnesses being cross-examined by a manic, triumphant, incompetent barrister, again played by me. I wrote it for a Smoker I was producing and the laughter that greeted it was the loudest I'd ever heard in the clubroom. By the end, I knew we had the big closing number for the 1963 revue.

My one problem at the time—apart from a sense of general misery—was that I was badly behind in my work. I hoped that my genuine enthusiasm for international law and jurisprudence could get me through those papers, despite the depression that made it so hard to focus. But real property and trusts and settlement, seemed very real threats. Could I summon up enough energy in the ten weeks that remained before finals to catch up and scrape a pass in these monstrous assaults on one's will to live?

13.	The New Boss Oddie	Oddie, Macdonald Johnny Lynn
14.	Watch Space McEwen	McEwen
15.	Championship Match Lewis	Gooderson, Ted Pater
16.	Alarming Buffery	Buffery
17.	The New Wave Dalrymple	Dalrymple, Mike Dornan
18.	Twisted trad.	Deb Croom-Johnson Fred Yeadon et al
19.	Dong Ding Riches	Riches, Blakemore John Cameron, John Day
20.	You Need Me Cassels	Jo Kendall Caroline Graham
21.	Sweet Varlets Heal, Beach	Heal, Beach
22.	Bought It Mankowitz et al.	Marion MacNaughton Caroline Graham
23.	The Little People Eyre, Shrapnel	Shrapnel, Richard Eyre
24.	Poor Mrs Palsgraf Cleese	Cleese, Stuart-Clark Brooke-Taylor, Buffery Cowell, Gooderson

Part of the programme for a typical Footlights Smoker.

And then I remembered *another* subject . . . evidence!

Aaaarrghh!!

I was dead. Stone dead. I had simply forgotten about evidence. My heart froze in horror. No pass in the evidence paper = no Cambridge law degree = no profession. QED.

Then . . . a moment of inspired madness. I'd heard that criminology was a relatively undemanding subject, and that the new Cambridge Criminology Department was short of students. So I hurried over to see the professor, explained that I felt I was wasting my time on evidence when I could be helping to get the crucial insights of criminology into the prison system, and that I was fired with enthusiasm. But was it too late to make the change, I asked?

I was expecting, "Of course it is. You're more than two-thirds of the way through the academic year. Are you out of your mind?"

Instead I heard, "It's late, yes, but not too late. Provided you can make up the visits to the prisons this vacation. And then there's the exam at the end of the summer, of course." At that moment, in an act of great kindness, he handed me a textbook and said, "If you learn what's in this book, you'll pass." I opened it. It was 254 pages long. The feeling of relief! I was in with a chance! "Thank you," I said, "I'd like to do criminology."

"OK," he replied.

With criminology in the bag I began my final term at Cambridge with one vital question consuming me: Should I do the revue this year, or should I save that time for studying?

It's shocking to think that my future career really was hanging on my answer to this. But it was a completely sensible question. I'd been interviewed and accepted by Freshfields (solicitors to the Bank of England, no less) at a salary of £12 per week for the first two and a half years *provided*, it went without saying, that I got my degree. So why would I bother to do another revue when I desperately needed the time to try to make sure I passed my exams? I dithered.

I took a look at the exam schedule and discovered the criminology exam was scheduled four whole days after all the others had finished. That was it! I would work like a fiend on the other papers, and then give myself ninety-six hours to cram up on the criminology textbook (which I'd skimmed and found very intelligible—a mixture of psychology and statistics, which I could do) . . . *and* I would do the revue.

For a cautious creature like me, it was a liberating moment.

To my delight Humphrey Barclay had been appointed director

of the 1963 revue. I liked him enormously: he emanated an air of good-natured, avuncular authority, which must have had something to do with the fact that he had been head boy at Harrow. He also seemed more organised and grown up than the rest of us. And if he was a bit bossy, well, directors are supposed to be bossy. What's more, having been with the Footlights for three years he was very familiar with the material from the Smokers, since he'd performed in all of them.

Tim Brooke-Taylor was clearly our strongest performer, because he could do any kind of comedy we needed: music-hall comedians, grande dames, silly-ass Englishmen, pompous twerps. He was also outstandingly good at physical comedy, using very precise movements but with tremendous energy and gusto. I loved working with him because we both enjoyed rehearsing, running sketches again and again. We also wrote some material together—the previous year, Chapman, he and I had written some fifteen minutes of the show—and we continued to do so for some years. But what was great about Tim above all was that he adored performing: he would really go for it—especially important on opening nights, when I was freezing up with nerves and having to fight my way through.

Bill Oddie was another natural star. He was a clown rather than a comic actor, but he wrote and sang some clever, funny and catchy pieces that gave our show a brightness and a variety far superior to the usual Footlights "point numbers." At the beginning of the year he was not a major figure at the clubroom. Then he suddenly exploded creatively and ended up contributing eighteen pieces to the show. He could be prickly, and slightly competitive—something that was otherwise absent from our group—but he was mostly jolly, energetic and a terrific natural singer.

Of the rest of the cast, I thought that the most interesting chap was a psychology postgraduate student called Anthony Buffery who was doing research on the memory of baboons. He was very bright, and I managed to learn quite a lot of academic psychology from our chats. He couldn't act for toffee, but he did weird solo acts that were extraordinarily original, and that he always invented on his own. His appearance helped his eccentricity: he was very tall and strong and upright, with a long, very pale face, huge eyes and a permanently surprised expression. An example of his work: he did a mime of a javelin thrower at an ancient battle who takes a long time before he actually launches his javelin . . . and then has nothing else to contribute to the occasion. Variations on embarrassment played a large part in Anthony's humour.

Chris Stuart-Clark, who was Tim's great pal, specialised in rather self-satisfied vicars and headmasters, and had an excellent turn of phrase; David Hatch could play anything from pompous to camp to sarcastic to cowardly, always straight-faced, but somehow conveying under that a mysterious silliness; and Jo Kendall, that year's Foot-lights "girl," was a delight: fun, relaxed, very experienced (she'd been in a lot of the big drama productions) and probably the first young woman with whom I felt (almost) at ease. I enjoyed rehearsing the Somerset Maugham take-off with her. As there was not a completed sentence in the whole scene, the timing was difficult, but we kept at it and parts of it began to feel really funny. Bill came up with a great idea: that now and again, during the continual anguished pauses, I should kill some dangerous tropical creature—a snake, a deadly spider and, at one point, a leopard. So Jo would ask me something . . . long pause . . . I would shout, "Look out," and beat a cobra to death with a stick . . . pause again . . . and then I would reply, "No." Jo also invented a great gag. At one point, she suddenly slapped me in the face . . . long pause . . . I slowly picked off my cheek the mosquito she had just killed and said, "Thank you."

I was coming to love the rehearsal process, and I knew it was having a positive effect on me. The previous year I had been a new boy, totally inexperienced, perhaps a little overawed, and consequently just trying to fit in and "get things right." This year, in the wonderfully warm and supportive atmosphere that the 1963 cast created, I started really to let go and be much more adventurous and inventive, developing personas that people would later recognise as characteristic of my work. And judging from the rehearsal-room reaction, I was getting a lot funnier.

Perhaps some of that extra sense of fun about rehearsals was that they were the only break we got from the heavy grind of studying for finals. When the exams eventually came round, I felt I did all right on the first few papers, so, following the plan I had devised, I then disappeared for four days with my criminology textbook for the most intense cramming session of my life. On the morning of the exam I walked over to the Law School, sat down, took a deep breath, and looked at the paper. Three seconds later I knew I had passed! They'd asked all the questions that I was hoping for! I had to hide the tears of joy and relief that welled up. After that I just sat there grinning. Then I felt a huge twinge of annoyance that I actually had to write the bloody answers down.

Two years later, I was told that I had got an upper second for that paper, and that the Criminology Department, realising how little time I had had to study for it, had been forced to hush the whole matter up. If law students ever found out that four days' work was enough to get a 2:1, you wouldn't have been able to get into the criminology building.

After the exam was over, I hurried off to a telephone box to call my parents. Mother answered. "Mum," I said, "I just wanted to tell you I've taken my final exam and I know I passed, so that means I've got my Cambridge degree!" There was a pause. Then she said, "You remember the greeny-brown pullover you took back at the beginning of term . . . ?" I thought of this years later when the screenwriter William Goldman told me about taking his mother to the premiere of his Oscar-winning *Butch Cassidy and the Sundance Kid*. At the end he turned to her and said, "Well, Mom, what do you think?" "Weren't the horses beautiful?" was her response.

As for our revue, which went under the unlikely title of *A Clump of Plinths,* the opening night was a great success and the ovation at the end for both Bill and Tim deafening: they were outstandingly the stars of the show. We all gathered in the clubroom afterwards and celebrated. For my part, I was surprised and slightly hurt that my best pieces did not attract much comment. It meant a lot to me when Chapman, who'd come up from St. Bart's Hospital, told me he thought they were the funniest things in the show.

So, mission accomplished. Exams passed, two weeks of the show at Cambridge, summer break, then on to Freshfields to begin my law career.

Except that a couple of nights later, two men in suits appeared in the clubroom after the show, invited me for a drink, said how much they liked the material I'd written, and asked me whether I would like to come and work in the BBC Radio Light Entertainment Department. I would be a trainee producer-writer, at £30 per week. Just like that. Humphrey and David Hatch received similar offers.

The extraordinary thing about the prospect of this complete volte-face was that it didn't feel at all dramatic or momentous. I just chatted quietly and sensibly with these two producers, Peter Titheradge and Ted Taylor, and in the course of our conversation it became quite obvious that the completely rational decision was to give up the law (for ever!) and join the BBC. After all, I'd discovered that I thoroughly enjoyed writing comedy and that I had a talent for it, and I thought I'd be much more at home in the relaxed, informal world of the arts than I ever would be in a law firm in the City. And I'd never really wanted to be a lawyer in any case. Besides, the BBC was offering me £30 a week to Freshfields' £12 ("How had I ever imagined I could survive on *that?*" I asked myself).

I made my mind up on the spot, but then asked for two days to pretend to think it over. I told my parents, who took the news surprisingly well: their view was that having a job at the BBC was like joining the civil service, with a pension and everything. After that I wrote to Freshfields. They responded with an exceedingly pleasant and courteous letter, wishing me luck. I remember thinking, "They must reckon that I'm mad."

8

Just days after I accepted my job with BBC Radio, an even larger apple dropped into my lap—or, rather, into our Footlights laps. One night after the show we were invited to sit down with a rueful, delightful, rather crumpled young man who told us that his name was Michael White, that he was a London impresario, that he thought our show was wonderful, and . . . that he wanted to put it on in the West End.

The West End?!

Michael had a theatre in mind called the Arts Theatre, just off Leicester Square. It was small—just 350 seats—but if we were successful he would transfer us to a larger one. The theatre wasn't free for a month so we would have to take a break—and we all felt we needed one—then we'd appear for a week at an arts festival in York to polish the show before opening in London. Oh, and *A Clump of Plinths* wasn't a good title for a London run. *Cambridge Circus* was better.

Nobody argued.

Before York we spent a week relaxing, and then got together to review the show, a process which proved unbelievably productive. Not being in performance mode every night helped to loosen us up; aspects of the acting that had become too automatic now seemed freer and more spontaneous. And we were in such a great mood that we became very playful and started to invent new "business."

For example, we started to elaborate one very simple gag in the courtroom sketch. In the original version the barrister I played called for "Exhibit A," and Tim, dressed as a fairly elderly usher, brought on a bassinet and stand, set it up and left. I then asked Tony Buffery as the witness, "Have you ever seen this before?" A pause followed; then Tony said, "No"; I said, "Thank you, m'lord"; and Tim came back, picked up the exhibit and took it away. It got a very fair laugh. But in York Tim played the usher ever older and more doddery each night, ageing from 65 to 115 during the week (he told me later he was just trying to make David Hatch, who played the judge, laugh). Milking his outrageous senile shaking for all it was worth, he took an age to set the bassinet on the stand, accidentally knocked it off, put it back on again, and only then picked it up and exited, quite genuinely exhausted by his exertions. What had originally been a fifteen-second piece now took about forty seconds. And the audience loved it. They roared. On the last night, David—out of pure naughtiness, knowing how knackered Tim was at that point—tapped his gavel and said, "Could I see that again, please?" Repeat performance, and hysteria all round. Just fooling around we'd stumbled on another sixty seconds of laughs for the London show.

Soon we were in London, doing technical rehearsals at the Arts Theatre. This is always an edgy experience for actors. The big night is coming up, you have to repeat everything umpteen times for the technicians, and soon you're not getting so much as a giggle from them. Then you start thinking, "This doesn't feel very funny," and your confidence can very easily waver. However, Michael was ahead of us.

He had arranged two "previews" before opening night, just so that we could get a real feeling for the London audience and for the theatre itself—not only the size of it, but its shape and "the pitch of the hall." And the first preview was good: a few little mistakes, but we knew that these could easily be corrected. The important thing was that the audience response was very warm; we were encouraged.

The second night's audience, by contrast, was the weirdest I'd ever played. They were abnormal from the very start, and when we found that we were not getting the laughs we were accustomed to, that threw us. Then some of the audience started laughing at things no one had ever previously laughed at. Once they roared at the set-up of a joke and then received the punchline in complete silence. We were bewildered, but struggled on desperately towards the final curtain, and when it came down we went into collective shock, trying to understand what had gone wrong. Michael was soon there with the explanation. Every ticket for that performance had been bought for the attendees of a conference that was being held in London. A conference of psychiatrists. There had been a shrink in every seat.

But, of course, by this time we had the reassurance of having done over thirty performances, and from the beginning of our first night the reception proved to be so warm and enthusiastic that we produced one of our best ever shows. The reviews were mixed, but sprinkled among them were some complimentary ones. *The Times,* for example, hailed it as "the funniest show to emerge from Cambridge for a long time" and picked out several of the sketches, including the final courtroom one, for particular praise.

One thing all the reviews told me: whatever this star quality was that Tim and Bill had, I certainly didn't. I'd already suspected this was the case.

As the show bedded down, we found ourselves playing to full houses in the evenings (despite our complete lack of any fashionable satirical content, as one paper pointed out). And we enjoyed their enjoyment. During the courtroom sketch, for example, there were a wonderful couple of minutes where I had no lines and so could just watch the audience reaction as they finally realised that the witness box they had assumed to be empty actually concealed a dwarf. It was glorious to observe their delight. One night, though, I noticed a young teenager in a rather grand party in the third row laughing so helplessly that his father leant across, tapped his arm and shook his head ("People of our class don't laugh like that"). I felt great sadness for the young fellow.

We also took delight in "corpsing"—laughing on stage when we weren't supposed to. And as we became completely relaxed and occasionally bored (usually at matinees) this turned into an ever more common occurrence. I was much the worst culprit. I knew it was unprofessional, but then there is an extraordinary sweetness to forbidden laughter, which we all remember from the classroom, church, pompous ceremonies and, of course, funerals. It's as though you get all the usual amount of pleasure from laughing, and then something indefinably special as an extra. I've never figured out why suppressing laughter makes it more joyful. What I do know is that I got a bit addicted, and had to be told off a few times by the production manager.

Now that I was performing eight times a week, I really had the opportunity to learn more about the rules of comedy, which, of course, are nothing more than the rules of audience psychology. When you are doing only a small number of performances, unless you have had weeks of rehearsal, your attention is primarily directed at remembering what you have to do: not just the words and the movements, obviously, but the emphases, the pauses, the pace, the volume, and then the gestures, the looks, the reactions, and so on. And to the extent that your mind is partially focused on all this remembering, you have less attention available to be "in the moment." But as the externals of your performance become more automatic, you can go beyond simply "trying to get it right," and relax into a greater awareness of yourself, the other actors and your situation, and that gives your acting an extra degree of freshness and spontaneity. And, of course, it also gives you a greater awareness of the audience's laughter. As I've said before, the laughter element is what can often make comedy trickier to perform than straight drama. If you're playing Macbeth you don't have to worry about treading on the laughs.[1] But

---

[1] Unless you were in the Peter O'Toole production at the Old Vic.

in comedy it's all too easy to get your timing wrong; listening to the audience enables you to pace your performance correctly.

The other function of laughter is, of course, to be the total arbiter of what is funny. It's so simple: if they don't laugh, there's something wrong, and you've got to fix it.

But just occasionally it's not quite as simple as that, which is why I found Tony Buffery's solos so fascinating to watch. At one moment in the show we pretended something had gone wrong: there was an awkward pause, and then Tony would be pushed on to the stage and would stand there looking embarrassed and confused. He was wonderful at this, as he had an astonishing range of distressed expressions, intensified by his alarmingly pale complexion. He now explained to the audience that he had been asked to "fill in" and that he would do so by performing some farmyard impressions. Then he did his impersonations of a cow, a cockerel and a sheep—and they were all absolutely awful. He apologised, but explained that those were the only ones he did. By this point the audience would be confused and uneasy. Tony now announced he would tell a joke. And he did. And again it was terrible. He apologised again, said he would try to do better and told another one—this time a fairly good one, and the audience laughed, partly out of relief. When they did, Tony jumped up and down with excitement and called to the wings, "They laughed! They laughed!" Then he thanked them for laughing, and said that as they had liked the joke so much, he'd tell it again. So he told it again, exactly the same way. Silence. Tony looked crestfallen. He looked at the audience, paused, and then said, "Please laugh." I have never felt such discomfort in the theatre. Then Tony confided in the audience, "Please laugh. My mother's in the audience tonight." By now, some people were trying to hide under their seats. Tony scanned the balcony for some time, looking for his mother, and then smiled sadly and said, "It's all right, she's gone now."

I thought it was wonderful, but only a small part of the audience agreed, and it used to take a while to cheer the rest of them up after Tony had finished. This just goes to show how much tastes in comedy vary. When members of the cast talked about the show, for example, we all felt that about twenty per cent was comparatively weak, but there was constant disagreement about which twenty per cent that was. At the time this puzzled and frustrated me, and it took me many years before I understood just how subjective each person's sense of humour is. Because laughter is infectious people tend to laugh together, but when they view the same production separately their opinions vary more widely than one would ever think possible. Even watching an audience view a film clip, as I do sometimes from the stage, reveals a range of reaction that is quite surprising, and absolutely at odds with one's assumptions that something is either funny or not funny. Another lesson I learned at the time came from watching a Marx Brothers festival at the Baker Street Classic cinema and realising just how much dross there was among all the brilliance: even the greatest comics, I concluded, frequently fail.

However much views of the individual sketches in our show varied, though, there was no doubt that it was working, because now Michael called us together to tell us that we would be reopening at a much larger theatre, the Lyric on Shaftesbury Avenue. With the move came a change in personnel. Tony Buffery went back to his academic career with baboons, and Chris Stuart-Clark took up his vocation, which was teaching (he eventually ran the Dragon School in Oxford, and then became a housemaster at Eton). In came Graham Chapman, who had been lined up from the start to replace Tony. He brought some of his best material with him, including a sensational series of mimes, where he became an espresso machine and a carrot and was finally dragged from the stage by a human magnet in the wings. He was also a very strong sketch performer, with an ultra-serious intensity that elevated the humour in whatever he did. Chris was replaced by Johnny Lynn, who had started with us on opening night in Cambridge as the drummer in the band. He was round and jolly and fitted in perfectly, especially as he already knew the show by heart.

The cast of Cambridge Circus: *me (lying down) and, from left to right, David, Jo, Graham, Bill, Chris, Tim (hiding face from real policeman), real policeman.*

We moved to the Lyric on August 14 and, despite the changes to the cast, the transition proved unexpectedly easy. I noticed only two major differences. First, the Lyric was much bigger and so required more energy, and much louder voice projection as, in those days, there were no microphones. Since none of us had ever had formal dramatic training, we had to figure out for ourselves how to be noisier.

The second change was the money. Since we'd moved to London, we'd all been getting £30 a week as performers and a small amount in royalties for contributions to the script. Now, with the big houses at the Lyric, my performance fee remained the same but my royalty payments shot up to £100 a week, three times what Dad had ever earned. It had not really occurred to me that this could happen, but it certainly transformed my fortunes. At Cambridge I had been living on about £400 a year (with the Bristol Education Authority contributing half of that), so by the time I came to London, I was about £600 in the red. But by October I had completely cleared the debt, had gone well into the black, and was also beginning to collect a salary at the BBC. For the first time in my life, at the age of twenty-four, I was able to buy clothes, eat in posh restaurants, take German lessons (at Berlitz, I learned more German in two weeks than in two years at Clifton) and look for proper accommodation (for four months I'd been living in a room that Graham had found me at the St. Bartholomew's Hospital student hostel; I kept a low profile at first, but after a time the staff assumed I was just another medical student). Soon afterwards Graham, Tim and I found a very workable flat off the top of Baker Street, about a hundred yards from Sherlock Holmes's old establishment.

We had a fourth flatmate, a delightful Hong Kong Chinese guy, who was one of Graham's medical-student pals from Bart's Hospital. Despite his impeccable manners, he rather upset us by being far more English than we were: he invariably wore an expensive and beautiful suit, complete with a waistcoat, smoked a pipe, spoke immaculate upper-class English with a slight Oxford drawl and knew much more about England than we did. He and Graham kept strange medical-student hours, and Tim and I didn't see much of them. In retrospect, though, one thing seems significant. I noticed that Graham, who had always been a very amiable, easy-going companion, would sometimes become strangely aggressive if he got home late after spending an evening drinking with his Bart's rugby teammates. I began to wonder if he was incapable of being assertive *unless* he'd had alcohol . . .

I was not really used to communal living, but only once did I annoy my flatmates. The first time it was my turn to do the shopping, I overindulged my growing taste for exotic food with a bagful of goodies like smoked elk's liver and chocolate-covered ants and mackerel-and-prune soup and curried walrus testicles. I'd sort of forgotten about the milk and the bread and the eggs. I was never allowed to shop again.

One of the huge advantages of our flat was that it was a mere thirteen minutes' walk from the BBC Radio Light Entertainment offices in New Bond Street. I had started there in September, in a beautiful old building with a marble entrance hall, and an atmosphere that reminded me of a prep-school common room: lots of pleasant, gentle people going quietly about work which they enjoyed, with a complete absence of anxiety, competition or any talk of audience figures. But I was also discovering the excitement of living in London. Like most of my generation, I had developed a very strong, highly emotional patriotism about my country, so the idea of being in its capital thrilled me. I was proud of what we had done in the war; I was aware of our long history and our centuries of empire. I was also confident of what I felt to be the basic decency and fair-mindedness of our culture, and wherever I went in London I would see a building or perhaps just a name inscribed somewhere that would remind me that I was a part of this deeply impressive civilisation. It may sound naive, but it brought a kind of significance to my life. Of course, I was embedded in a very particular middle-class culture: it was fundamentally well educated, well mannered and orderly. And as I slowly learned more about all its various faults—its sexism, its racism, its bottomless class-consciousness—I also felt an optimism that things would inevitably and inexorably improve.

At the BBC I was assigned a rather boring little job writing material for an early-evening magazine programme. The only challenge was to avoid clichés; sadly, any surreal attempts to do so were rewritten by others. The greatest pleasure was getting to know many of the producers of famous radio comedy shows, some of which (like *The Navy Lark*, *The Clitheroe Kid* and *Beyond Our Ken*) had been running for years. The golden age of radio had ended when television took over, but what I found was that there was a collective delusion among the older producers that television was essentially a passing fad, that its attraction would begin to fade, and that the audiences would then drift back to their real first love—radio. It was an astonishing fantasy but it showed me what even apparently sensible people can believe if they really want to.

I was still performing at the Lyric and about six weeks before the end of the run I had what should have been a wonderful experience. One night I did, as near as dammit, a perfect show. I got every laugh, never missed a beat, my timing was exquisite; I was relaxed, disciplined and hilarious. There had been nights when I'd got most of the sketches dead right, but never before had I done the whole show impeccably. I was superb. (Please remember we did about 180 performances and this happened just *once*.)

The result: exhilaration. And then, the next day, depression. Because I realised I'd never do it so well again. Every night from now on I would go on stage and do it less well than I was capable of—it was going to be downhill all the way. And for a week or so after that, doing the show became a struggle: I was having to push myself through an emotional sound barrier, going on stage to do an imperfect performance that was going to dissatisfy me. It was a ridiculous expression of perfectionism but it made me belatedly realise that that's why I always called myself a writer-performer: I wanted to write something, perform it perfectly just once and then move on. Of course, I eventually found the right professional attitude: keep it as fresh as possible every night, and take pride in your discipline, but it now always felt like work.

When the run came to an end in November, we were, all of us, rather relieved, which meant that the last-night party seemed rather downbeat. We were proud of what we'd achieved but we also knew it was a passing phase. Two days later, to celebrate my first free week-day evening for five months, I treated myself by taking a good book to a fine fish restaurant on Baker Street. I ordered my meal, started to read—and then began to feel uncomfortable. I couldn't work out what was unsettling me, but I knew I was becoming more anxious by the minute. I'd started to sweat and my chest was tightening up, and now—a flash of alarm—my heart was pounding hard. Very hard. I took several deep breaths. What the hell was happening to me? I glanced at my watch. It was eight o'clock! Curtain up! The moment I realised what was going on, the symptoms disappeared. The weird-est part of it all was the fact that this happened to me not on the Sunday that followed the end of the run, but on the Monday when we would have been performing. My subconscious knew the difference.

THE LIGHT Entertainment Department now assigned me my first major project—a Christmas one-off for Brian Rix and Terry Scott called *Yule Be Surprised*. The first draft had been crammed full of the most ancient and enfeebled jokes; my job was to cut the worst ones. The main problem was leaving anything in the script at all. It was not the most creative start to a BBC writing career.

More encouraging was that Peter Titheradge, who had recruited Humphrey Barclay, David Hatch and me to the Light Entertainment staff as trainees, now persuaded the BBC to make three audience comedy shows, based on the *Cambridge Circus* show and cast, which turned out to be the prototype of our long-running radio comedy show *I'm Sorry I'll Read That Again*. I enjoyed recording these enor-mously. In radio, technology is at the absolute minimum: just a microphone between the performers and the audience; a studio audience which becomes an ally in the conspiracy to entertain the listeners; and a script in your hand which removes any possibility you might forget the words. Perfection. And it was lovely to be working with the team again, with Humphrey producing the shows under Peter's mentorship.

And, in the New Year, at last a proper writing job, producing two or three sketches weekly for a couple of comedians a generation or so older than me: Dick Emery and Deryck Guyler. This was the first time I had worked with professionals. We'd meet at ten in the morning, read the script through a couple of times, do some rewrites, take a break, and then record the programme at lunchtime. Emery was very good at playing broad comedy characters, but I always felt that he was not a classy performer, though he had his own immensely popular TV series for nearly twenty years. He never seemed to stretch his abilities, and that may be why he's not remembered as one of the greats. Guyler, on the other hand, was a top-class comic actor, but one who never became a "star." Their attitudes to our show were revealed by the first two minutes of rehearsal: Dick would slit open the envelope containing the script he had been sent; Deryck's script was already covered with little marks, like musical annotations. Dick's performance would be OK; Deryck's superb.

For the first time in my comedy-writing life I now had to produce scripts on a regular basis, and this brought with it a simple problem: I would start the morning with a blank sheet of paper, and I might well finish the day with a blank sheet of paper (and an overflowing waste-paper basket). There are not many jobs where you can produce absolutely nothing in the course of eight hours, and the uncertainty that produces is very scary. You never hear of accountant's block or bricklayer's block; but when you try to do something creative there can be no guarantee anything will happen.

And this is why Peter Titheradge suddenly became such an important influence. In his time he'd been a distinguished writer of West End revue material, and he was able to calm my incipient panics when fruitless hours were passing. He got me to understand that, if you kept at it, material would always emerge: a bad day would be followed by a decent one, and somehow an acceptable average would be forthcoming. I took a leap of faith, and my experience started to confirm this mysterious principle.

He also clarified something that had been slowly occurring to me: how very, very rare it is to find a great punchline which both surprises an audience and pulls the main threads of the sketch together in a satisfying way. He showed me that I was wasting hours of my time trying to discover the ideal punchline when the conditions for one simply didn't exist. You just needed to find something that was "good enough" to resolve the piece. I sometimes wonder whether Peter's radical insight helped me six years later towards the Python punchline solution—"Don't bother with them."

In addition, Peter helped me to edit what I had written, removing whatever "fat" my dialogue had on it, whether it was a repetition, a redundant phrase, an unnecessary adjective—even a single syllable. I'd half-realised some of this, but not the ruthlessness it required. Finally, of the many things that he taught me, I still remember this: always put the key funny word in a sentence at the end of it, as this will give it maximum impact; any words that follow it will soften its effect, causing the audience momentarily to hold back their laughter so that they do not miss what is still to be said.

I was fascinated by Peter's expertise, and I asked him why he had stopped writing. "When the war was over, I ran out of malice," he replied. I'd never met a man so free of malice as Peter. He padded his way round the corridors of the Aeolian Hall, where the BBC had some of their recording studios, dispensing whatever executive expertise was necessary, and people were invariably delighted to see him coming. He was always immaculately dressed; I teased him by calling him "dapper." He exuded a mixture of wisdom, charm and empathy that made him loved throughout the department. I've never met a more admirable human being.

Yet his remark about "malice" bothered me. Was humour essentially malicious? It was certainly in some way critical. You can't make a joke about people behaving intelligently and generously. A TV executive once said to me, "Show me a sitcom about St. Francis of Assisi and I'll show you a bummer." Jokes are about stupidity, greed, vengefulness, anger, obsession . . . all things of which we should disapprove. But is this disapproval malicious? I think it really depends on the frame of mind of the joke-teller. Think of teasing: there can be nasty, spiteful, hurtful teasing, and there can be affectionate, even loving, teasing that gently reminds someone of an aspect of their behaviour that needs attention, but that does so in a way that is entirely accepting of them, and it. But then what about a joke like "Why do the French have so many civil wars?" Answer: "So they can win one now and again." We don't laugh because we hate the French, yet there is nevertheless a hard-edged quality here, as there is in all laughs that involve cultural stereotypes. Perhaps the problem could be solved if each year the United Nations voted that one country should be the butt of all the insult jokes for the forthcoming twelve months. My proposal when it's Sweden's turn: "How do you get fifteen Swedes into a Volvo?" Answer: "Throw a krona in the back."

AFTER A few months in the new job, the BBC very kindly gave me six weeks' leave to tour New Zealand with *Cambridge Circus*. It was something that Michael White had arranged. He'd called us to his office and said he wanted to take the show on tour. We assumed he meant round Britain, but he said, "No, here," and showed us on a map. We agreed like a shot. I think we were intrigued by the sheer pointlessness of the idea. Anyway, it would certainly be fun.

Getting ready for New Zealand. From left to right: me, Johnny, David Palmer (musical director), Graham, Mrs. Palmer, Master Palmer, our hosts Lady and Lord Crathorne, Humphrey (sitting), Jean Hart, Bill, Jo, Tim, David, Peter Titheradge, and Ann Hatch.

In July 1964, therefore, we all boarded a BOAC airliner and flew to New Zealand, where it was the midwinter of 1922. Our first hotel was a good indication of what was to come. Modelled closely on Norman Bates's motel in *Psycho,* it was run by two sour, unobliging old bats who were clearly put out by the whole idea of accommodating overnight guests. Registering, an hour or so after landing at the airport, caused endless difficulties, during which we were asked, "How do you like New Zealand so far?" "Very promising," we lied. "We're a happy-go-lucky people," one of the old bats explained, rather grudgingly.

We soon discovered that the country was basically completely clueless. Bill Oddie walked into an ice-cream parlour and ordered a banana split. The chef took a banana, peeled it, split it in half and presented it to him. Graham caused consternation by ordering a "three-egg omelette." "A three-egg omelette?" "Yes," said Graham, "a *three*-egg omelette. Made with three eggs . . ." He received a large omelette with three fried eggs on the top. At Sunday lunch I saw "Colonial Goose" on the menu. I love goose, so I ordered it. When it arrived, it tasted like lamb. "This is Colonial Goose?" I queried. "Yis." Graham tasted some. "It's lamb," he said. I called the waitress back. "I'm sorry, but this tastes like lamb." "Yis," she said. "But I ordered Colonial Goose." "Colonial Goose *is* lamb," she explained.

Fortunately the shows were well received, but even in the theatre ineptitude ruled. During one performance, a loud bell started ringing at regular junctures, which distracted the audience badly. At the interval, Humphrey, who had taken over as stage manager, since we could find no one else in New Zealand who was up to the task, raced round to the front of the theatre, found the theatre manager and angrily asked him to find out who was ringing the bell.

"It's me," replied the manager.

"What?" cried Humphrey.

"I'm ringing it," explained the manager.

"Why?"

"It's the fire bell."

"Is there a fire?" Humphrey demanded.

"No."

"Well, why are you ringing it?"

"I'm testing it."

"But we're doing a *performance*!"

"I'm only doing my job."

Perhaps the most bizarre moment came when we went to Dunedin. On the way in by car we noticed cinema posters advertising *Zulu.*

We'd heard it was a great film and got excited about the prospect of seeing it during our stay. As we checked in at the hotel we noticed we were being scrutinised rather closely by the proprietor. Conversation seemed stilted; eventually she posed the question on her mind: "Are you the Zulus, then?"

Another extraordinary phenomenon. In an attempt to reduce the dangers of alcohol, it was illegal for public houses to serve drinks after six in the evening. So people would race to the pub after work, and line up six pints of beer which they would then drink in the next thirty minutes, rendering them all legless by the time the pubs closed. This was known as the "six o'clock swill."

When you encounter a culture totally uncontaminated by logic, it eventually undermines your reliance on reason. For example, Johnny Lynn walked into a department store in search of cufflinks. "Where do I find cufflinks?" he asked. "Try the tobacco counter." "No," said Johnny, indicating the cuffs on his shirt, "cufflinks." "Yis. Try the tobacco counter." "OK," thought Johnny. "After all, this is New Zealand." So he strolled over to the tobacco counter. "Excuse me, do you have any cufflinks?" "This is the *tobacco* counter!" was the reply.

When we talked to New Zealanders of our own age we found a complete dichotomy between those who had never left their country and those who had spent a year or so abroad. The former were very happy with their lives; the latter now viewed New Zealand from a wider perspective and spent their waking hours plotting how to escape again.

Nevertheless, our gang—Tim, Bill and his girlfriend Jean Hart, Jo Kendall, Graham, David, Humphrey, Johnny and I—travelled happily by coach around this beautiful country with its small centres of population separated by vast tracts of countryside and sheep, being treated with great friendliness and laughing all the way.

So relaxed did I become that I made an important breakthrough: I started to feel comfortable in the company of women. Up until now

I had faced a seemingly insuperable hurdle: the feeling that, when I was on my own with a person of the same sex as my mother, I had to put on some sort of act. I had no clear idea of what the act needed to be, just a deep intuition that there was some mental button which, if I could ever find and press it, would shove me into a more male persona—one that was quietly impressive, strong, manly, effortlessly sexual, masterful, ironic and whatever else it was that James Bond exuded. Until this button had been located, the best I could do was to hint that these secret-agent qualities existed deep inside me, albeit skilfully camouflaged by my extreme good manners and self-deprecating humour.

But in the six weeks that I travelled around New Zealand in the company of Jo Kendall, I underwent a sea-change. I am not for a moment hinting at a romance with Jo; it was just that the experience of being around a cheerful, chatty, undramatic friend-who-happened-to-be-a-girl nudged me in the direction of being a little more "myself"; partly, no doubt, because my "act" was too demanding to maintain for hours on end, so weariness produced more authentic behaviour.

And a few weeks later I was presented with the surprising offer of a chance to lose my virginity. The New Zealand girls were a wholesome and cheery bunch and I must have been losing my stiffness and rigidity (I speak metaphorically) because in Christchurch I met a girl—we'll call her Ann—with whom I felt really relaxed and who thought me hilarious. She found my impersonation of a mouse the funniest thing she had ever seen. We enjoyed a couple of evenings of entirely lust-free meetings, and off I flew to Auckland for the last stage of the tour. I was embarrassed that I still was unable to drive a car, so to fill my afternoons usefully, I arranged some driving lessons, but then received a phone call from Ann, making it quite clear that she was coming to Auckland the next day, and would be staying with me at the hotel. The message was unequivocal, even to dopey old me. Intimacy would be taking place.

The next day, trying to anticipate what normal human beings did when faced with romantic encounters, I decided that apart from flowers in the hotel room, I should buy Ann some scent, to create the right atmosphere. So I visited the perfume department of the local store, but found it difficult to find a scent that I liked, which meant that it took me some time before I could hurry off to my driving lesson.

Arriving late, I was shown into the driving seat; the instructor sat next to me and started introducing himself; and then he froze, snatched his hand back, flattened himself against the passenger door, stared with a look of horror straight out of the windscreen, and went white. I looked at him and saw fear. I explained that I was not a complete beginner. He nodded but would not look at me. I was bemused. I put my hand out for the keys, but this caused him to bang his forehead on the visor. Did he think I was an escaped psychopath? Then I noticed he was covertly opening a window and I finally got it. He'd read about actors—worse, English actors—and I smelled like a direct hit on a perfumery. This so-called "driving lesson" was clearly a prelude to something much more intimate—an act so alien to New Zealand culture that it was probably punishable by ritual disembowelment during half-time in a rugby match.

I immediately started talking about my "girlfriend" who was arriving that afternoon, and how I was thinking of proposing marriage, but it was to no avail. A travesty of a driving lesson now took place, as I jerked the car around, stalling it at ten-second intervals, and then just got out, apologised and walked away . . .

After that, the evening was a relative anticlimax, thank God. Ann and I had a few drinks, went upstairs, and she made it easy for me, bless her. I had no idea how to please her, but she seemed perfectly happy, and there was affection, and she only asked me to do my mouse impersonation twice.

This took place at the Station Hotel, Auckland, midwinter, 1964, and I was nearly twenty-five years old. When I was in New Zealand in 2006, I met Ann again, and I was pleased and proud that such a lovely and kind woman had been my first love. Thank you, Ann.

WHILE WE were in Dunedin we were hugely surprised to receive an official, entirely serious invitation to take our show on to New York. We were bewildered. Who in America knew about us? We stared at each other, shrugged . . . and agreed. It made no sense, but then that seemed the normal state of affairs in New Zealand. To my relief, my notional employers, the BBC, proved very relaxed about when I might return. The arrangement was that we would fly to the States when we finished in Auckland, and open three weeks later on Broadway.

Just before we set off, the New Zealand Broadcasting Corporation invited us all to see the TV recording they had made of our last performance in Auckland. I had never seen myself on videotape (or film) before. This may seem hard to believe, but the world back in 1964 had few replay facilities: if you missed a film when it was on in the cinema, there was no way of seeing it again, unless the studio decided to re-release it fifteen years later; there was no way you could record TV shows for later viewing; and the only video recordings in existence sat in the vaults of TV companies on the off-chance that they wanted to repeat a programme after it had first been transmitted.

So to see myself on screen for the first time was the most terrible shock. I had had no clue how awkward and strange I looked, and I shuddered to think that West End audiences had nightly watched this weird apparition. First, when I spoke I had such a stiff upper lip that I scarcely moved my mouth: I resembled a third-rate ventriloquist; then my hand and arm gestures were so cramped it looked as though my elbows were stapled to my hips; and, silliest of all, when I hurried across the stage, the lower half of me floated about like a hovercraft, while my top half swayed to and fro, giraffe-style.

It was almost impossible to believe this "thing" was *me*. But once I had got over the shock, it proved to be the most useful feedback I ever received. I immediately started working on all my movements: exaggerating and relaxing my lips when speaking, enlarging my gestures, and learning how to walk more conventionally. I had only three weeks before my American debut, but I practised hard and my mirror told me I was improving. Nobody noticed, of course, but at least I knew that I was on my way to behaving a little more normally. On stage, at any rate . . .

9

Two days later, we got back on a BOAC airliner and headed for New York, where we were allotted rooms in a slightly cheesy hotel just off Times Square, the noisiest, busiest, most crowded acre of seething humanity we'd ever set eyes on. I thought London was cosmopolitan, but what amazed me about Manhattan was the unbelievable variety of faces on the sidewalks. It made Soho look like Cheltenham. And everything was so huge—you looked down Park Avenue towards the old Pan Am Building and the scale of the skyscrapers so dwarfed Regent Street you felt you were on a different planet.

We soon started rehearsals. No one at the theatre seemed to know much about the show, but we felt relaxed and confident, with a long London run behind us (and rave reviews from New Zealand, ha ha). It therefore took us about two hours before we sensed something was wrong. We had been casually rehearsing different parts of the show for the benefit of the stage staff, when we noticed several shadowy figures moving around in the stalls, having rather loud conversations. This was not rehearsal etiquette, so we asked for quiet while we were running dialogue, but we got none. When we enquired who the interlopers were, we were told, "The backers"—meaning the investors in the show. And apparently they were rattled. Word had filtered back that the show was "too English." A full rehearsal was requested the next morning, before we had the chance to have the requisite full technical rehearsal. We pointed out that they could assess the show better if it had been rehearsed properly but their panic had taken over. We were bewildered. Why had they invited us to Broadway if they knew nothing at all about the content of the show?

Nobody can remember what really happened next, because the following few days were so panicky and frenzied that everything became a blur. The investors let it be known that about twenty-five per cent of the show had to be replaced—a *quarter*!—in the few days we had left before opening. I was not too badly affected, as all but one of my sketches ("Regella") were deemed acceptable; but Humphrey, Bill, Tim and Graham had to go into an inspired creative frenzy. We got permission from some Oxford guys called Terry Jones and Michael Palin to use a sketch they had written that we'd come across where three stooges illustrate various slapstick jokes involving planks and custard pies, while a lecturer explains the mechanics of the jokes (a sketch which finished up later in the *Python* stage show); Graham remembered an old Footlights wrestling match where one wrestler fails to turn up, leaving the other to fight himself (also to become a standard *Python* routine); and best of all, Bill, Johnny, Tim and David came up with a wonderful Beatles version of the "Hallelujah Chorus," which turned into an absolute show-stopper. We dug up a few other old sketches and quickies from the past, cobbled them all together into a radically new running order in an insanely short period of time and somehow managed to produce out of our maelstrom of nerves an opening night that received a tremendous reception. It was such an extraordinary achievement given the time available that we stood at final curtains soaking up the applause, but also stunned that we had pulled off this theatre miracle. Our only regret was that we had to admit that the "investors" had actually helped us make the show better. Bastards . . .

So off we all trooped to Sardi's, where Broadway opening nights were traditionally celebrated, popped champagne corks, and generally behaved in a very un-English orgy of relief and astonishment and self-congratulation; and then the volume of noise began to fade,

ever so slowly at first, and then to a murmur, a hush, and—finally—
silence. One man, with a long, long face, was standing in the middle
of the room holding up a sheet of newspaper—it was an early, smug-
gled version of the review of our show in the *New York Times*. People
gathered round it and fell silent.

The review was not good. In fact, it was pretty dismissive. "The
visitors behave," the critic wrote, "as if they are sure that what they
are doing, singing or saying is hilarious, but what emerges seems
obvious or purposeless."

I have never seen a party pooped so effectively. The crowds
melted away and the cast, lost and dismayed, asked, "But surely there
will be other reviews that will reflect the audience's enthusiasm?"
And, indeed, there were. But we were Brits; we didn't understand. A
bad review in the *New York Times*—in New York that spelt D-E-A-T-H.
The situation was not recoverable.

The next night the audience was even better—tremendous! But,
so what? The decision to close the show in three weeks was taken.
The best critic in New York, Walter Kerr, wrote a rave review of the
show to try to keep us alive. It appeared the day after we closed.

Twenty-four years later another *New York Times* review all but
killed off a film of mine. "It's not easy to describe the movie's ac-
cumulating dimness or to understand what went wrong," the critic
wrote, before concluding, *"A Fish Called Wanda* seems to have turned
into a private joke to be enjoyed only by the members of the cast and
crew who made it." Fortunately, this particular enterprise survived
the critical mauling.

However, things can move very fast in New York, and no sooner
was the show declared dead than it was being revived. A Washington
Square supper-club theatre called Square East invited us to perform
the show there, and we reopened just four days after we closed on
Broadway. It was a delightful, warm, rather classy club, where people
dined as they watched a shortened version of our performance, and
after the usual rushed transfer and rehearsal period—the stage itself

GRAHAM CHAPMAN.

A 23-year-old medical student, he has
made frequent appearances in cabaret at
various London night-clubs, and though not an
original member of the cast he joined the
revue when it transferred to the Lyric Theatre in London.
His friends and enemies alike describe him
as a gangling pipe-smoker. Gangle, gangle, gangle
he goes, smoking his pipe.

JOHN CLEESE.

Bluff, slate-faced and gimlet-eyed, he
prefers to be known as Otto and lives in
a light-weight cupboard. He worked
as a script-writer for the BBC until released
by them for this tour, and is an
amusing 24. He gives his hobbies as
photography, football, food and slumber
— but (he adds) 'I am utterly trendless.'

Two of the cast of *Cambridge Circus*.

Cambridge Circus cast members as photographed by me
(anti-clockwise from top): David Hatch, Tim Brooke-Taylor,
and Jonathan Lynn.

Other members of the cast: *(above)* Humphrey
Barclay; *(below)* Bill Oddie; *(right)* David and
me, fooling around.

Cambridge Circus sketches: *(above)* Jo Kendall and me
in a take-off of Somerset Maugham; *(below)* my withering
cross-examination of a terrified Graham Chapman.
David Hatch is the judge.

The "Chinese Song": unforgivably racist now but deemed
acceptable in 1963.

(Above) Tommy Steele and Polly James in *Half a Sixpence;*
(below) a pointless production still with me and a dancer.

The Frost Report: (from left to right) Nicholas Smith, Julie Felix, Tom Lehrer, Ronnie Barker, me, Ronnie Corbett, Nicky Henson, and David Frost.

(Right) Pretending to be coppers; *(below)* the "Class" sketch. Ronnie Corbett has just made me laugh.

Connie.

Gra.

was much smaller and the staging of the show much simpler—I discovered to my surprise I much preferred performing there to playing at our Broadway theatre.

In retrospect this may seem absurd but I think it says quite a lot about my attitude to show business. For a start, the strict rules of "legitimate" theatre did not apply, so I was able to change into my performing outfit in my hotel, walk twenty minutes to the theatre, arrive five minutes before the show opened and more or less go straight on stage, without any of the nonsense about make-up. Best of all, the much smaller room required far less voice projection, and allowed a more naturalistic performance, free from the slightly operatic exaggeration of expression and gesture that seemed necessary in a 1,100-seat theatre. It took me a few performances to adapt to this new style (almost by a process of osmosis) and by the time I had, I noticed that I was enjoying doing the show more than I ever had before. This more relaxed mode of comic acting chimed in with my natural aesthetic instincts in a way that I'd not expected; and because the venue felt less demanding, performance anxiety was reduced to an absolute minimum. I've never had so much fun. I also began to sense that I was becoming funnier.

Of course, I may well have been the first actor in history to have preferred being Off-Broadway to being On it, and I suspect that says a lot about my lack of performing ambition. For example, it never occurred to me to take lessons in acting (or in singing, or dancing). I did not view the world as an actor does, and I never thought of myself as one, although I certainly enjoyed getting laughs from the audiences at Square East. But I saw no future in it. As far as fame was concerned, it never crossed my mind. I did not know where my life was taking me and, looking back, I seemed to be quite unconcerned about it. After all, I had a job waiting for me in BBC radio, writing and producing, and if that went askew, I could always fall back on teaching.

I certainly liked New York, and I loved the feeling of freedom it gave me. It's hard to explain, but I felt anonymous in a way that was completely liberating. Why had I not felt this in London? Nobody knew me there either, but *there* I seemed to carry some vague feeling of being watched—of needing to be on my best behaviour so that I would not be reported to . . . to whom? Perhaps it was just a lower-middle-class anxiety about respectability. But it certainly vanished in New York.

One morning, after I had been in New York for a couple of months, I woke up in my hotel on Lexington Avenue and 48th Street (where I was paying $30 a week for my room), worked out in the hotel gym, had a swim in its pool, and then wandered out to buy a *New York Times* to catch up on the world. I skimmed the front page and something caught my eye—the date. It was Tuesday, October 27, 1964. My birthday. I was twenty-five. So I went off and had a lovely celebratory lunch at my favourite restaurant. I was perfectly happy to be on my own. While I enjoyed company, I didn't seem to need it, and I saw little of the *Cambridge Circus* team each day until we came together in the evenings to perform.

When I did socialise, it was with people I'd met in New York; and two of them were to become very important in my life. The first was a management consultant called Nick Walt, whom I met at a party; he worked with the Boston Consulting Group, although he was from a different Boston, in Lincolnshire. He was insanely polite and overbearingly considerate, but when you could trick him into talking about himself, he revealed an intriguing and offbeat way of looking at life, which included, for example, making graphs of his romantic relationships. When he analysed things—which was all the time—they took on an exponential complexity; I told him that if he wrote a report for the Boston Consulting Group about what he had for breakfast, it would come out resembling a Russian novel. But what I liked—indeed, loved—about this man was that he was a passionate supporter of the Somerset county cricket team. Now, to conjure up genuine enthusiasm for the antics of such a comprehensively hopeless bunch of underdogs and ne'er-do-wells was hard enough for someone born and brought up in Somerset; but to choose them *voluntarily,* when there was absolutely no kind of geographical loyalty involved, was an act of such utter pointlessness that I felt rather in awe of Nick. I had been reading about existentialism; here was someone living it, someone who accepted the concept of an act of Free Will in a Meaningless Universe, and was taking it to a new level.

Given Nick's take on the world, it was with some surprise that I learned that he was about to attend the Harvard Business School. But then I realised that, in a meaningless universe, going into business makes a lot of sense. When all values are in doubt, even Pascal might agree that making money is the best bet.

I had, however, misunderstood Nick's motives. He was learning all the precepts of business so that he could turn his back on them. Having once described to me how Harvard taught him what a brilliant "operation" McDonald's was, with its universal standardisation carefully eliminating any trace of individuality or spontaneity, he went ahead and bought . . . an artists' materials shop in London, L. Cornelissen & Son, which he has run ever since.

For anyone who has not yet got Nick's joke, I should explain that artists' materials resist attempts to standardise them more strongly than any other products known to man. *This* pigment, called Russian Real White, is made in Vladivostok by frying the wings of the White Admiral butterfly with mugwort pollen and ermine fur, in an oil made by crushing a rare kind of gravel found only in the Bering Strait; this other white, next to it, and apparently indistinguishable from it, called Butterworth Raw White, is a mixture of bleached Umbrian pasteurised talcum powder and fossilised Etruscan snow, baked in meerschaum clay over a mesquite grill and then frozen for twelve years in a glacier; and this white (the shade of which is halfway between the whites already described), which is called Not Off

White, can only be obtained by importing it from mines on one of the outer moons of Neptune. So Nick, who has spent the last forty years trying to systematise the storage of over 7 million of these pigments, has in fact merely been thumbing his nose at Harvard and its money-grubbing Brush Salesman culture. I think you can see why I love him.

And there's another reason, too. I have to thank Nick for my first proper romantic relationship. Let me swiftly explain, before you get the wrong idea.

Early on in our friendship, Nick took me for lunch to a restaurant on 3rd Avenue called the Living Room. It was rather dark and loungey, but it offered a very good buffet: "All You Can Eat: $3.49." As I was living on $15 a day, the place was a useful "find." But I couldn't get Nick to concentrate on our conversation because he kept glancing at, and making admiring comments about, my future bride. Eventually she came over to see if we needed more iced water, and chatted briefly to us, and went away, and I agreed with Nick that she was very charming and attractive, and then I agreed with him again, and a third time, and then did my best to discourage him from proposing when she brought the check.

However, a few days later, for a reason that now escapes me, I went back to the Living Room to splash out $3.49 on lunch, and found myself chatting with Connie Booth again. I learned that all the waitresses there were looking for acting work, and so we talked about theatre and I mentioned the show I was appearing in at Square East. On my next visit—the following day—I took a book called *Laughter* by Henri Bergson because I thought I might impress her if she saw me reading a French philosopher. (Remember I was painfully naive.) Finally Nick and I had another lunch there together and we invited Connie to see the *Cambridge Circus* show.

The evening she came did not start well. The opening number of the show involved all the cast running out on to the stage and singing a jolly end-of-the-pier song:

It's the end of the show!
It's time now to go,
We hope we've brought you laughter and joy,
So until we see you all . . . next year!
It's goodbye, goodbye, goodbye.

And then we all bowed and waved and left the stage, except for David Hatch, who stepped forward and said, "Well, as you can see, there have been one or two changes in the running order of the show," which I always liked, as a silly, upbeat way of getting things started.

Connie took one look at me as I stood there, "singing" and "dancing," and—as I later learned—thought to herself in horror, "Oh no! Oh God! He's *terrible*!" And, of course, I *was* terrible—absolutely terrible, since I have no musical ability at all; indeed I was so aware of my ineptitude that the results of my natural lack of talent were made even worse by my acute self-consciousness about it.

So as I pranced about the stage like a wounded heron, Connie started making plans to escape the dinner that we had arranged for afterwards: perhaps she could just disappear, leaving a note that her mother had been hit by a bus in Jakarta and that she didn't know when she would be back; perhaps she could feign an attack of lockjaw when we arrived at the dinner table; anything, *anything* to avoid the moment when she would have to make some comment about my performance skills.

And then, as she sat there enduring an agony of embarrassment, I reappeared on the stage to do a sketch with David Hatch (when I vetted him for a job with the Secret Service) and my battiness made her laugh a lot, and so everything was all right in the end, even though at dinner afterwards she hardly understood a word Nick and I said, because we "talked so fast in our English accents" . . .

And so, with great decorousness, Connie and I started to see each other regularly. We loved talking together and I think we both knew we might be in a serious relationship.

I remember that I was surprised to learn how much of Connie's time was taken up by auditions. In the fourteen months since I'd left Cambridge I'd never done one, so I was very amused when, two weeks later, I was asked to read for a role. Although the *Cambridge Circus* cast had been represented by a New York theatrical agency while we were on Broadway, we were sure that none of the agents really knew who we were. But one of them called, and told me I'd been invited to audition for a British show that was coming to Broadway in the New Year: *Half a Sixpence* with Tommy Steele. I just laughed and laughed and felt I couldn't resist: the idea that I could tell Bill and Tim that I was auditioning for a Broadway musical was going to be well worth the humiliation involved. Unlike Dudley Moore's one-legged man auditioning for the role of Tarzan, I was not expecting to land the job.

So I went along to the theatre and hung around backstage until I was called, at which point I walked to the lighted part of the stage and gave my name. A stage manager joined me and we read out the four or five pages of dialogue I'd been given when I'd arrived. I got a few laughs from the blackness in the orchestra stalls, because I was playing the part of a snooty upper-class English twit of the kind guaranteed to amuse Americans. And then I handed the pages back, and a voice asked:

"Could you sing something?"

"No."

This got a laugh. Pause.

". . . Just sing anything . . ."

"I don't know anything. I cannot remember tunes." (This was not quite true. I could remember tunes, I just couldn't sing them. But I was keen to end the audition as soon as possible.)

A pause. Muttering in the stalls. Then:

"Well . . . could you sing your national anthem?"

"All right. How does it go?"

This got a big laugh, but they persisted, and so I gave in and sang

"God Save the Queen" so appallingly it should have been renamed "God Help the Queen." I went home, giggling, and that night told Bill and Tim that I'd auditioned and got the part. They didn't believe me, although I swore it was true.

The next morning the agent called to tell me that I'd been given the role.

The degree of my flabbergastedness beggars description: I was dumbfounded. My mind jammed. I had never even bothered to consider whether I wanted the job.

"Don't you?" asked my agent.

"Er . . ."

"It's $200 a week for six months if it runs, which it probably will. You'll rehearse here in New York, and then do a few weeks in Boston and Toronto, and then on to Broadway . . . Hello?"

"Er . . ."

"Your show in Washington Square closes in a few weeks, doesn't it? What are your plans?"

I didn't want to admit that I didn't have any, and, yes, it felt as though *Cambridge Circus* was winding down and didn't seem likely to be going on far into the New Year.

"Have you ever been in a musical before?"

"Not exactly."

"It'll be an interesting experience then."

And that's what got me. True, it was only a very small part, and even someone as inexperienced as me could tell that there was nothing very special about the writing. The show was adapted from H. G. Wells's novel *Kipps* about an orphan working as an apprentice in a draper's shop, who has a childhood sweetheart named Ann. By a stroke of good luck, Kipps comes into a fortune and then falls for an upper-class girl, whose brother, Walsingham, a stockbroker (possibly played by John Cleese), offers to take over the management of Kipps's money, swindles him and disappears, leaving him a pauper again. Kipps now discovers that money isn't everything and, in a superb plot twist, returns to his childhood sweetheart, Ann, marries her, and they live happily ever after.

I learned all this from the script which was sent to me while I made up my mind. I also met with the producer who told me they'd heard that I was a writer, and that if I cared to rewrite any of the dialogue, they would be very interested to see what I might come up with. I was rather excited (and flattered) by this, especially as I thought the ending could be made more interesting if, when Kipps and Ann returned from the wedding at the church, he dismembered her with an axe and invited all his old apprentice friends round for the barbecue.

So I accepted the role, both for the experience and for the chance to help with the writing, without worrying at all about its minuscule size. I'd discovered that I had about twenty lines altogether, most of them spread over four group scenes in the first act, and the rest delivered in the first scene of the second act, which meant that I could then go to my dressing room and read until I was required for the final bows. I'm amused that the Wikipedia entry for *Half a Sixpence* says that I played "a small but crucial role." "Small" I wouldn't argue with; but the "crucial" aspect of my role—the swindling and the absconding—took place in its entirety after I had left the stage and gone off to read, and so I wouldn't claim much credit for it.

With my future income now assured, but with several weeks to kill before rehearsals, I found myself working on a new version of *Cambridge Circus*. The two guys who ran Square East, Murray Sweig and Charles Rubin, both of whom we all liked very much, noticed that audiences were falling off slightly, and asked us if we could put on a new show with different material. Since Graham needed to resume his studies at St. Bartholomew's Hospital, and Jo Kendall and Johnny Lynn both wanted to get back to London, this suited us, and those who were left therefore started thinking about new sketches. I decided to try writing on my own, and found it hard to get started because, without Graham there to reassure me, I was uncertain whether what I was putting down was funny. But I stuck with it and began to come up with some material, which I got the others to assess when I went in to do the old show each evening. We also dug up some old skits from Cambridge days and kept a couple of numbers from the Broadway show: the Jones and Palin "Humour Lecture" and the "Beatles Hallelujah Chorus."

After a while we started rehearsing, and, for the first time since we had opened in London, some of us began to get a bit ratty with each other. Humphrey had done a terrific job moulding the original *Circus* and then holding it together, but now I wanted more say in the shaping of the new show, as I was coming up with half of the material for it, but, on the other hand, he was still the director, and so the arguments went back and forth. Disagreements about the script were nothing new, and they were to persist through *I'm Sorry I'll Read That Again* and *At Last the 1948 Show* and Python TV shows to *The Meaning of Life*. But this was something slightly different. We'd been together for some time, and when that happens everyone starts to develop their own style, and sometimes the styles, which originally blended well, begin to diverge and produce genuine "artistic differences"—a phrase which people use to paper over far more serious conflicts (as when Emperor Hirohito described the attack on Pearl Harbor as being due to "artistic differences with Franklin D. Roosevelt"). That said, the squabbling never got too personal and I continued to work with Humph over the next thirty-five years.

The only other thing that I remember from the rehearsal period was that I started smoking: menthols at first, but within a few months I was on the hard stuff—Larks and Parliament.

The new show opened in the middle of January 1965, without any kind of fanfare, and got surprisingly good reviews in the New York papers. Jean Hart had come into the cast in place of Jo Kendall, and she sang some jazzy numbers as well as funny ones, and Bill had written several good new songs, so the musical side of the show was exceptionally strong; the buffoonery was largely in the hands of Tim,

David and me. I hugely enjoyed performing with these two because we had been doing sketches together long enough to have developed a real comedic rapport. They had great timing, and good energy too, and were very generous, always thinking about the overall effect of a moment, and not just about their own contribution. In one sketch, which we had great fun with, we played three top RAF officers who are briefing bomber crews for a raid over Germany (during the war, of course, though it now occurs to me that it might have been funnier if it had been set in peacetime). The theme was British inefficiency and unpreparedness: at one point the crews are asked to consult their maps and instructed to fly over Gaul and drop their bombs just above the "R" of Holy Roman Empire. Watches are then synchronised with the words "In exactly five seconds from . . . *now!* . . . it will be a few minutes after ten."

In another skit, I played a BBC presenter who has carefully prepared his questions for an interview with a deep-sea diver. When he discovers that his interviewee is, in fact, an insurance salesman he has to improvise.

> BBC PRESENTER: You're *not* a deep-sea diver?
>
> INSURANCE SALESMAN: No.
>
> PRESENTER: I see . . . well, if I may ask you some questions about . . . being an insurance salesman . . .
>
> SALESMAN: Certainly.
>
> PRESENTER: When you've been . . . selling insurance . . . have you ever been attacked by any large fish . . . like sharks?
>
> SALESMAN: . . . Not really, no.
>
> PRESENTER: . . . That's very interesting! And may I ask . . . what is the . . . greatest depth at which you've ever worked?
>
> SALESMAN: Sub-basement level, I should think.

PRESENTER: Really! Sub-basement, eh? Well I never! And
    finally . . . have you ever experienced "the bends"?
SALESMAN: The . . . *what?*
PRESENTER: "The bends" . . . it's something that happens
    to . . . deep-sea divers sometimes . . . though probably
    not to insurance salesmen . . .
SALESMAN: No . . . I'm afraid not.
PRESENTER: I just wondered . . . you know, on the off-
    chance.
SALESMAN: Sorry!

We also unearthed an old Footlights chestnut, and were delighted when Jean Hart produced a powerful performance as Henry V, exhorting the English troops before the battle of Agincourt.

> In peace there's nothing so becomes a man
> As modest stillness and humility:
> But when the blast of war blows in our ears,
> Then imitate the action of the tiger;
> Stiffen the sinews, summon up the blood,
> Disguise fair nature with hard-favour'd rage;

Henry's army, played by Bill, Tim, David and me, were in thrall to their monarch, and would loyally obey his orders, no matter what they were told to do.

> Then lend the eye a terrible aspect;
> Let pry through the portage of the head
> Like the brass cannon; let the brow o'erwhelm it
> As fearfully as doth a galled rock
> O'erhang and jutty his confounded base,
> Swill'd with the wild and wasteful ocean.

These instructions were followed to the letter, and produced some acting that would have distressed Lee Strasberg. Especially Tim's.

> Now set the teeth and stretch the nostril wide,
> Hold hard the breath and bend up every spirit
> To his full height.

As we tottered off stage on tiptoe, I don't think anyone in the audience would have put money on the English army.

One other sketch I recall with affection. David played the head keeper of a zoo where most of the animals have gone missing.

> HEAD KEEPER: And where are the giraffes?
> ASSISTANT: They were all there on Friday, sir.
> HEAD KEEPER: Well, have they been *stolen*?
> ASSISTANT: Oh no, sir! I think people just borrow them, and
> forget to give them back.

After about a month of the new show we found that the audiences were getting smaller again and we all sensed that end of term was approaching.

By now I had moved out of the Lexington Hotel and was staying with an old Footlights friend called Nick Ullett. He'd been a regular performer in the clubroom Smokers, singing his own songs to a guitar, and when he left Cambridge he went to America, where he teamed up with Tony Hendra to form a successful comedy-musical double act. By now the two of them were making regular appearances on late-night talk shows, including Merv Griffin and, especially, Ed Sullivan. I'd reconnected with Nick through Tony, who'd been to our opening night on Broadway. (Tony, you may remember, had been in the Footlights 1962 revue with Graham, Tim, Humphrey and me; he was still slightly outrageous and formidably well informed, with a thumb in many different writing pies.)

Nick had a quite roomy apartment at 10 West 65th, right next to Central Park and two minutes from Columbus Circle. I remember sitting there with him at the end of January, while we listened to Winston Churchill's funeral on the radio.

By now I'd been in New York for about six months and I recall writing down the impressions I'd formed of the people. I've lost the original, but can still reconstruct the gist.

1. America had what seemed to me an extraordinary reverence for anyone with lots of money. In England, to appear to be very interested in the old spondulicks was, as I said earlier, considered vulgar and a sign of peasant ancestry. But in America, untrammelled money-grubbing was a way of life—nay, a *raison d'être*. Furthermore it didn't matter how the rich made their pile: waste disposal, trailer parks, sex toys, plastic forks, rubber doorstops, pornographic magazines, torture equipment, edible goldfish, mines, contraceptive sheaths, trading in widows-and-orphans, it . . . just . . . didn't . . . matter. A journalist friend of mine lost his young wife to a chicken-wire magnate. However your fortune was made, you had paramount status, with just a whiff of moral superiority about it. You'd *made* it!

2. Slightly different, though allied to this: success needed to be visible. Visitors to NYC wanted to see the theatrical "hits." If you told them that you'd seen such-and-such a hit, and that it was really dreary and predictable and crass and vacuous, but that there were two productions that nobody knew about that were brilliant and original and exciting . . . regretfully, they still wanted to see the "hit."

3. New Yorkers weren't rude so much as tense. If I went into a tobacconist and started with my public school patter, "I'm so sorry to bother you but I'd rather care to buy some cigarettes, so if you'd be so good as to allow me to intrude upon

your time . . . ," they'd shout "Whaddyawant?" as though
you'd insulted them. But if you strode into the store, fixed
them with a look of pure hatred and hissed the word
"Larks!," they'd smile and chat and tell you why they'd just
left their wife.

NOW I turned my thoughts to *Half a Sixpence*. On the first day of
rehearsal, I turned up very early and asked to speak to the musical
director. My agent had assured me that the producers all understood
about my lack of singing talent, but I wanted to clear the air with
the man who mattered. Accordingly, I was led over to meet Stanley
Lebowsky. He was short and plump and pleasant, but he was clearly
a busy man and had lots to do that day.

"Mr. Lebowsky, this is John Cleese. He wants to tell you something."

"What can I do for you, John?"

"Mr. Lebowsky—"

"Stanley . . ."

"Stanley . . . I need to tell you something . . ."

". . . What?"

"I can't sing."

He laughed.

"I told them at the audition. Really."

He put a reassuring hand on my shoulder.

"John, let me tell you something. I've been working on Broadway
for forty years. *Everybody* can sing . . ."

He took me over to a piano, hit a key and asked me to sing the
note. I did so, to the best of my ability. I think for a moment he
thought I was trying to make him laugh, but then he saw from my

face that I was in earnest. He hit the key again very deliberately. I made the same noise. He just stared. I think he quite genuinely could not believe his ears. He hit a different note. I made another noise. He looked a little shaken and then nodded a lot.

"John," he said. "You're right. You can't sing."

"Sorry, Stanley."

"Never mind! Just learn the words, and *mime* . . ."

Because, of course, I was only in the chorus numbers, surrounded by trained singers, so who would ever know?

I wandered back to the main room and was astonished to see just how many people had gathered. A Broadway musical requires a small army. Then I was taken over to meet the director, a dear little Texan who looked like a bushbaby, called Word Baker.

For the first two weeks, rehearsals proceeded at a surprisingly gentle and undemanding pace. After all, I was in scenes solely for the purpose of explaining the plot. I had no big laughs to get, so, as Noël Coward put it, my only requirements were to remember the lines and not fall over the furniture. I therefore became rather relaxed, except when I had to go and rehearse my one and only mime-and-dance routine (which opened the second act). The miming was no problem; the words were simple to learn; all I had to do was to ensure that I made no sound whatsoever. (Stanley Lebowsky could detect a fly clearing its throat, at fifty paces. When, three months after the show opened, I had a rush of blood to the head and actually started singing quietly, pianissimo, at the bottom of my voice, I found him waiting for me as I emerged from my dressing room at the conclusion of the evening's entertainment. "John," he said, "are you *singing*?" To a passing backstage visitor it must have seemed an odd accusation, but he'd caught me at it, fair and square. "Only a little bit, Stanley," I offered, in extenuation. He looked me right in the eye. "Don't!")

So far as the dancing was concerned, my work needed work. This was the only choreography in the show that involved non-professional dancers so I had high hopes that there would be a couple of basket

cases to keep me company. No such luck. The other actors had all
clearly done this sort of thing before. I felt a flash of panic, imagining that on opening night I would stand out so badly from everyone
else on stage that after the first few steps of the routine I would have
caught the audience's exclusive attention, and that they would then
spend the rest of the number staring at my efforts, trying to work
out what could possibly be wrong with me. So from that moment I
dedicated my waking hours to trying to narrow the gap between me
and the next-least-talented dancer. The routine was based, unfortunately, on the polka, which involves leaping sideways at unpredictable intervals while moving in circles, and smiling as though this is
an enjoyable experience. I gathered it was a Polish form of musical
exercise, though what it had to do with dots I never found out. Beads
of cold sweat, maybe?

I rehearsed my steps for hours, with the help of an assistant chore-
ographer, but I could never enact this strange Slavic routine with any
kind of confidence. I would sometimes find myself polkaing away
for a few seconds quite fluently, but then the thought "My God, I'm
doing it!" would flash into my brain, creating a neurological inter-
ference pattern which immediately transformed my prancing into
an imitation of a man in battle trying to avoid one of those chariots
with nasty sharp knives sticking out of their wheels. The real trained
dancers, fine athletes to a man and woman, were extraordinarily
kind and patient and encouraging, even though I sometimes caught
them watching me with the same fascination people display the first
time they see a duck-billed platypus. The only thing I didn't like
about them was that when they themselves danced, they counted out
loud the whole time, which I found very distracting. I didn't know
why they were counting, and I was too embarrassed to ask what they
were adding up. The number of steps they were dancing, perhaps? "I
danced 50,112 steps today." "Hey, that's great!" "How many did you
dance?" "Only 43,694. But I'm going to do another 7,000 after supper."
A prima ballerina told me that dancers have very little conversation

(except about dancing), so perhaps they were just practising *not* talking about dancing.

During this early rehearsal period Word Baker would drop in now and then to watch and make suggestions. I learned that he had directed a long-running musical called *The Fantasticks* which had already lasted for five years Off-Broadway. (It continued playing until 2002, by which time it had set the world-theatrical-long-running record of forty-two years.) It was a very charming, sweet and tuneful production and the producers obviously believed that this flavour was just right for *Half a Sixpence*.

The other person we saw regularly was our star, and leader, Tommy Steele. He had made his reputation as Britain's answer to Elvis Presley, and he proved a tremendously pleasant chap to work with, exuding an easy cheerfulness, cockney elan, unfailing energy and total informality that made running through scenes with him actually fun. It was OK to make a mistake, provided you learned from it. But his relaxed demeanour hid an unwavering commitment to making the show as good as it could be, and when he felt anyone was slacking, or not fully concentrating, he could hand out a good ticking-off, never losing his temper, but telling people firmly and forcefully what they had done wrong. It was interesting to me, with my lower-middle-class embarrassment about showing anger, that anyone who received a scolding from Tommy always felt it was fair: they never felt resentful, because it never became "nasty." This aspect of Tommy's character was thoroughly helpful for the production.

Provided one worked hard and remained focused, then, a lighthearted approach was acceptable. This extended, incidentally, to the actual performances themselves. There was a moment quite early in the show when my character was first introduced to Tommy's Kipps, and we shook hands. Now this scene took place downstage of the front curtain (while stagehands behind it were arranging the set for the next scene), so there wasn't much room, and, as I shook Tommy's hand, I had been directed to cross downstage of him. A couple of weeks into the show proper, as I was shaking his hand, he locked my wrist and gently propelled me towards the orchestra pit. This was only about four feet away. Of course, he didn't try very hard, but I found it particularly funny because he carried out his dastardly plan with that famous cockney grin of his plastered across his face. Such innocent glee at the prospect of damaging several musicians tickled me pink, and so this dicing-with-death routine became a regular part of the show. The audience had no idea what we were up to; if they ever had, it would have disappeared from the show forthwith.

All in all, then, the first two weeks of rehearsal went smoothly. But when we arrived on the Monday of the third week, we were told there had been a *coup d'état*. Word Baker was gone, never to be seen again. In his place was Gene Saks, an actor-turned-director, who told us that so far as he was concerned there was still a lot of work to be done, and that we had better be getting on with it, since we were opening in Boston in two weeks. We dispersed to the rehearsal rooms in a state of mild shock. At this point I suddenly discovered that I had a new mother. The first Mrs. Walsingham had been played (or, rather, rehearsed) by Charlotte Rae, a jolly, outgoing musical-comedy trouper; but she had now been replaced by Ann Shoemaker, a formidably grave figure, who reminded me of a less feminine version of William Gladstone. Joining Charlotte and Word Baker in outer darkness was the producer who'd wanted me to have a shot at rewriting some of the scenes. So that was the end of that idea. As someone remarked of this theatrical purge, "In the beginning was Word, but only for a fortnight."

Rehearsal now took on a slightly sombre tone, partly because of a general anxiety that we didn't really know what was going on, partly because we all suspected that if we did make a joke we would have to send Ann Shoemaker a written explanation for our misconduct. I learned she had been a Hollywood film actress for the last thirty years, so perhaps she regarded this musical-comedy lark as a bit of a come-down. As the actress playing her daughter (and my sister) Carrie Nye remarked, "Apparently, when you break the ice with Ann, there's a lot of cold water underneath." I liked Carrie enormously. She was a true Southern belle in real life with an astonishingly languid manner and a wicked dry sense of humour; she also happened to be married to Dick Cavett, who later went on to host his own talk show, the wittiest and most intelligent one I ever watched.

I couldn't really understand what changes Gene Saks was making to the show, because when big musicals are being rehearsed the key elements are kept separate until the final stages: we had the dancers in one room, the singers in another, the actors out of earshot in the third, and Tommy Steele in all of them; out of eleven song-and-dance routines, he was in ten. Mind you, the show had been written specifically as a vehicle for his talents, so he only had himself to blame (in the original London production there were several numbers without him, none of which were as good as the ones he was in, so they were cut out of the Broadway show). Consequently he was hardly ever off stage, for which, again, he only had himself to blame. How he found the energy I shall never know. But he clearly loved what he was doing.

So, anyway ... in this rather serious and uncertain atmosphere we all travelled up to Boston where we were opening at the Colonial Theatre in just five days, and this was when Saks started putting the show together for the first time. We all gathered in a proper theatre at last and started to run the show from the top, very haltingly, as mistakes were made and corrected and unforeseen problems identified and discussed, and transitions between scenes practised, and I was able to sit in the stalls and watch the songs and the dance numbers and picture in my mind how it was all going to look.

And, of course, I was watching Gene Saks like a hawk, seeing as how he had the power of life and death over me. Up until now he had been a rather remote figure; when he watched the dialogue scenes, he had made few comments, though I had the feeling that he was rather put out that he had inherited me from my previous owner, when he would never have cast me in the first place. But he hadn't made any critical remarks so I was not sure where I stood. Certainly he seemed a rather formidable figure: tallish, strongly built, decisive, and not overburdened by any sense of fun. It never occurred to me that *Half a Sixpence* was only the third Broadway show he'd directed, that when he took it over it was an impending train wreck, that he had been given a paltry fifteen days to sort it out, and that, like any other human being in his position, he must have been pretty fucking nervous.

And I realised that *I* was getting nervous, as my first scene was steadily approaching, when I would have to walk out on stage and deliver a few lines towards Gene, and some producers and cast, who were scattered around the stalls. I was to make my entrance right after a big rambunctious song-and-dance called "A Proper Gentleman," involving Tommy, all the apprentices and all of the singers and dancers. The scene comprised a conversation with Mr. Shalford, the owner of the milliner's shop where Kipps worked as an apprentice. He was a tyrannical boss, played by Mercer McLeod, an extraordinarily sweet and kind old actor who had been in show business for fifty years, but who had obviously undergone a dozen or so facelifts, so that he resembled a very, very tall baby. He and I met in the wings and got ready for our entrance immediately after the "Knees Up Mother Brown" routine ended.

And it does. And we walk out together and I say my first line.

"Ah, Shalford, I wonder if I might have a word with you. This business—"

"Stop!"

It's Gene.

"Louder, John!"

"Oh, sorry! OK . . ."

We leave the stage; the singers and dancers have gone out front to watch Mercer and me re-enter, and I say, loudly:

"Ah, Shalford, I wonder if I might have a word—"

"Louder!"

"Louder?"

"Yes, *much* louder!"

"*Much* louder?"

"Yes! Again, please . . ."

I leave the stage, bewildered. Last time was pretty loud and now he wants it much louder than *that*? I am getting a bit embarrassed, too. Enter Shalford and Walsingham, who says, very loudly, as though he is a fairground barker:

"Ah, Shalford! I wonder if I might have a word with you!"

Wow! That's the loudest I've ever spoken in my life! If I ever spoke like this in a restaurant, people would run for cover! Town criers would cower in submission! So I continue . . .

"This business about—"

"LOUDER!!!!"

What? Louder than *that*? Suddenly I begin to see red mist. Is this man insane? Why is he putting me through this ridiculous humiliation? Did the British hang his mother? So, calmly and with just a hint of mockery:

". . . Louder than *that*, Mr. Saks?"

"Yes!"

All right! My dander has been approaching the vertical for the last few seconds and now it is right up. He wants it "loud"? Fine! He shall have "loud," then. I will try to create a sound wave that will damage him for the rest of his life. To frighten him to death will not be enough. I want BLOOD to come out of his ears!

I walk calmly off stage, I take a couple of deep breaths, mutter to Shalford:

"Turn away . . ."

And I walk back on stage and (with the sole intent of making

Mr. Bloody Gene Saks say, with a deprecating laugh, "Oh, I didn't mean as loud as that!") I scream:

"AAAAAARHHH!!!! SHAL!!!! FFFFORD!!!! I!!!! WONDER!!!! IF!!!! I!!!! MIGHT!!!! HAVE!!!! A!!!! WORD!!!! WITH!!!! *YOU*!!!!"

Take that, you bastard, and *die*! I'm glad we burnt the White House down, you power-crazed Yankee schmuck!

I stand there, breathing heavily, and triumphant.

And Gene calls out:

"That's it!"

Well! You could have knocked me down with one of those huge balls that are swung backwards and forwards from cranes to demolish buildings! I am so stunned I forget the next line.

"Once more, please . . ."

And the awful thing was: he was right. What Gene taught me in about sixty seconds was the vital importance of brute energy. The dance number Mercer and I had to follow was so noisy and exuberant and boisterous that had I spoken in a normal loud voice my presence would have scarcely been detected by the audience. I had to find the same level of energy or all the life would have drained from the scene. Years later, when I was directing one of the Amnesty *Secret Policeman* shows, I had the same problem with any sketch that followed a stand-up comic. I had to put Ben Elton on at the end of the first half, because he delivered his very funny routine into a hand mike at a half-shout and with such "attack" that any comedy performers coming on right after him to do normal sketch material didn't stand a chance, not even Peter Cook. Only another stand-up could have survived, and then we would have had the same problem with the act after that. If I'd been smart enough to have enlisted more musical turns I could have used them to drop the level of energy for the benefit of the next sketch, because music can accomplish this without feeling anticlimactic.

So after this right-angled learning curve, my life on stage became pleasantly straightforward. I had only to turn up half an hour before the show, deliver my infrequent lines, make sure I stayed out of the orchestra pit, avoid becoming too conspicuous during the polka (a feat I managed by the time we opened on Broadway), and retire to my dressing room to read Damon Runyon and Scott Fitzgerald and James Thurber.

10

After our first few days in Boston (when Gene tweaked our scenes a bit, and I put in some hard work on twirling around, Polish-fashion), I had plenty of time to look round the city, and to socialise with the cast. Boston appealed to me, with its comparatively historic buildings and constant associations with 1776. And earlier, too: in one cemetery I strayed into (I enjoy a nice graveyard now and then) I found the 1660 tombstone of a Quaker who had been hanged for heresy by the Puritans. I'd always thought that the *Mayflower* crowd had invaded New England to establish religious tolerance, but I suppose they must have decided that you can have too much of a good thing. After all, you've got to draw the line somewhere. God knows what would have happened if these God-fearing people had caught a Catholic. All they would have then needed was a couple of witches and an agnostic and they would have had enough entertainment for an entire weekend.

The parts of Boston round the universities were very pretty, with coffee shops and bookstores and little theatres; such sights never failed to remind me how happy I always believed I could have been in academia, if only I could have discovered something academic that I was halfway good at. I pictured myself studying a subject that fascinated me, and slowly building a real understanding of it; teaching it to bright, enthusiastic young people; being surrounded by brilliant colleagues who would happily condescend to discuss interesting topics; endless good coffee, and thoughtful walks in dappled sunlight (so not in England); all of this uninterrupted by the need to turn up and say exactly the same thing every night to the same people in the same way, while pretending to be someone else. I soon began to experience the whole theatrical process as mildly insulting to my intelligence, ungrateful wretch that I was, but at least I kept these feelings to myself, not least because the pleasant and friendly people around me were joyfully expressing their *raisons d'être*.

I know now, fifty years later, that though I have developed some of the skills of an actor, I have never possessed an actor's temperament. Even back then I realised that when I felt I was not learning anything from my work, my spirits began to droop, so that it then required an act of will to try to make sure I did not let the audience down. I suspect that several of the *Cambridge Circus* crowd felt something similar, and that it was for this reason that we often fooled around on stage, changing the words and trying to make each other corpse: when we broke up it immediately became fun, which injected a fresh, frisky energy into the performance and seemed to have a positive effect for the audience, too. It certainly cheered me immensely whenever Tommy Steele tried to introduce me to the orchestra pit.

However, although I was getting bored on stage, I didn't appreciate how much I was learning off stage. This was, after all, the first time in my entire public-schoolboy life that I had spent a lot of leisure time around girls and gays. Since leaving Cambridge, I had, in my own exquisitely poised and asexual way, dated a small number of girls, culminating with the Main Event itself at the Station Hotel, Auckland, and by now had met Connie. But I had still not lost the ingrained belief that most forms of affectionate physical contact were likely to be interpreted as sexual. Consequently, to find myself suddenly embedded in a group of young American dancers and singers who had no inhibitions at all about touching each other, hugging, kissing, and generally displaying spontaneous physical affection of the kind that someone from Weston-super-Mare would have des-

ignated "brazen," was definitely startling. Then, after about ninety
minutes, it became strangely reassuring and appealing. Moreover, to
my surprise, they accepted me as one of them, even after they had
seen me dance. My sense of freakhood was diminishing.

Along with this behavioural reconditioning, there was another
major shift taking place in my social attitude system. From the first
day of rehearsal, back in the days of Word Baker, I had begun to
notice something else that was unfamiliar in the streets of Weston-
super-Mare. A number of males in the cast seemed to be on particularly friendly terms with each other—more so than, say, the Scottish
rugby team would have considered the norm. And their interaction
was distinctly more playful than would have been expected from
their Gaelic counterparts. So much so that it gradually began to
dawn on me that it was not beyond the bounds of possibility that
one or two of them might, to be blunt, occasionally bat for the other
team. A discreet enquiry and much giggling later, my lovely friends-
who-were-girls explained that, contrary to Broadway custom, the
dancers were straight (except for one), while the singers were very
largely of a different persuasion. Whatever traces still persisted in
me of Clifton College's steadfast belief that homosexuality ranked
somewhere between regicide and treason were now eroded rapidly
by my observation of their good nature and sense of fun; and today it
is rather horrifying to think that in England at the time their behaviour could have landed them in jail—a state of affairs that continued
for two more years, until 1967.

The everyday camaraderie of these girls and gays did a lot to advance my emotional age. I was also coming to realise that I was more
adaptable to circumstances than I (or my friends) had thought; my
failing was a lack of boldness and initiative in stepping outside my
comfort zone, both emotionally and physically. (Especially the latter:
I do not understand why anyone should want to seek out experiences
that involve any kind of discomfort. I find mountaineers and polar

explorers and cage-fighters deeply mysterious. Why should people voluntarily take part in these slow-motion suicide attempts? If they want to end it all, why don't they just get it over with, quickly? When I was young Dad told me about a man who used to bang his head against a wall because it was so nice when he stopped. Even at that age I was puzzled by why he had started it in the first place. Terry Gilliam has spoken scathingly about my preference for physical comfort. I have come to the conclusion that this is very much his problem.)

Apart from my informal socialisation classes, I had one other learning experience in Boston. One Sunday morning I woke up with a very painful toothache. It was so bad I couldn't cope, and eventually I found a dentist who was prepared to provide emergency treatment over the weekend. As I sank gratefully into his chair I envisaged an end to my suffering. He advised an X-ray, took several, and disappeared to process them. After a time (during which the pain had not diminished) he reappeared, and put the various X-rays up on an illuminated screen, and then invited me to come and view the screen with him, which allowed him to point to the number of procedures that I was going to need—some crowns, a couple of bridges, a root canal or two, and so forth. When he was finished he offered me his hand and asked me to call his secretary to make a schedule of appointments so that he could carry out this intensive programme before I left Boston.

I was astounded. The fact that the sound of cash registers had completely obliterated from his mind the reason for my visiting him in the first place appalled me. When I reminded him, instead of profuse apologies, he quite casually commented, "Oh yes," and glanced rather pointedly at his watch—it was a Sunday after all—before injecting me and starting on the drilling. I began to suspect that the American professional classes had a different interpretation of the word "vocation" from the one I was used to. And this was before I'd met any of their lawyers.

THE MOVE to Toronto brought a surprise or two. Although the opening night's performance was well received by the audience, the next morning's reviews were savage. I was shocked that our show, which had been well liked by the Boston public and critics alike, was now dismissed as a dreadful, talent-free disaster. Yet on my arrival at the theatre for the matinee I noticed that everyone was carefree and blissfully unaware of the impending disaster that was going to be our Broadway first night. When I finally plucked up the courage to mention the reviews to one of the producers, he laughed and told me, "Oh, the Canadian critics are always like that. You see, nobody pays any attention to them. So they write vicious stuff to try and get noticed." I wondered if this was just bravado, but, sure enough, three weeks later *Half a Sixpence* opened in New York to really rather good reviews from the so-called "Butchers of Broadway." Meanwhile the cast contented themselves with the thought that it was reassuring to know that there were, after all, some mean people in Canada.

I was still a little shaken by the thought that a critic of a proper newspaper would be allowed to use such a base and unethical way to advertise himself, but then I realised that from a journalist's point of view the great advantage of writing abusively is that it takes no talent; the sad thing about it is that the English sometimes mistake such taunting for wit.

I found Toronto an immensely likeable city, spacious and gentle and slightly dignified, but in a low-key, friendly way. The only people who didn't seem to think much of it were its inhabitants, who could hardly wait for you to ask directions, because that gave them the perfect opportunity to apologise for it. What they were apologising for I never understood. I think they felt uninteresting, compared with America. I took the opposite view; I remember reading about the doctrine of American "Exceptionalism" and thinking that what

I liked so much about Canadians was that they consider themselves *un*exceptional. This modest, unthreatening attitude seems to produce a nation that is stable, safe, decent and well respected. It's just a shame that for seven months of the year it's so cold that only Canadians would put up with it.

Still, they have one compensation for their climate. Hockey (or as we would call it, ice hockey). My God, they love it!

During one of the first performances of *Half a Sixpence* in Toronto, I was on stage when I heard the sound of muffled cheering coming from the wings. I could not believe it was connected with the scene we were playing, so the moment I got off stage, I hurried to its source and found a large group of stagehands glued to a TV set. They were watching the semi-finals of the Stanley Cup, where their beloved Maple Leafs were taking on their arch rivals, the dastardly Montreal Canadiens. It was gripping stuff, and by the end of the show the entire cast had got involved, rushing over to the TV the moment they completed a dance number to cheer for the Leafs and then racing back to the stage for the next spurt of hoofing. (With the exception of Ann Shoemaker, who appeared quite unmoved. Rumour had it she was a Black Hawks fan.)

The semi-finals consisted of seven games, so by the time the decider was reached, the cast's devotion to the Leafs had reached fever pitch and people were missing their entrances, and leaving scenes earlier than usual, lest they missed a crucial goal. And when the odious Canadiens (who couldn't even spell their own name correctly) scored the winner in the very last minute of the seventh game, the show-stopper that immediately followed had a despairingly bereft and forlorn quality that was quite contrary to the director's intentions. Luckily, Gene was back in New York by then. And the next day, we were also heading there, to our loved ones and to our Broadway opening.

Fortunately, my first-night nerves did not seem as bad as usual, probably because we'd done plenty of performances and were confident we had a pretty good show, and also because, unless I fell over, nobody was going to notice me. But just before I made my first entrance I went to stand in the wings and saw, sitting in the box closest to the stage and about fifteen feet above it, Tim Brooke-Taylor and Bill Oddie. It was not just their presence that unnerved me; it was their demeanour: they were leaning over the edge of the box with an expression of gleeful, bloodthirsty anticipation, like a couple of vultures excitedly waiting for their supper to expire. I noted, for future reference, how the possibility of my public humiliation gave them great joy, and the promise of a better life, and this suddenly ignited in me a fierce determination: a steely, warrior-like resolution not to fall over.

And though I say it, who shouldn't, my performance was a triumph! Not only did I not come a cropper, I circumnavigated the Polish lateral-springing-about with fewer than usual mistakes, my miming was lip-perfect and my dialogue scenes were so inconspicuous that I avoided any mention *at all* in the reviews. I spent the next month imagining Brooke-Taylor and Oddie slinking away from the theatre with their tails between their scrawny legs. Friends! I never encountered such treachery again.

Until the Pythons, of course . . .

Half a Sixpence became a decent-sized hit, and I found I had a lot of time on my hands. As usual, I did nothing to advance my showbiz career, but I did find other ways to occupy myself. One, strangely enough, was journalism. While *Cambridge Circus* was still on Broadway, I was waiting on a subway platform when I was recognised by one of the very few people in New York who'd ever seen the show: a *Newsweek* journalist called Everett Martin. We chatted, I told him how interested I was by international politics and, on the spot, he invited me to my first Thanksgiving dinner. I had no idea what an important occasion it was for Americans: especially for Everett, who met his next wife that evening. After that we lunched a few times. I loved the way he was so well informed; in fact, I told him how useful and honourable the job of a journalist seemed to me: to try to understand a situation, and then describe it interestingly. Just before I left for Boston, he asked me to contact him on my return, because the foreign editor at *Newsweek*, Bob Christopher, wanted to see if I might care to join the staff for a trial period, contributing light-hearted, more humorous pieces, at least to begin with. So now I had another iron in the fire, over and above my song-and-dance career. I studied *Newsweek* carefully and discovered that I preferred its style to that of *Time*. I also noted that the foreign-affairs articles usually started with a remark made to the journalist by a cab driver, followed by a second paragraph that began: "However, by the end of last week it was becoming abundantly clear that . . ." How difficult could it be? I thought. Therefore I spent a lot of time reading about world politics. There was something about seeing the world and understanding how it worked that excited me.

For the first time in my life, I also made regular visits to art galleries. I was staggered by the abundance of great paintings that I could see at the Met, MoMA, the Frick, the Guggenheim, and all the commercial galleries scattered all over Manhattan. I dutifully stared at them for longer than most people; it seemed to me that I had a rather slow eye that simply didn't take in visual information quickly; that I had a poor memory for it. I also discovered that I couldn't abide paintings with plump angels with spindly trumpets serenading even plumper ladies with wispy underwear, and that most of the more schematic modern art left me unaffected and puzzled, in a dissatisfying way. But now and again I would find something I could hardly tear myself away from, that made me tingle and even shiver with delight: probably a Bosch, or a Brueghel, or a Caravaggio, or a Vermeer, or a Rembrandt, or a Courbet, or a Manet, or an Impressionist, or a Cézanne, or a Fauvist. Best of all, I noticed that whenever I walked home from an exhibition I felt calmer and saner than when I'd gone in.

Talking of great artists brings me to the subject of Terry Gilliam, because he liked them too. He had approached me after he'd seen me in a performance of *Cambridge Circus*. At the time he was working for *Help!* magazine, founded by the (apparently) legendary Harvey Kurtzman, who had made *Mad* magazine (apparently) famous. Terry asked me if I would work with him on a story for *Help!*, told in the form of "fumetti"; this meant that in place of drawings there would be photographs, but ones with speech balloons coming out of the characters' mouths. Terry explained that what he'd liked about my acting was the "faces that you pulled." This was rather flattering, because what I had long admired about Sir Laurence Olivier and, on film, Marlon Brando, was that they pulled the best faces that I had ever seen—much better than the faces pulled by, for example, Ingrid Bergman or Cary Grant, or Dame Sybil Thorndike, who couldn't, frankly, pull faces to save her life. Terry, being so visually gifted, was terribly good with faces; it was only what was going on behind them that mystified him.

Trying not to let Terry's praise go to my head, I agreed and we embarked on a two-day photo shoot in which I played a young husband who discovers one day that a Barbie doll that his young daughter has been given is surprisingly realistic; he is strangely attracted to it (her); he becomes obsessed, until one night etc., etc. It was a pleasant, stress-free shoot and Terry seemed happy with most of the faces I pulled. When I saw the results I thought he had told the story well, but I found it slightly distasteful: perhaps my Westonian prudery was asserting itself, but then I have never shared Terry's deep conviction that the main purpose of Art is to rub people up the wrong way; or perhaps I was just worried that having it away with a very small figurine might suggest that I was rather sparingly endowed. Anyway, Terry and I met up occasionally, although neither of us would have bet heavily on the prospect of another professional co-operation. It's odd to think he was the second Python with whom I worked.

Meanwhile, Connie and I picked up where we had left off. Quite unlike me, she kept busy with acting and singing lessons, and a regular flow of auditions. She was looking for roles in "summer stock" productions, and to our excitement, she landed a great one in a comedy called *Never Too Late,* which was set to tour parts of the East Coast that summer. The lead was played by the comedy star Bert Lahr, who was best known for his role as the Cowardly Lion in *The Wizard of Oz.* Connie had a decent-sized role, and she played most of her scenes with Bert; when I took a train down to Pennsylvania to catch a matinee performance, I was proud to see her standing toe to toe with Bert's considerable presence. It's odd again to think that ten years later I would be writing a successful sitcom with her, and that thirty-five years later she would be marrying Bert's son John.

I could only attend her matinees as I was still required briefly each night at the Broadhurst Theatre, where, apart from the occasional moment on stage, I was managing to get a lot of reading done; it was such a gentle routine that $200 per week seemed more than my due. One performance morphed into another and the months passed without leaving any trace on my memory.

Except when things went awry. All funny theatrical stories are about disasters, and when a large number of singers and dancers are involved, the sight of them all trying to keep a straight face becomes risible in itself, especially when they deliberately start dancing off stage, where they can collapse into laughter for a moment, before taking a deep breath and capering back in front of the audience again.

One evening a very competent dancer called Bill, having just completed three spectacular leaps with legs at full extension forward and back, was walking round to start the next part of his performance, when he inexplicably fell in a heap. It was so sudden, and unexpected, and delightfully simple, that it was gloriously funny; and even more so when Bill then got back on his feet and tried to laugh the whole thing off. This, for some reason, turned out to be a terrible misjudgement. If he had gone straight on dancing, the audience might have been able to overlook the lapse, but in trying to share the joke about his pratfall, he reduced them to depths of embarrassment I had rarely before witnessed. They writhed, they hid their faces and they started to read their programmes. Meanwhile poor Bill, realising that he had actually made things worse, just stood there contemplating hara-kiri while the rest of us danced around him, trying to keep straight faces and failing badly.

An advertisement for VAT 69.

The paradox, of course, was that we were the ones who should have been embarrassed. There's a similar phenomenon when comedy is going badly. There you are, going for it, and failing, and the sound of a very little, rather forced laughter coming from an audience that is trying to encourage you truly makes you want to end it all; but when you are knocking yourself out, and the response is total, dead silence . . . it can suddenly tickle you insanely pink. Maybe it's because you have in fact died, so it doesn't matter anymore.

The most surprising thing that you begin to learn from audiences is just how much you can get away with. All sorts of mistakes and accidents and horrendous confusions will be happily accepted by the paying public: they will assume they missed something, or that they were being a bit thick, or that the accident was always intended to happen. You apologise that they had to come to see you the night that someone in the stalls had a fit, and they say, "Oh, we thought that was part of the show." I sometimes wonder why we bother.

Just such a moment occurred during the run of *Half a Sixpence*. There's a scene in the show when Tommy Steele's childhood sweetheart, played by Polly James, realises that she has lost his love to Carrie Nye, and, in horror, drops the tea tray she is carrying. Well, obviously she can't drop a proper one, because there might be broken crockery where the dancers have to prance around thirty seconds later, and there won't be enough time to clear it away. Initially, therefore, the crockery is attached to the tray with wires; but some of it still breaks, so plastic tea things are substituted. Now the problem is that the falling plastic makes the wrong sound: instead of a loud crash, there's a tiny rattle; so now a stagehand has to stand in the wings with a large metal tray with metal plates on it, and he has, on a cue from Polly, to drop the tray at the same time that Polly drops all the plastic in order to make it sound as though the resulting crash comes from the on-stage tray. (Yes, I know you're ahead of me.) One matinee, the stagehand misses the cue when Polly drops her tray, and it therefore lands silently. There's a moment of panic as everyone on stage freezes. Meanwhile the stagehand faces the most difficult decision of his entire life. After some thought, he decides "Better late than never" and drops his tray, making the normal startling clatter. We peep out at the audience surreptitiously: they are staring contentedly ahead and continuing to enjoy their afternoon. There is not the tiniest ripple of surprise, nor a nanosecond of mystification: everyone knows that sound travels slower than light, and if it was rather slower than usual today, well, this *is* a matinee. On stage we can't believe their calm acceptance of the miracle. And then . . . from the back of the stalls, from my old friend Tony Hendra, who has chosen to see the show this very afternoon, peals of laughter that continue for several minutes, puzzling the audience no end.

By the time I prepared to leave the show I was bored to death with my role, but while I was relieved at the prospect of being shot of it I still felt a pang of sadness. I was genuinely fond of the cast. I thought Tommy Steele was splendid: his talent, his charm and charisma, his professionalism, his cheerful friendliness were all terrific. Even the great Shoemaker had unbent a little over time; and the rest of the cast gave their best every night and were easy to be around.

One of the odder things about show business is that you grow quite close to people during a production, and then may literally never see them again. Despite all my affectionate memories of the show, I can only recall three occasions on which I have bumped into my old *Sixpence* friends since 1965: I encountered Polly James at a London party in the late '70s; I made the mistake once of playing a charity squash match against Tommy; and in 2009, to my surprise and delight, Gene Saks recognised me in a New York restaurant. I was touched, since forty-four years had passed, during which he'd directed countless Broadway hits and had enjoyed a twenty-year collaboration with the great Neil Simon, on both stage and screen, including some of the classiest film comedies of that period, such as *The Odd Couple, Brighton Beach Memoirs,* and *Barefoot in the Park.* He's ninety-two as I write this in 2014, and still working. Perhaps he's got a part for me . . .

Although *Half a Sixpence* was a wonderful experience from a personal point of view, it was a surprisingly useless one professionally. I don't think I learned a single thing that was subsequently helpful to me. Even though Gene's tutorial on energy was interesting, it never really applied to my TV or film work. And musicals don't appeal to me, by and large, since I look for funniness, wit, intriguing plots and a degree of subtlety that are strangers to most productions. Worse still for me, most musical comedies aren't really comedies. I think, therefore, that I had a tendency to underrate *Half a Sixpence:* in reality it had a lot of good tunes, some tremendous upbeat show-stoppers, a few touching moments, an enthusiastic, talented cast and a real star. Let's not forget it got eight Tony nominations, too, including Best Musical. So if I've sounded a bit snotty, I apologise.

BY NOW my relationship with Connie had progressed to the point where we had decided we wanted to live together. I therefore took a small apartment at 213 East 81st, and Connie moved most of her things in. It was a likeable, slightly quirky area, neither smart nor run-down, with strong Czech and Hungarian communities and restaurants. It was here that I discovered just how many good beverages there were around. I'd always been mystified by the paucity and sheer dreadfulness of traditional English drinks: Indian tea, Scotch and bitters all tasted awful to me. But slowly I stumbled upon China tea, and Lowland malt Scotches, and now, Pilsner—especially as brewed by the Germans. What a selection! Light and dark! A new world had opened up.

I was also tentatively making my way in my new career as a journalist. By way of background work I now read the *New York Times* dutifully, along with *Time* and *Newsweek,* noting with surprise how much space the *Times* devoted to Asia and the Middle East, compared with what it gave to Europe, but impressed by the thoroughness with which they approached their stories. (I would say "seriousness," but then many British journalists reading this would assume I meant "boring.") My day at *Newsweek* started with a meeting where Bob Christopher and eight or so writers, including my friend Everett Martin, discussed what was going on in the world and what the magazine should be covering. For me, it was like the perfect seminar, because it was jam-packed with good information about significant world events. At the same time, it was conducted with a relaxed good humour, and my occasional questions were kindly treated. I soon realised that they all had a rather disapproving view of British journalists, who, they felt, were too invested in their writing, and not sufficiently concerned in what they were writing about—"long on opinion, short on facts" just about summed it up. They also once or twice discussed journalistic ethics, which in England is an oxymoron. But what impressed me was that, above all, they were always trying to make clear the distinction between reporting the "facts" and the process of "evaluating" them.

After a few days, though, during which I penned a couple of lighter-hearted stories which were heavily rewritten, disaster struck my infant journalistic career. I had not been too worried about finding an acceptable way of turning out a few of these minor stories while I was learning my craft, because my mentor Everett was there to guide me. But he was suddenly dispatched to cover a crisis in the Dominican Republic, and I was left to fend for myself. Clearly they didn't think much of my next efforts because I was soon asked to prepare an obituary for President Sukarno of Indonesia, who had been running his country for twenty years and was looking good for a few more. I took the hint and wrote a letter of resignation to Bob Christopher, to spare him the embarrassment of having to fire me.

So there I was, that Friday evening, jobless and, indeed, directionless, having dinner with Connie in an open-air restaurant and wondering what on earth I was going to do next. Not that I was worried. Connie was very supportive and I knew I had enough money to eat for a week or two, so the world was my mollusc and I mused about the exciting opportunities ahead. I needn't have bothered. By Sunday afternoon I was back in show business, and I've never looked forward since.

We'd arranged to have lunch that day with one of my new acquaintances, a young producer I'd met recently, called John Morris. He had a deal, it turned out, with the Establishment Club which Peter Cook had founded in Soho in 1961, the year of *Beyond the Fringe* and the start of the Satire Boom. By making his club a members-only place, Cook was able to avoid the censorship laws of the time, and put on shows that would have upset the Lord Chamberlain. Morris had acquired the rights to a couple of these for performance in North America, and hearing about me via *Newsweek,* he asked me if I wanted to join the cast of a show he was about to send off on a mini-tour of Chicago and Washington. The group of four included Peter Bellwood, who had been president of the Footlights in my first year at Cambridge, and who was an immensely likeable and amusing fellow. I knew it would be a pleasure to work with him, so I said "Yes" over the coffee, and agreed to start rehearsing the very next day.

In a way it was a stroke of purest luck, because having sacked myself on Friday, it meant that I was back earning my crust by Monday morning. But I sometimes wonder what might have turned up if I'd had the nerve to hang around for a time, before snapping up the first offer. Yes, I know about gift horses, but I'd been chatting about banking with two old Cambridge friends who worked at Citibank and had asked me if I might be interested; I could have enquired through Terry Gilliam about writing for *Mad* magazine; then again I always thought I could work in advertising, and, after all, Madison Avenue was at its sparkiest at that time. But my constant companions, good luck and Westonian cautiousness, decreed otherwise. In fact, I think there have only been about four occasions in my professional life when I have shown any real initiative: suggesting to Graham Chapman that we should contact the other four Pythons-to-be; arranging to write a sitcom with Connie; proposing to Robin Skynner that we should write a TV series about basic principles in psychology; and initiating and shaping *A Fish Called Wanda*. The rest of the time I have just accepted the next interesting offer, or continued in a pattern already created.

So we gathered at the producer's house and read through the Establishment script, which was pretty good if a bit conventional. British satire was only four years old, but there had been a glut of it, and so it had already developed its clichés. Still, as we only had ten days to rehearse we didn't rewrite much other than cutting some of the more specific British references and replacing a few weaker sketches with ones from other shows we'd been in. It was a mixed bag, but the tone was eighty per cent satirical, with sketches about the Queen, birth control, the Labour Party trying to use subliminal sex messages in their advertising, the Church of England, and so on. What seemed rather standard stuff to us, however, was greeted by the critics and audiences with delight. In those days Americans were not used to political satire: one comedian told me that satire was "what closes Saturday night," so what we were doing seemed very fresh to them. The critics were surprisingly enthusiastic about our performances, too, singling out Peter Bellwood in particular. He had a very engaging, relaxed style, with a wry affability that concealed his precision. Marion Grey, also English—noticeably so—was very well mannered, considerate, almost quiet—until she got on stage, where her work was strong and funny and quite effortless. She did a good Queen ("Philip, what is an anachronism?" "You've been reading again, haven't you?"). And then there was the shaggy, charming, playful Irishman, with a wonderful purring voice, Joe Maher, who seemed to be acting for a few weeks just for the fun of it, but who somehow went on to pick up three separate Tony nominations for Best Featured Actor in a Play.

We opened in a small theatre in Hyde Park, just off the University of Chicago campus, in July 1965. The audiences were young and quick and enthusiastic, and the four of us almost immediately found a loose, slightly boisterous style which suited the material. It's a good feeling when you find a rhythm that chimes in with everybody else's and the shows become real fun. Luckily we were there for the two weeks in the fall during which the Chicago weather is pleasant, marking the transition from sticky to freezing; so we strolled everywhere and decided Chicago was a proper "great" city with a proper river and proper big newspaper offices and lots of theatres and lots of friendly Midwesterners making jokes about how dim the Poles were. It had never occurred to me that Polish folk were remarkable in this way, so I was mystified when I was asked for the first time how many Poles it took to change a light bulb. My questioners were equally thrown when I asked them why anyone would use a pole for this purpose.

I found a pool hall and managed to beat a pool shark. He offered me a return match for $20. I declined: I was wise enough to know that I would never beat him again; I wasn't wise enough to know that I wouldn't have won the first game if he hadn't wanted me to. I was still hilariously naive. So naive, indeed, that I went to the Playboy Club and bought drinks and felt rather racy. Someone there then told me about a wonderful Peter Cook incident: he'd arrived for dinner at the club and they apologised that his table wasn't ready yet, so he had a drink and waited quietly. Then some big-shot local politician turned up and blew his top when they asked him to wait, too. "Do you know *who* I am? Do you have *any idea* who I am?" Peter got up and took over. "Does anyone know who this man is? Can anyone help this poor man? He's forgotten who he is . . ." The jerk was so perfectly deflated that the only course left open to him was to leave. On the rare occasions Peter was angry about something, he could be magnificent.

Thanks to the new show, I had to visit an immigration office in Chicago to extend my work visa, and it was here that I encountered my own local big shot. Unlike Peter, though, I came off worse. It was, of course, meant to be purely a routine matter: I filled the form in carefully and presented it to the immigration officer, a guy in his mid-fifties. The ensuing dialogue went as follows:

"Are you British?"

"Yes."

"What's this then?"

"Oh! That's my citizenship."

"You said you were British."

". . . I'm sorry?"

"Are you Ukrainian?"

". . . Ukrainian?"

"It says here 'UK.'"

"Oh! No, that's the United Kingdom."

"The what?"

"The United Kingdom. England, Scotland, Wales and—"

"UK is Ukraine."

"Um. I don't think so. You know when they have debates in the Security Council, the British ambassador has a little sign in front of him which says 'United Kingdom.' UK . . ."

"UK is Ukraine."

"I promise you, I did international law at Cambridge, and—"

"Are you Ukrainian?"

". . . No, but—"

"Change it, please. There's a law against giving incorrect information."

Remember that the person I was talking to was a fully trained, experienced officer of the United States Immigration Bureau, a man whose life had been devoted to interactions with foreign nationals, some of whom, over the years, must, statistically speaking, have been citizens of the United Kingdom. And he did not just *believe* that UK was an abbreviation of "Ukraine"; he *knew* it to be the case with the same degree of certainty he had about the reality of his own existence. Here was a uniformed idiot of the highest possible ranking: a man who even in his own chosen specialised area of expertise had managed to remain pig-ignorant; and not just ignorant (which can easily be remedied) but so incomparably dim-witted that he had not the faintest inkling . . . just how prize-winningly, cat-frighteningly stupid he really was. And so, realising that I must not challenge his authority (as it was the only thing he possessed) I did as I was told and, breaking the law about giving incorrect information, crossed out UK and wrote "Great British." Thus my visa was renewed.

In a way I was disappointed that our show became such a hit in Hyde Park, because it extended our run by a week, and I found that I was missing Connie a lot. I wanted to get back to New York and make plans about our future. I was therefore relieved when, after our last performance, we finally bundled ourselves into an old van and Peter drove the 800 miles back with hardly a pit stop.

But I had scarcely settled back into our little apartment to enjoy the autumn when I got the most important phone call of my professional life.

11

The call was from David Frost. Ever since he'd used a little of my material in the 1961 Footlights revue, and then some of my sketches in *That Was The Week That Was,* he had kept in touch with me. He'd seen *Cambridge Circus* in the West End, and again during our brief time on Broadway, and when he was in New York doing the American version of *That Was The Week That Was,* he'd occasionally call, just to "stay in touch." Of course, I always left these contacts to him, because he was hugely famous and insanely busy on British and American television. So, as usual, he greeted me with great cheeriness and warmth, and after the usual thirty seconds of banter he said he was doing thirteen half-hour sketch shows for the BBC in the New Year, and would I like to be part of it? This extraordinary offer was presented so casually that it felt almost like the natural next development in our relationship. Before the immensity of it had sunk in, I told him I'd love to, and he whinnied, "Oh! They've just called my flight! Got to go! Call me when you get to London! Bye-ee!," and he was gone. And the next phase of my life had been settled, just like that.

I'd always assumed I would return to London, eventually, but events were moving faster than I had anticipated. I told Connie about Frost's call and we started making plans about our future together. We'd been talking for a while about getting married. Now, I realised, getting hitched sooner rather than later had a practical aspect to it:

Connie's career was very important to her, and I wanted to be sure that if she followed me to England she would readily be able to get a work-permit.

In the middle of all this rather exciting planning I had to leave for Washington, and the second leg of the Establishment "tour." This time we were appearing not in a theatre but at a nightclub. As the facilities were rather limited—a slightly raised stage at one end of the room—and as we were expected to do two performances a night and three on Saturday, we cut the show down to forty minutes and happily relaxed into the nightclub atmosphere. The sober members of the audience were very appreciative, but I found myself facing a new challenge on stage: how to get through sketches with a fellow performer who started the evening one sheet to the wind, and regularly added a fresh sheet; with the result that by the third show on Saturday night he was several more of them to the wind than the customary three, *and* increasing their number at a rate of knots, causing our scenes to tack in unexpected directions.

For example, we had a "quickie" which went like this.

Lights up. I am standing in the middle of the stage. Enter Joe Maher, with a policeman's helmet on. He marches up to me and announces:

"Irish stew!"

"Irish stew? What about Irish stew?"

"Irish stew in the name of the law!"

Joe then frogmarches me off the stage.

It was so quick and silly we got away with it. But on the Saturday night (the third performance) it went like this.

Lights up. I am standing in the middle of the stage. Enter Joe, wearing a policeman's helmet at a strange angle. He marches up to me and announces:

"I arrest you!"

Hard to know where to go from there, really. "OK" or "It's a fair cop" doesn't open up a vista of comedic possibilities. If I tried,

"What's the charge?" he could have said, "No charge. I do it for free!" but, looking into his eyes, I didn't think he'd get my drift, so I just burst into tears, which at least made him laugh. A few minutes and another sheet later, Joe had to start a sketch with a rather long speech. He embarked on it with quiet determination, getting a fair number of the words correct, if not exactly in the right order; but as he reached the midpoint of the monologue, he began slowing, like a huge lorry approaching the brow of the hill, and such words as he did manage to emit bore very little relation to each other, although he had increased their loudness considerably, as though to compensate for their scarcity. I tried to interrupt, to help him out, but he would not yield. He was going to finish this damn speech or die in the attempt. On and on he went, as members of the audience tried to get their checks, or at least another drink. And at that point I did something naughty. I asked him to wait a moment, walked off stage, picked up a chair, brought it back on stage with me, sat down on it, and then thanked him and asked him to continue. He looked at me, his face slowly crumbled, and he started crying with laughter, sending out great sobs of mirth as he took the chair from me and sat down on it himself, spreading himself over the back of the chair, shaking and shaking with the wonderful helpless convulsions of a man who has come to the conclusion that nothing, absolutely *nothing* . . . matters. And by this time the rest of the room had joined in this glorious, pointless merriment. They knew not why, neither did they care. It is said that laughter is infectious. Well, several people nearly died.

He was something special, that Joe Maher.

One other thing from my time in Washington sticks in my mind. After the show one night we were carousing in a bar when a fellow drinker offered to read our palms. He stared at mine for some time and then said, "This is very unusual. Your logical, thinking side balances your creative side. Almost everyone has one side stronger than the other." This caught my curiosity, and over the years I came to the conclusion he was right, because the people who were more creative than me didn't seem very strong at analysis or construction, especially when it came to plot and to the careful building of emotion within a scene; whereas the ones who analysed well were good at verbal wit and parody, but seemed very constrained creatively, unable to make the non-logical jumps (or even hops) over to where the richest comedy lay. Perhaps this explains why some witty people aren't very funny, and why some very funny people can't think straight. I'm not top class in either department but I can switch back and fro between them, so I can sometimes get to something good if I rewrite enough (*A Fish Called Wanda* took thirteen drafts).

And so our harmonious little Establishment interlude came to an end and we went our separate ways. Many years afterwards, Joe contacted me when he was visiting London. I threw a party for him, and we vowed to stay in touch, but the next thing I heard was that he had died of a brain tumour. He had teased me mercilessly in London for not realising he was gay; I pointed out I had not missed that he was Irish, because he'd been so refreshingly open about that.

With my American perfoming days behind me, Connie and I now had time in New York to make plans for our life together; and so we went to our favourite haunt, the Ginger Man on West 66th Street, where they made the best omelettes I'd ever tasted, and she told me that she didn't feel that she was ready to get married. A few days later, she added she didn't really feel she was up to coming to London with me either. It was all very civilised. Of course, we both expected that we would get together eventually, and that in the meantime we would visit each other regularly. But it was my first experience of disappointment of "real world" romantic hopes, so I got very glum. I gallantly tried to hide my woe (though not so hard that it didn't show just a bit) and became the star of my own B-movie, written, directed by and starring me, in which I exulted in my suffering, knowing it to be very, very special—and all because, at that time, I didn't know any better. When I got back to London, I sent Connie a postcard wishing her "Happy Christmas," signed it, added the afterthought "all alone in the London rain," and posted it at the Trafalgar Square Post Office and then did my final close-up brilliantly.

Now I went down to Weston-super-Mare to spend Christmas with my parents and to catch up with them. And there was a lot of catching up to do, because since my arrival in New York I have to admit that I'd made no attempt to write or phone them. I know this sounds extraordinary, and it's not that I ever took a decision to stop communicating: it's just that the longer I didn't, the easier it became not to do so. Obviously a psychiatrist could write several chapters on this, "the final severing of the umbilical cord," but the odd thing was that I went from being quite dutiful, to American silence, and then back to being dutiful again as though I had never made my Unilateral Declaration of Independence. It must have been due to the sense of freedom I'd been experiencing in America.

I soon discovered that Mother's interest in my life abroad was perfunctory: once she'd listened for a couple of minutes to my Broadway adventures she started asking me questions about when I would be able to come down to Weston again. This was her invariable modus operandi, but after an *eighteen-month* separation, I thought it funny: I envisaged a sketch where a young monopod returns home from war to be greeted by his mother, diary and pen in hand, eager to establish the exact date and duration of his next visit, and the one after that, too.

Dad listened to my adventures, but our conversations weren't meshing as they used to: now he seemed to want to do most of the talking, and often gave me advice on matters about which I was better informed than he. This frustrated and puzzled me, until I realised that when I was younger he had loved his role as "Daddy," the wise, all-knowing advisor; and he was now trying unconsciously to resurrect the relationship we'd had back then. When I finally figured this out, I felt rather sad that he couldn't accept my growing up, and our moving to a relationship of equals, because it stymied any kind of deeper communication. Of course, being English, it never occurred to us to talk about it.

I was also a bit surprised that my parents showed so little interest in what I told them about Connie. Mother, I suspect, felt uneasy that she would have to compete with another woman for my attention, while Dad seemed almost relieved to hear of the hiatus in the relationship. He had always, in his heart of hearts, hoped that I would marry the daughter of a duke. This was not pure snobbery, by any means. As I've said before, Dad's brush with the upper crust just after the Great War, both in London and in India, had convinced him that they were the most impressive and admirable of human beings. So if I had managed to get hitched to someone with blue blood, it would have been heaven for him. In fact so determined was he that I should make an advantageous match that when I told him, two years later, that Connie and I had finally decided to get married, he groaned out loud. Not the textbook reaction, I remember thinking. But I know he always loved me, and genuinely wanted me to be happy; he just didn't know what made the adult me tick. Which made two of us, I suppose, though I had a clue or two, and Dad didn't.

The days passed quite slowly when I was down in Weston. Breakfast and the newspapers dominated the morning. Around midday I would escape for a walk, if I could come up with an acceptable excuse. Then Mum would present a tasty lunch and, once that was out of the way, Dad would have an afternoon nap, and at about four o'clock we would settle down and wait for the evening. And it was worth waiting for, because in those days British television was so consistently good that every night there were programmes we really wanted to see. Dad and I would start watching, and Mother would soon join us and knit or stroke the cat or remove stains from a tea cosy, keeping an eye on what was happening on the screen, and occasionally commenting on the action. One night we were watching the final episode of a thriller serial, and at the particularly tense moment when the villain walked in holding a gun, Mother remarked, "Oh, look, he's got a nose like Uncle Eric's." She specialised in these off-the-wall remarks. If the Prime Minister had suddenly appeared on our screens to tell the nation that we were declaring war on Russia, she would have remarked upon the colour of his pullover.

One morning, in a desperate attempt to enliven the hours till television-time, I suggested that we might go and see a film that afternoon. It was fascinating to observe the alarm, verging on panic, that this caused; it was as though I had proposed that we invade Poland. Father was instantly at the window, peering towards the Quantock Hills, noting clouds, comparing his observations with the newspapers' weather forecasts, remembering the car was low on petrol, checking that our raincoats had not been stolen overnight, and starting to make a list of things we would need to take with us. Mother, meanwhile, stood in the middle of the room, her eyes staring, repeating, "Well, will we go before tea, or after tea? Will we go *before* tea or *after* tea?" I got them both seated again, but there was fear in their eyes and they could take nothing in. I tried to calm them by talking to them about the happy times we'd had at the cinema in the past, but when I ran out of these—after about twenty seconds—they were still looking as though they had seen a ghost. They had had a perfectly good, workable schedule for the day: not to do much until, at seven o'clock, we started to watch television, and then bed at ten. Now their plans lay in ruins.

I therefore agreed that it was a bit late to change everything, as we'd already finished breakfast, but that perhaps we could start thinking about going to the pictures on my next visit. Thus calm was restored. So much so that by lunchtime, Mother was asking me when I thought my next visit might be. There were times when "never" would have felt too soon.

A rather revealing aspect of this moment of high drama is that the one question that was never addressed was, if we *did* decide to take the risk, what film were we actually going to see? The priorities of my parents' generation defied comprehension, at least for someone who had just spent an extended period of time in the US. If, for example, we were going to have a meal "out," then the main criteria for choosing our restaurant would be its state of cleanliness, the temperature of the plates and the food, and the size of the portions (not too big); but the *taste* of the food would play no part in the selection process. Thus my parents' favourite restaurant was the Copper Kettle because here the napkins and tablecloths were "spotless," the plates "lovely and warm," and the food "sizzling hot" and not "oily" or "rich" or "spicy" (especially garlicky). The highest praise for food (other than hotness) was "plain." There was a hint of xenophobia here: the unspoken purpose behind English cooking was that the results should not damage you. Vegetables had to be boiled to death, because goodness knows what could be hiding in there, ready to pounce on you; meat and fish were more demonstrably dead, and so safer, but they still required the *coup de grâce*. The sight of someone eating a steak tartare would have occasioned a call to the Samaritans.

Where was I? Oh, yes. Films. It is hard to believe that my parents' generation would walk into a cinema when it suited them, without paying any attention to what film it was that they were going to see. Indeed they weren't even concerned whether the film had just started, or was halfway through, or was in the middle of the final chase sequence. They would just happily settle into their seats with their sweets and cigarettes and start trying to decipher the plot, and who was the villain, and why everybody was in Hamburg, and then the film would end, and they would sit patiently through the advertisements and newsreels, eat an ice cream, and then the film would begin again, and they would finally discover who everyone was, and why they had all gone to Hamburg, and at exactly the moment when they'd understood what the hell was going on, and could now enjoy the denouement, they'd all shout, "Oh! This is where we came in!"— and leave. How are you supposed to write for an audience like that? The great farce-writer Ben Travers once told me that in the '30s, posh "country people" would invariably arrive in their seats at the back of the stalls about twenty minutes late (to show that they were not bound by the trivial conventions of the proletariat) and that he therefore always added a brief summary of the plot at that point, so the toffs could get up to speed. But Ben at least knew *roughly* when they'd be arriving. Did the "Oh! This is where we came in!" brigade ever consider *why* they liked watching a movie in the wrong order? Well, not my parents, anyway. "Theirs not to reason why . . ."

I eventually tore myself away from Weston, and raced joyfully to Notting Hill, where Tim Brooke-Taylor had offered me a bed in his place in Ledbury Road while I looked for somewhere more permanent. I learned that when he, David Hatch, Bill Oddie and Jo Kendall had got back to the UK from their stint at Square East, Humphrey Barclay, who had resumed his job in BBC Light Entertainment, had gathered them up and created a programme along the lines of the handful of radio shows we had done before we had all set off for New Zealand, which we'd called *I'm Sorry I'll Read That Again.* In my place he had hired Graeme Garden, another Footlights stalwart we'd all known at Cambridge, who was a particularly good "voice man" and mimic, as well as a witty and prolific writer; and he had then produced and directed a full series of thirteen shows, largely written by Graeme and Bill. It had been successful—or "promising" as the powers that be put it—and so they were doing thirteen more and . . . they wanted me to join the cast. Another little apple had dropped in my lap.

I was so chuffed that, after I'd called David Frost and established that nothing was happening on his programme for a couple of weeks, I persuaded Tim to join me on a quick trip to the Canary Islands to get some sun. And in Tenerife I had a glorious experience, spread over several days: I read Kingsley Amis's *Lucky Jim.* In my entire life I have found only two novels which have consistently made me laugh out loud, to the point where it starts to hurt. *Three Men in a Boat,* so beloved by Dad and Captain Lancaster, was the first. Now I discovered in *Lucky Jim's* hero, the academic manqué Jim Dixon, a character I could love and sympathise with because he reacted to the people and events around him a little as I did, but much more consciously and clearly and boldly than I would have ever dared. The scene where Jim's lecture on "Merrie England" goes wonky under the influence of alcohol, or where he takes a *slow* bus journey to the station, or where his cigarette burns a hole in his hostess's blankets are hilarious in an expertly sustained way that is rare—indeed, endangered.

When I got back to London I was contacted by my old Cambridge friend Alan Hutchison, who had just returned from a long trip abroad that had taken him to places as far-flung as Japan and South America. He was now about to take up a job as foreign correspondent with Reuters, and had found a very pretty little flat in Logan Mews, just off the Earls Court Road, which he suggested we might share for the next couple of years. I jumped at the offer. The flat was just big enough, with two small bedrooms and a living room and a tiny kitchen, and the mews was wonderfully quiet considering we were two minutes' walk from the Cromwell Road, with its endless supply of taxis, and only five minutes from Earls Court tube station.

Alan's travels had proved far more exotic than mine. At one point, after spending some time in Tokyo, he had decided to visit areas where Westerners had not yet trod. Realising that from now on his English was going to get him nowhere, he asked a fellow traveller to teach him the Japanese for "I'm sorry to bother you, but could you tell me where I could find accommodation?" Then he set off. Immediately the weather turned against him: rain bucketing down, thunder and lightning, the full works. Fortunately, a few rather small dwellings came in sight, so he approached one, knocked, and when the door opened, repeated his Japanese phrase. The householder looked very surprised, gathered himself, smiled, bowed three times and closed the door. Mystified, Alan decided to try again at the next cottage, with the identical result. By now he was soaked to his skin but since he had no Plan B all he could do was to keep on and on, repeating the scenario, until at last he found a woodshed where he spent the night. The next day, to his relief, he stumbled on a Japanese-style youth hostel, where the owner spoke some English. Alan asked

him if he would translate into English the phrase that he had so carefully learned. The owner agreed, listened and explained that it meant
"May I take this opportunity to wish you goodnight?"

How dismaying it must have been for those poor people to have
been roused from their beds, to find, standing at their front door,
towering over them, the first non-Japanese being they had ever set
eyes on, a creature probably of aquatic origin, and moreover one who
had chosen to make a special excursion to their home in the midst of
this torrential downpour, simply in order to wish them goodnight.
In fact so implausible must this have seemed, that, as they lay tossing in bed, these Japanese can have only come to the conclusion that
extraterrestrials were busy reconnoitring their neighbourhood, and,
under the cover of offering blessings and asking, "May I take this opportunity to wish you goodnight?," were estimating the strength of
their defences. It says much for the legendary politeness of the Japanese that they did not band together to hunt Alan down with hoes
and pitchforks.

I WAS now preparing to join David Frost in what was to become *The
Frost Report,* and was also meeting all the key personnel. Thanks to
David's relaxed and cheerful manner, and because I knew no more
about them than they did about me, we mingled easily without
any jockeying for position. It never occurred to me that at least fifteen of this friendly, amusing, low-key group would become major
professional collaborators over the next twenty years. I think our
easy harmony was helped by the fact that it was effortlessly clear
who was in charge: David, the director, and Jimmy Gilbert, the
producer—a delightful Scot whose judgement we all instinctively
respected, and whose calm confidence was infectious; his quick

and clear thinking allowed us all to relax, knowing he was always on top of things.

When David had called me in New York, he had mentioned that he would be doing the show with two people I hadn't come across before, Ronnie Barker and Ronnie Corbett. Now I got to meet them. Ronnie Barker, I learned, was a top-class character actor: he could play anything from a general to a yokel, and he'd done a good deal of television, so audiences recognised his face even if they didn't know his name. He was obviously going to be one of the principal performers and yet he was the least actorish actor I'd ever met; he seemed more like a jolly uncle, oozing with bonhomie and good jokes. Ronnie Corbett similarly had a real presence about him, even if he was only five feet tall; he'd done a lot of children's television but his background was more in cabaret and some music hall. He could go out in front of an audience as himself, without needing to be in character. He was also a great raconteur, so there was always laughter around him. That said, he had a highly tuned bullshit detector, and behind some of his funny remarks there was often a wickedly accurate observation. Both Ronnies were some ten years older than the rest of the performing team, who were in their mid-to-late twenties and who included Sheila Steafel, Nicholas Smith and Nicky Henson.

My first day's work for British television, at the end of January 1966, involved Nicky and me being driven off to a park in West London, where we dressed up as park attendants and were filmed as we stood, bewildered and powerless, watching Ronnie Corbett dancing around on the grass—the joke being that the signs read, "Do not *walk* on the grass." It wasn't exactly an inspired idea, and its execution wasn't helped by the fact that I had no idea what I was doing and got my sight lines wrong; but fortunately it was saved by Ronnie's performance. Nicky and I hit it off straight away and have been the closest of friends ever since. He tells the best actor stories I've ever heard, and also has a wonderful barking guffaw, which I constantly try to activate. I love the connection, too, that I feel through him and his actor and producer father, the great Leslie Henson, to the legendary Aldwych farces, starring Tom Walls and Ralph Lynn, and written (mostly) by Ben Travers, which were the funniest plays in England in the '20s and '30s. Dad saw several and he always told me he'd never heard laughter like it.

The cast and writers of The Frost Report. *In the front row (left to right): Marty Feldman, Sheila Steafel, David Frost, Jimmy Gilbert, Julie Felix, and Ronnie Barker, with five Pythons and assorted writers and dogs bodies behind.*

The piece Ronnie and Nicky and I filmed was for a pilot that Jimmy Gilbert had arranged, so that he and David could see what a *Frost Report* would actually look like. The format was very simple: David introduced the show and then set up a series of "quickies" and sketches; at the end of each item, we cut back to David for more of his CDM—Continuing Developing Monologue. Writers, being the sneakily subversive snarky bunch they always are, also called it Cadbury's Dairy Milk, and OJATIL—Old Jokes and Totally Irrelevant Links.

In reality we saw surprisingly little of David during the rehearsal days before the pilot, partly because his material was quite separate from ours, partly because, after the initial selection of sketches, he was happy to leave everything in Jimmy's hands while he just disappeared, as we used to say, "to continue running the world." I wasn't particularly nervous about the pilot: I knew that nobody outside the BBC would see it, and the rehearsal-room atmosphere always seemed friendly and relaxed.

But on the day of the shooting, when I went on to the floor of a proper TV studio for the first time, things began to feel much odder. It bothered me, for example, that when we rehearsed sketches for the cameras, there was no laughter at all: I didn't realise that the crew were so focused on learning to shoot this new show that the last thing they had time for was listening to the jokes. And when I came to do a monologue straight to camera, I got very spooked: talking to another actor while a camera is shooting you is pretty much like normal acting, but speaking straight at a camera for the first time felt so artificial, so weird, so utterly unnatural, that I immediately became very self-conscious and tightened up, losing my timing, and feeling rather rattled. Nobody seemed concerned, however, so I didn't say anything, and I was relieved to find that people seemed pleased with the overall performance and clearly had no doubt that the format would work.

There was a gap of a month between recording the *Frost Report* pilot and the evening when we transmitted the first show live, and it coincided perfectly with my reintegration in the cast of the *I'm Sorry I'll Read That Again* radio show. We began a new series in mid-February, and over the next eight years Tim, Bill, David, Jo, Graeme and I went on to make over a hundred more shows. Bill and Graeme were writing more and more of the scripts, although, to begin with, I wrote a little of the material, too.

I have to confess, though, that my relationship with *I'm Sorry I'll Read That Again* was a complicated and conflicted one. The problem for me was not with the cast, but with the style of the programme itself. Radio shows in those days could be immensely popular. After lunch on Sundays, families would gather to listen to, say, *Round the Horne,* and laugh themselves silly. But the majority of radio shows were pretty uninspired, relying almost entirely on puns and catch-phrases and stock characters and, worst of all, stock characters *with* catchphrases. When the writers of these dismal shows ran out of funny ideas, which was most of the time, there would be the sound of a door opening, followed by a sadly familiar "funny voice" say-ing something like "I won't take my coat off, I'm not stopping" or "Hello everyone, I'm back!" or "I still haven't found that scarf I lost" or "Anybody want a kipper?" or (if it was a female voice) "Young Doctor Hardcastle? He's *lovely!*" or "I'm blushing on all my cheeks" or "Those fucking rats have eaten my frock again" (well, perhaps not "fucking"; in those days it would have been "bally" or "flipping" or "blooming"). And what passeth understanding is that these ap-parently factual statements would be greeted by the audience with a crack of laughter and whoops of joy, followed by interminable ap-plause and a hint of cheering. What were they cheering? Why were they applauding? Had somebody done something clever? It defeated me as a teenager and still does. And I used to feel really annoyed that audiences were being fobbed off with this dross, and that writ-ers would stoop to such easy and, indeed, despicable tricks. And yes, I was rather snotty and condescending and puritanical about what was, and what was not, good comedy, but to this day I still believe writers ought to work for their money. Quite recently I went to see a well-known American stand-up comedian at an arena in San Jose and the audience cheered *every* joke. They hardly laughed, they just cheered, and punched the air triumphantly. And it occurred to me what a clever young man he was. He had come up with comedy for people with no sense of humour.

Back to British radio . . .

My conflict over *ISIRTA*, then, was between the exceptional warmth I felt towards the rest of the cast and the production team and a certain disdain that I couldn't quite hide for the material which they were performing with such enjoyment. After all, David Hatch and Tim Brooke-Taylor were among my closest friends, as were the producers, Humphrey Barclay and Peter Titheradge. Bill Oddie could be a bit obtuse sometimes, but I was genuinely fond of him. I didn't know Graeme Garden so well at that point, but you couldn't imagine a more agreeable, amusing and skilled colleague, and I'd always got on well with Jo Kendall. But when I suggested changes to the script, nobody else really shared my sensibilities (the aversion to puns, for example), so I found myself continually outvoted, and since I took the whole business far more seriously than I should have done, I'm sure I regularly came across as carping and elitist, since consistently criticising material that everyone else is happy with is implying that your artistic standards are higher than theirs. In addition I felt I was an ingrate, because Bill and Graeme wrote all the scripts, and there I was, moaning about doing them, while eagerly snaffling the £28 fee we got for each show (plus fifty per cent for repeats).

I apologise for the offensive remark I am about to make.

The audience was to blame.

When we *Cambridge Circus* people did our first few radio shows, they were based on the stage-show script which was of quite a high standard, and the audiences were suitably responsive. By the time I returned from America they had become a football crowd. With their wild applause, thunderous laughter, cheering of catchphrases, groaning at puns, friendly booing and general OTT enthusiasm they had become part of the show—or rather, they had pretty much taken the show over and made it a mini-phenomenon in the radio world. And the audience at home loved it, too. So my attempt to move *ISIRTA* an inch or two back towards its earliest incarnation was Canute-like, and totally inappropriate.

WHILE ALL this was going on, David Frost proposed that I help him, as writer and performer, record a comedy album to be called *Frost Over Britain*. It was set up at great speed; David wanted to incorporate a few of my old sketches, which we performed together, as there was no one else from the *Frost Report* pilot involved; the other material was all David's, though in the sense that he had gathered it rather than actually written it. It was to become a great joke among the *Frost Report* writers that in the final credits of the TV show every week the words "Written by" were closely followed by the words "David Frost" in large letters, and then, after a slight gap, by the word "and" in smaller letters, and finally, in even smaller letters, the names of a couple of dozen writers (relative unknowns like Denis Norden, Marty Feldman, Tony Jay, Barry Cryer, Dick Vosburgh, John Law, Frank Muir, David Nobbs, Peter Tinniswood, Willis Hall, Barry Took and Keith Waterhouse).

The general public must have wondered why so many of these so-called "writers" were needed to fill in the occasional gaps in what David had crafted. Those closer to the programme would sometimes speculate whether there was any single word which David could have been said in any meaningful sense to have "written." Dick Vosburgh summed up the general consensus when he pointed out how greatly David had always improved our punctuation.

David was endearingly shameless in matters such as these, and the question therefore arises: why was he so little resented for it? After all, writers normally get rather touchy about matters of contribution.

Part of the reason, I think, was that we all felt real affection for him, and were grateful to be part of the enjoyable groups and quasi-families he assembled. There's no doubt, too, that we admired his strengths as a producer: he was brilliant at spotting talent and trusting it, and while he occasionally shaped a project in helpful ways he seldom interfered unnecessarily. But I think another major factor was that he was one of the few people I've known who was "pronoid."

I have borrowed this word from the late, great Rob Buckman. He explained to me that whereas a "paranoid" person believes delusionally that people hate him and are out to get him, a pronoid person believes, on no reasonable grounds whatsoever, that people like him and want to help him (I use "him" rather than "her" because the pronoid folk I am acquainted with are all male). There used to be a saying—"What's good for General Motors is good for the USA." Well, at some level, David had a similar deep faith that what was good for DF was good for the whole UK, and that everyone who could be helpful to him would want to be. And this belief of his, that everybody wished him well, was largely true of the people with whom he interacted all the time. The people who didn't like him (and he did attract a lot of criticism—there's no question about that) tended not to know him personally, and he had the happy knack of simply tuning their negativity out, so that he was never drawn into responding to it. It is an extraordinary thing to say, but in a fairly close friendship of fifty-three years I never heard him make a mean remark about anyone. Those who envied him so much should have envied his pronoia, too.

What they actually envied was, of course, his success. England is quite an envious country: look at the tone of lofty, snide denigration that so often characterises media coverage, or consider how much people like to see others taken down a peg or two. But David was lucky enough to be immune to this. Moreover, as was said at the time, he was unusually extroverted in the sense that he took his values from the outside world to a much greater extent than the English normally do. He wanted to know whether one of his shows was "successful" rather than whether it was "good." He was simply not concerned with any of those internal qualms about quality that bothered most of the people I worked with. I remember him once attending a cabaret performance that I gave in a Chelsea restaurant over a bank holiday. It was not a success: the audience was rather drunk, and a bit noisy, led by a sozzled journalist who greeted my appearance by chanting "Cheese! Cheese! Cheese!" for some time. I got a few laughs, but I allowed the shouters to unsettle my timing, some of the material was too gentle, and at least a couple of pieces laid complete eggs. At the end I felt embarrassed that I had done such a bad job, sought out the guy who'd hired me, apologised, and asked his opinion about what had worked, and why some things hadn't. David intruded with great good humour, said how well it had all gone, and then took me aside to tell me off in the kindest and warmest way possible, asserting that I should never, under *any* circumstance, admit that *anything* was *any* kind of failure, but always claim how well it had all gone and how the audience had absolutely loved it. His advice, needless to say, came from his essential kindness. But . . . I just can't do this, although I can see the advantages of such a strategy. And David couldn't *not* do it. This essentially extroverted orientation on his part often got under the English skin; at the time someone remarked that if he'd had an American accent his success would have been more easily forgiven.

One final thought. David was very intelligent, but not temperamentally intellectual. He was extremely well informed on anything to do with the world he inhabited as an interviewer or businessman: he knew everyone who was anyone and he absorbed what they told him; he took a briefing incredibly quickly, grasping the essentials and the overall picture, and then could use this knowledge, thinking very fast on his feet. Added to his social skills, which were considerable, this all made him a remarkably able man of affairs. But his skills and talent were not those taught or valued much by Oxbridge types, who felt their ability to write clever essays on Yeats or Walter Bagehot or "The Influence of E. M. Forster on Flemish Wardrobe Design" should have earned them greater prestige and money and, let's face it, *fame* than this transatlantic chancer deserved. Their cultural perspective prevented them from recognising David's strengths. The idol of this snotty coterie, Malcolm Muggeridge (with whom I was to cross swords over his view that *Life of Brian* was blasphemous), once pronounced that "Television was not invented to make human beings vacuous, but is an emanation of their vacuity"; and it was his wife Kitty who made the most celebrated anti-Frost jibe, that David "rose without a trace." Well, if so, he nevertheless continued to leave more of one than she did. (Look her up online if you have a spare twenty seconds.)

All that granted, though, David's many admirers would never have accused him of a neurotic perfectionism; and the recording of the *Frost Over Britain* album was pretty slapdash. David did a number of monologues (some from *That Was The Week That Was*), and he and I performed three of my old sketches (the zookeeper who had lost all the animals, the interviewer of the non-deep-sea-diver, and a parody of an inter-school general knowledge competition) and one new sketch which Graham and I had written for the *Frost Report* pilot (a prep-school headmaster's speech). But David was never a top-class performer of comedy and this time I wasn't on form either, the audience seemed rather unresponsive, and the whole album sounded as though it had been recorded in a church hall by a couple of church wardens. I was embarrassed that it turned out so amateurishly, and I was genuinely grateful that it attracted no attention and soon sank, like Kitty Muggeridge, without trace.

But I also regretted that it was not approached with more love and attention because in those far-off days, a really good comedy album (for the gramophone!) could almost reach the status—and the longevity—of a work of art. Records were, after all, along with books, the only form of comedy material that one could enjoy at will. As a schoolboy I had prized recordings of live performances of the likes of Flanders and Swann, Victor Borge and Noël Coward (at Las Vegas!). Then George Martin (of Beatles fame) started producing studio comedy albums which were superb, most of them featuring

Peter Sellers and combining his extraordinary vocal prowess with top-class, specially commissioned scripts. Then I added albums by Peter Ustinov and the casts of *Beyond the Fringe* and *That Was The Week That Was;* and by this time I was also listening to some very clever material from America, where nightclub acts like Nichols and May, and Shelley Berman and Bob Newhart existed in record form. On my return to London I learned that Peter Cook and Dudley Moore had just done a couple of wonderfully funny series called *Not Only . . . But Also* and I listened to their records over and over again, even setting myself exercises in which I tried to write their sketches out from memory, carefully checked what I had written against the recordings, and then tried to recall them again from scratch. I like to think I learned a lot about sketch construction from those two.

I was always less interested in funny songs, but I did love Tom Lehrer, the Harvard mathematics teacher whose numbers some-times contained much blacker humour than I'd heard before—about nuclear war, and venereal disease, and poisoning pigeons in the park. I was exhilarated by his stuff: I found it liberating, and very funny and oddly good-humoured, and I was excited by the prospect of meeting the man himself, because David Frost had the excellent idea of having one of his songs on each *Frost Report* we were about to transmit. Tom duly came over to London, sang a song in the pilot show and then taped another dozen songs. (Each of these was then played in a subsequent *Frost Report,* with David introducing him as though he were in the studio, live.) I had a few drinks with him and liked him hugely. He was very tickled by his "fame"; it literally never occurred to me that I would suffer a similar fate. But the beginnings of all that were only a few weeks away . . .

The first stage of my new life, rehearsals in the church hall on Crawford Street, just off the top of Baker Street, was fine: basically a rerun of the material we'd used the month before in the pilot, along with my performance of a headmaster monologue that I knew backwards. My nerves seemed under control. But on the day of the show, when we went into the TV studio at Shepherd's Bush to re-hearse with the cameras, I sensed that tension was mounting. The show was due to be transmitted at half-past eight and by six o'clock I was feeling very tight and scared, though I was just about able to hide my alarm from the others, who, to add to my fright, seemed to be enjoying themselves. Then we broke for supper in the canteen, but I funked it and hurried to my dressing room where I sat and watched the second hand on the wall clock as it steadily ticked off the final moments before 8:30. And what I was now feeling was TOTAL DREAD. I started to wonder how on earth I could have got myself into this horrific predicament when I could be working in a nice tea room somewhere in Somerset without a care in the world and living in a little flat in lovely Weston-super-Mare, with a dear little kitty cat, doing jigsaws and eating toasted crumpets . . . At which moment the door opened, a sweet production assistant smiled at me and an-nounced, "Make-up!"

I managed to stand and lurch down the corridor to the make-up room where everyone was cheery and excited and joking, and I began to think how lovely it would be to have a nice quick heart attack and be done with it all. No such luck, unfortunately, and I sat down while base and powder were applied. It struck me I could still make a run for it just before the opening music, take a taxi to King's Cross and on to Holyhead, and catch the night ferry to the Isle of Man, with which I fancied the UK had no extradition treaty. News of this plan must have leaked, however, because now our floor man-ager was standing by me. He led me on to the set and showed me my mark on the floor—I think he may have offered me a blindfold—and then the music began, they ran the opening credits, I could see the studio audience watching on the monitors; and then David greeted the audience at home, and we were started, and I fainted. Metaphori-cally, that is, because at this point my mind stopped and I switched one hundred per cent on to automatic, as had happened before on opening nights: you do all the things you've practised, like soldiers attacking a machine-gun nest, you switch your mind off and something takes over and does it all for you, provided—PROVIDED—you don't think. Or even think about thinking. So when I was cued for my first line, the something did it for me. I was then taken to stand on my next mark, and when it was time for me to speak, it did my line for me again. At which point I was taken and put in front of another camera, and told my headmaster monologue was coming up in ten seconds and "Just look into the lens," and I stared at the Cyclops-like eye of this weird pile of ironwork, and the first line popped into my head, and the floor manager waved to cue me, and whatever it was started doing my lines for me.

> HEADMASTER: Good morning, boys! I'd like to welcome
> you back to a new term, and I hope it will be a very
> happy and successful one for us all. Who did that?

It passed, I heard a laugh from the audience, and something about the laugh jolted me, and I made the mistake of starting to think. I thought, "My Auntie Vera in Plymouth is watching me AT THIS VERY MOMENT!" This seemed such an extraordinary fact that I could think of nothing else, although the monologue was continuing without my missing a beat. Auntie Vera was actually watching me NOW! VERA! In Plymouth! This cannot be happening! I stifled the impulse to wave to her, knowing that it would not fit the sense of the words that were being said for me.

> I would like to welcome four new members of the
> staff this term, but unfortunately I could only find
> two. Mr. Jones, who is a grammar school man—STOP
> LAUGHING!—will be taking the middle school in all the
> subjects nobody else wants to teach, and I'm sure he will
> be an invaluable member of the staff. And in time, a valu-
> able one . . .

Is she laughing? She doesn't know much about prep schools. Perhaps Uncle Eric is explaining it. AS I SPEAK!

> Next I would like to welcome to the staff Mr. M'Boko.
> Now this is the first time that our curriculum will have included Swahili, but we hope to resume French again next term. Incidentally, you may be interested to know that until last week Mr. M'Boko was Prime Minister of Chad.

She won't understand that. I'm not sure he will either. I wish I'd chosen a different monologue for them.

> And so on Monday mornings he will be teaching the sixth form Swahili. And on Thursday afternoons they will be teaching him English.

OH MY GOD! Is MOTHER watching? Is my HAIR TIDY? Can she see my socks? She'll be knitting, but WILL SHE LOOK UP? Surely Dad will POINT ME OUT to her. How will I explain this to her, my being on television? She'll think it's a *trick*!

> That's all. Dismissed.

I'll call her when I've finished. Oh! I *have* finished! For Bernard Thompson, our lovely, calm, warm, endlessly amused, utterly efficient floor manager, is leading me gently out of the way of Julie Felix's upcoming song, and leaving me to recover my wits in the wings.

It took me so long to come to myself that when it was time for me to speak my next line, and David said the introductory phrase and the camera cut to me, I wasn't there: there was just an empty frame. I didn't even realise I'd missed my entrance because I was still in the wings, celebrating my survival.

Anyway, at some point the show apparently ended, because I

found myself being bustled along corridors and past *Frost Report* personnel, all of whom seemed to think my headmaster piece had been OK. I found it hard to believe, but the fact is I know now that if you have learned your words really well, then the mechanical part of you remembers not only the words, but also the correct timing and gestures. The memory of what you have rehearsed is a memory of the whole gestalt.

The purpose of all the bustling was to get me into a waiting car, which was to take me to the BBC TV Centre to be interviewed on *Late Night Line-Up,* an arts-oriented discussion programme that ran for many years during the '60s. I was to be questioned by Michael Dean, who introduced me by reference to that night's *Frost Report* and went on to ask me a few questions about myself. I then gave the worst performance of my life; because in this, my first ever experience of being interviewed, and interviewed *live* on BBC TV, on a programme well watched by bright people . . . I had no automatic to fall back on.

I can remember nothing of it, except that I sat there trying to hide in my chair, stammering out defensive half-truths and evasions, as though I had fallen into the hands of an experienced KGB interrogator. Why was I so stilted and overawed and graceless? In part, I suspect, it was because I was taking this whole new interview business absurdly seriously, feeling that everything I said was "on record," and so being acutely afraid of making any remark that might not be one hundred per cent factually correct. To make matters worse, I had felt all my life that my opinions were pretty worthless as I lacked the information, the life experience and therefore the authority to pronounce on anything, whether a play or a glass of wine or an idea or even a football team's performance, so I was not going to start making pronouncements on television. Just as critical, I now see, was the fact that there were *so* many areas of my emotional life where I was muddled and unresolved and therefore ripe for horrendous embarrassment that I was pointlessly guarded about *everything.* The lurking fear that I might accidentally give away something I did not want to reveal resulted in blanket self-censorship. I think the *Late Night Line-Up* people must have wondered what was wrong with me; somehow they got me safely into the taxi home.

So I went back to the Logan Mews flat, turned the lights on, and sat quietly, trying to review the events of the past few hours—definitely the most stressful episode of my life since my travails in Mother's birth canal. One thing I knew for sure: my life seemed to be spinning off in an unfamiliar direction, and I sensed I was beginning to lose control of parts of it, although it took me years to realise the whole spectrum of effects that celebrity has on one's existence.

12

I was now able to settle into a regular, if anxious, routine where many kind and comedically experienced people seemed to be happy to reassure me that my most recent performance had been "all right." On Fridays, the day after the show, Graham would get time off from St. Bart's and we would write a sketch for the show after next, feeling very complimented that our effort would almost always be included in the script. On Saturday mornings there would be a big read-through at the Baker Street church hall, with all the performers and many of the writers, when we would discover what material Jimmy Gilbert and David had chosen for next week's show. At the end of the reading, we would start to "put it on its feet," that is, Jimmy and the cast would work out the right positions and moves for the performers, and start running the sketches, scripts in hand. Sunday was a *Frost*-free day, but I would set off mid-morning for the studio where we were going to record *ISIRTA*, and spend the day with David, Tim, Graeme, Bill, Jo, Humphrey and Peter Titheradge. Here there was always a pretty relaxed, matey atmosphere, and after the show was over, we would adjourn to the pub, although I usually had to leave early because I had lines to learn for the *Frost* rehearsals on Monday. I looked forward to these because they were a priceless opportunity to study the two Ronnies at work. Ronnie B appeared to be able to switch character and accent at the press of a button, but he made it all seem so effortless that I couldn't see what I could learn from him; however, I watched Ronnie C like a sparrowhawk, because he played with his timing, sometimes taking risks by extending pauses longer than I would ever have dared, and I noticed how, by waiting this fraction more, he would build the tension just before he triggered his line, and get a bigger laugh as a result (just watch what he does in the famous "Class" sketch when Ronnie B has said, "I look up to him [Cleese] because he is upper class, but I look down on him [Corbett] because he is lower class," and Ronnie C has to follow with "I know my place").

On Tuesdays I was usually picked up and driven either to the BBC's Ealing Studios, to film "quickies" that were too ambitious to be done live at Shepherd's Bush, or to a location to shoot longer out-doors sketches, which, I began to notice, were usually written by a couple of young Oxford guys, whom I had met briefly in the past and were now regulars at the Saturday morning script read-through: Michael Palin and Terry Jones. Wednesday mornings brought a sec-ond day of rehearsal, which was all we needed, because although it was a half-hour show, a large proportion of it—David's CDM, songs from Julie Felix and Tom Lehrer, the filmed items and the opening and closing titles—did not require input from the performers on the day of transmission. We only had to do the "quickies," which required minimal rehearsal, and two or sometimes three sketches. Not a lot, when people like the two Ronnies were involved.

Not a lot, but this did little to ameliorate the Fear Factor. And the second week of the series actually turned out to be more terrifying than the first. Graham and I had written another monologue, which by default I was chosen to perform. It was a good piece, I thought, in which we created the image of a charabanc hurtling through Europe on one of those "See Twenty-two European Capitals in Eight Days" tours while I stood beside the driver shouting instructions to the cowering passengers:

COURIER: Now then . . . in twenty minutes we will be leaving Italy and entering Switzerland, which is a *different country*. So finish your spaghetti, throw the cans out of the window, and put the Primus stoves back under your seats. You may now open your souvenir plastic bags marked "Not to be opened till Italy." You'll find a small green plastic replica of the Tower of Pisa . . . don't try and stand it up, it's *made* that way. Right, now in half a minute we'll be crossing the border. You don't need your passports yet, we've got a special arrangement: they just stamp the coach. We're in Switzerland . . . *now*! Switzerland is famous for its mountains, cheese, clocks and chocolate. Nothing else. Open your plastic bags marked "Switzerland." You'll find a small piece of chocolate . . . eat it up quickly, we're not here long, it's a small country.

It was a riot at the read-through. Everybody loved it. All I had to do was . . . *remember* it. And the big problem was that it had to be delivered at breakneck speed. Doing your lines very fast is ten times more difficult than delivering them at a normal pace; there is no time to think what the next line is—it just has to come out right (and in front of 14 million people, live, in my case). So I learned the words even more diligently than usual, and practised them at speeds even greater than I was intending to deliver them. By the time I went to bed the night before the show, I felt I had mastered them, and I ran through the lines twice before I fell asleep. After a couple of hours, I woke up, turned over, ran the lines again and suddenly realised I wasn't sure whether it was "Next, as advertised in the brochure, the midnight bathe in the crystal clear waters of the Swiss lake, so get your swimming costumes on now" or "Next, the midnight bathe in the crystal clear waters of the Swiss lake as advertised in the brochure, so get your swimming costumes on now." This bothered me, so after a time I got out of bed, checked the script, and found it was actually "Next, the midnight bathe in the crystal clear waters of the Swiss lake as advertised in the brochure. The coach will be passing *through* the lake in thirty seconds. So get your swimming costumes on now." I then got back into bed, did the lines once more and then one final time, just to make sure, and made a mistake where I'd never gone wrong before. This was a shock, and it made me nervous. Now as I repeated the lines to reassure myself, I made new errors, fluffed lines, and then went blank. I had not yet learned that the main cause of forgetting your words is starting to think that you may, in fact, forget them. And I was, indeed, soon believing that I was *almost certainly* destined to "dry" in front of Auntie Vera, Uncle Eric, Dad and Mum, Mr. Bartlett, Mr. Tolson, Mrs. Tolson, the entire casts of *Cambridge Circus* and *ISIRTA*, Billy Williams, every TV critic in Britain, possibly the Queen, and 13,999,961 other people. After all, if I couldn't get my performance right now, in the security of my own bed, what chance did I have tomorrow, addressing an unfamiliar camera machine, in front of 14 million people?

I scarcely slept. Whenever I woke I immediately started rerunning the lines, and getting something wrong. Eventually I was forced to crawl out of bed and dress; I somehow sleep-walked through the day in the studio, smiling bravely and pretending I was still alive, until the dreaded moment came when I stood in front of the huge forbidding camera-dinosaur-THING . . . waited until the little red light went on . . . and did my big monologue really well. Correction! I stood there without fainting and my automatic pilot did the "Courier" sketch really well for me. Big laughs!

The show ended, people congratulated me, and I came to the half-stunned realisation that I had done all right, that I had not let everyone down. There was no hint of triumph on my part, just a profound liberating sense of relief, and a recognition that my life could now go forward. It was a little like a last-minute reprieve, except that I had done something that was definitely good *enough*. To put it bluntly: I had not been a failure.

As the series progressed, my fear diminished a little, at the rate of about one per cent per show. This was helped by the fact that Graham and I never again wrote a monologue for me. I don't remember this being intentional, but I suspect that the largely unconscious part of me that had performed the monologues also played a major part in the decision not to risk any more of them.

It's odd to recall that up until *The Frost Report,* Graham and I, though we thought of ourselves as a writing partnership, had in fact produced very little together. Apart from co-scripting (with Tim) four sketches for the 1962 Footlights revue, I cannot remember writing anything with Graham until I returned to London at the end of 1965, at which point we gravitated towards each other at great speed, starting a regular collaboration that lasted, on and off, for twenty-seven years, until the Python's last film, *The Meaning of Life,* in 1982. He was now in his fourth year of study at St. Bartholomew's Hospital—three months to go—but on that one day each week he was able to escape and come over to Logan Mews, to write our three- or four-minute sketch. Most of what we came up with was pretty good, but very conventional and not terribly funny.

Graham and I often had wilder and funnier ideas, but we soon realised that they were never going to make it into the show. If "wacky" ideas were suggested at the table readings, the other writers would usually laugh and so would Jimmy Gilbert, but he would then say, with a rueful smile, "Very funny, boys, but they won't get it in Bradford." We never argued. We were very well treated, but we also knew that we were right at the bottom of the batting order, decision-wise. Nevertheless, there was a wonderful camaraderie in the room, and I took particular pleasure in the company of the writers there, several of whom were to become great friends.

One who particularly intrigued me was Tony Jay, a charming and utterly non-snotty intellectual, who had done Classics and then philology at Cambridge (and got a first in both), before joining the BBC as a humble researcher. He swiftly ascended the ranks to become the producer of *Tonight*, the hugely loved and respected early-evening magazine programme that offered a wonderful fresh mixture of the serious and the light-hearted. He'd ended up as head of the Talks department before going freelance. David spotted his talents immediately, the greatest being originality of thought, clarity of expression and wit, and he asked Tony to write a point-of-view piece on the theme of each week's show, solely to guide the writers. Graham and I read them, enjoyed them, and ignored them, as did the others, so far as we could judge. But I loved chatting to Tony and I was flattered that someone as bright and distinguished should take an interest in my thoughts—perhaps he was intrigued by my ability to make people laugh. Some five years later he invited me to become one of the founder members of Video Arts, and we went on to write a score of training films together, before, in 1980, he embarked on *Yes Minister* and then *Yes, Prime Minister,* both witty masterpieces of clever plotting which he co-wrote with Jonathan Lynn. These programmes famously became Margaret Thatcher's favourite entertainment—a rather dubious or back-handed compliment, if you ever saw her attempt to reprise the "Dead Parrot" sketch at the 1990 Tory Party Conference, with reference to the Lib Dems (her foreign-policy advisor Sir Charles Powell told me that rehearsing the Iron Lady for this speech had been a fairly slow process).

The other person at the *Frost Report* table to whom I was drawn was one Marty Feldman. I hasten to add that my interest in him was platonic: in fact when I first met him, I was rather shocked by his physical appearance. Dressed only in black, heavily suntanned and very fit, he looked like an Armani gargoyle. This was the script editor? Then I discovered his writing credits: *The Army Game, Bootsie and Snudge* (one of the very few top-class ITV comedies) and then several years of *Beyond Our Ken,* the nation's favourite radio half-hour. I found him instantly likeable: a little anxious, tentative and over-eager to please, perhaps, but brimming with ideas and immensely quick and funny, as he puffed on Gitanes and blinked a lot. We swiftly became friends and I discovered that his looks were not the only exotic thing about him. He'd been born in the East End of London to a Ukrainian Jewish couple, had left school at fifteen and had gone straight into show business as a stooge to an Indian fakir who performed on Margate Pier. Apparently, and for reasons I never entirely understood, Marty's role was to fire (blunt) arrows into the fakir's stomach. He seemed a lot older than me (even though there were only five years between us), because he'd been a successful writer for years, knew his way round London, went to jazz clubs and fancy restaurants, had exotic holidays and generally seemed like a real grown-up. Moreover, he was married—to a woman called Lauretta, an attractive, dark-haired protector with a wonderful husky voice and nicotine-infused chuckle who exuded goodwill and stability and fun. I started spending a lot of time with them, learning cockney rhyming slang and back-slang, discussing life and comedy, and laughing a lot; and later that year I invited them to stay with Graham and me in a holiday villa in Ibiza that the two of us had decided to rent for a couple of months.

THE FACT that Graham and I were now able to contemplate living on this rather grand scale was entirely due to the patronage of David Frost. We ourselves were not adult enough to plan ahead: we simply reacted to offers; and that meant that David effectively planned for us. He had come up with the idea of a film in which an intelligent but unscrupulous pollster uses his professional skills to become Prime Minister, and now he suggested that the two of us write the script of what was to become *The Rise and Rise of Michael Rimmer*. This was miles more ambitious than anything we had attempted but we jumped at it, not least because David offered us an enormous fee: £2,000.

To put this sum in context, you need to remember that on *The Frost Report* I was getting £70 per week as a performer, and perhaps another £30 for writing. That fee of £2,000, then, represented our first sniff of *la dolce vita*. That was why Graham and I decided that we would take a fair-sized villa in the sun—our plan being that we would enjoy a holiday recovering from, respectively, medical exams and performance anxiety—that I would then return to London to watch England host the 1966 World Cup, and that, finally, we would settle down back in the villa, me with my nose to the typewriter and Graham with his to a sunbed, and knock out a first draft of the film *in five weeks* (about the same time as it takes me nowadays to make coffee, sharpen my pencils and get comfortable at my desk).

So far, so good. But a bit further, even better; for David now took me aside and told me he was about to do a late-night show on ITV for Rediffusion, and he invited me to be his sidekick on it. I was delighted to sign on to work with someone with whom relations were always warm and easy, and who was offering me a job that guaranteed an income throughout the autumn, a not too prominent position on air, and, it was hinted, the possibility of being involved in some of the more weighty discussions that were planned for the new show (a final flicker of my *Newsweek* aspirations).

So off Graham and I went to rent a place in Ibiza (which I should explain did not, in those days, have the Bacchanalian image it subsequently earned; it was regarded in 1966 as a smaller, cheaper, less crowded Majorca), and various friends, like Tim, Humphrey, Marty and Lauretta, came to stay. This was where I started reading the *Daily Telegraph* obsessively, memorising names and dates, and looking up economic and political terms I didn't know, so I would appear well informed in the serious interviews I might soon be doing, exactly zero of which ever happened. After a few days Connie arrived from New York; she'd visited me in London once already, but now we could have a proper holiday, and we started to explore the island together.

We noticed that a bullfight was advertised. Neither of us had ever seen one before, and although I suspected that Ibiza might not be the most auspicious place to be initiated into the toreadorean culture, we decided to go along. And it was terrible: inept and embarrassing, especially when the second bull turned out to be a practitioner of Gandhi's creed of non-violent resistance, completely ignoring attempts to make it cross, and trotting methodically round the ring in search of the exit. Connie's inclination—as was mine—was to support the underdog, but her cries of support for the bull alarmed me, as I thought members of the toreador's family might take exception to them. Both of us, though, cheered loudly when our bull was awarded a draw and allowed to live not to fight another day; and we were about to leave when a new toreador suddenly rode into the ring on a beautiful black stallion, followed immediately by a bull of a different stripe: a huge bilious piece of cattle with an *idée fixe*, which was to toss the horse a few feet in front of him out of the arena, even if it took the entire afternoon.

Connie was soon supporting the horse, while I watched mesmerised as the toreador slowed the horse a little, and then, as the bull almost caught up, leant backwards in the saddle, placing two long darts in the bull's shoulders, and accelerating away in the nick of time. The manoeuvre was repeated again and again, the toreador always succeeding by the tiniest of margins; I came to the conclusion that, as a way of earning a living, this was more stressful than live television comedy. Eventually, the bull slowed right down, and the bullfighter dismounted, took a cape, and carried out a series of wonderful passes, so varied and spectacular that we found ourselves cheering. Finally, everything stopped. The bull, cross-eyed and quite bewildered, stood looking at the man with the cape twelve feet in front of it, as though it couldn't quite remember what was supposed to happen next. The toreador now lowered the cape, walked slowly and deliberately up to the massive creature, stopped in front of it, reached out and gently touched its nose, and then, to our astonishment, turned his back and walked slowly away from it, to the sound of a deep, all-embracing silence.

At which point Connie cried out at the top of her voice, "Behind you!"

I'm pleased to report this got a laugh. One. From me. The rest of the stadium gasped. The toreador turned slowly round and stared. Did this strange woman *really* believe he had an acute short-term memory problem? There was, of course, no question that Connie's advice had been offered with the best of intentions. But the sudden loudness seemed to rouse the bull from its torpor and into the slim-hipped toreador positioned right in front of it, bringing the scores level at Spain 1½, Bulls 1½. (I'm lying about this last bit.)

Connie subsequently maintained that what she had actually shouted was "Look out!" I record this, as I want to include both sides of the story, but I'm sure it was "Behind you!" Either way, it was, to be blunt, a redundant remark.

I feel I should balance this by telling a story against myself. Although I had a facility for ball games (provided they were not too rough) and I could balance umbrellas and billiard cues on my nose or my foot, I had always known that I was awkward and spindly when it came to anything that required a combination of strength, agility and physical courage. So I decided to set myself a challenge. I was now spending a lot of time on the beach for the first time in my adult life, and I soon became aware how irritated I was by waterskiing. Not only did it encapsulate all the skills I lacked, causing feelings of inadequacy and resentment (otherwise known as envy), it also seemed to provide dedicated narcissists with a ridiculously simple way of showing off. There they all were, with their flowing blond hair and suntans and lean bodies being dragged through water by a boat. If any of them had been pulled along a road by a car, people would have thought them unhinged, but at sea they could parade their rather narrow range of skills to an appreciative packed beach, provided only that they were beddable.

So I decided to take some waterskiing lessons, not because I wanted to waterski, but because I wanted to prove to myself how easy and therefore pointless it was. The only problem was the potential for public humiliation, but by booking a lesson first thing in the morning, I reckoned I could get it all over before people began arriving on the beach. Except that on the appointed day the water was too rough, so I had to wait three hours for it to become calm enough, and by the time I was eventually able to start, the throngs had arrived.

I was now acutely aware that I was the only visible entertainment, but had the idea that if I could convey the impression that I had previously suffered an injury, spectators might, out of a sense of tact, not watch me too closely. I therefore acquired a sudden limp, which rather puzzled my instructors (though they might later have thought that it explained my subsequent performance). I donned the skis, sat down into them, grasped the ring by which I was to be towed, obeyed the instruction to sit up as the motorboat accelerated away, but then failed to lean back enough, with the result that I simply disappeared head first into the water in front of me, having gained about two feet. When I'd finished expelling the surprisingly large amount of seawater that my body had acquired during this first trip, I tried again, but because I was now consciously trying to lean back more as the boat surged forward, my skis shot straight up in front of me, and I spun backwards, landing with an enormous splash. By the time I was ready for my third effort, every eye on the beach (except one of Marty's) was focused on me. This time, as I steeled myself for my third and final attempt (a lesson, thank God, consisted of only three goes), I cleared my mind, remembered to pull on the ring and lean back, but not too far, and to stand up, keeping my back straight and my arms half-braced, not at full stretch, as the boat pulled away, and to relax, above all to relax, and to try to take the full weight of my body on my thighs, and to keep my head up. And the boat surged and I was up, up, UP for about a yard when I let go of the ring, toppled sideways with my arms flailing, and produced the biggest splash of that summer. As I staggered to the shore, believing that my misery was at an end, I became aware of the crowd, who were standing applauding and laughing, with several of them offering my instructors money to buy more lessons for me.

Connie was very sweet to me when I got back, but Marty, Graham and Tim drifted away almost as though they didn't want to be seen with me. I suspect they were envious of the laughs I'd got.

Marty, who was always amused by my painful politeness and inability to shake off people who were being a pest, had developed an annoying habit since his arrival. Every morning, after we arrived at the beach, he would wander off on his own, chatting to people at random, until he came across someone—always a man—whom he judged to be outstandingly boring. He would talk to him until he had ferreted out his pet subject—or better, hobbyhorse—and would then say, "What a coincidence! I'm here with my best friend, John, and he's also just crazy about badgers/garden sheds/postage stamps/ potholing/model railways/plastic forks. You simply must meet him!" Then he would bring the megabore over and introduce him to me. "You're both crazy about brass rubbing/moths/flying saucers/ Tranmere Rovers/folk music/bestiality. You'll have so much to talk about!" And then he'd retire to a safe distance, and snigger. On one occasion, to his delight, the only way I could escape from a Scrabble fanatic was by swimming further out to sea than he could.

I asked Marty to stop, but unsuccessfully. He passionately believed that the highest form of practical joking was to waste someone's time. Years later, it occurred to me how many of his sketches involved an annoying man (usually called Mr. Pest) doing exactly that.

There was one other incident which I should mention, since, according to Connie, it revealed an aspect of me that was new to her. I'd happily assigned any further involvement with waterskiing to my next reincarnation, but I'd come to the conclusion that there was one other physical skill that I did need to come to terms with—riding a bicycle. I'd never asked my parents for a bike, because it had never occurred to me that I might want one. But the moment we arrived in Ibiza, all the others hired them and were incredulous to find I didn't know how to ride one. I could get away with not being able to drive, but my inability to cycle provoked an unprecedented level of banter. So one evening I crept away, stole a bike, took it about a hundred yards from the house, and on a rough track in semi-darkness, mounted it, and started falling off. For two hours I persevered, using a cold fury to keep me at it, until I could actually travel a reasonable distance between each crash. Then I went back to the house to look for Savlon and plasters, and discovered that Connie had been observing my struggles. She'd never glimpsed this intense bloody-minded determination before and she said that she now felt she understood me better. Mind you, I've never had a *lot* of it on tap, but it does occasionally emerge, usually to help me to get work done. In other aspects of my life it's largely absent, except in occasional tussles with crosswords and sudoku. I wish I could focus this intently on my non-professional interests, but making a real effort always seems to interfere with taking things easy, and so I remain a perpetual dilettante.

Graham and I had taken things very easy since getting to Ibiza, and we'd done little to advance the film script. And now, to add further delay, the World Cup loomed. I had tickets for all the games, so, leaving Graham behind, I returned to London, along with Tim and Connie, and then put Connie on a plane back to New York. It was a moment of sadness, neither of us sure when we would see each other again. Once Connie had gone, I sought to pull myself together, and then settled down to the demanding process of watching England play football, beginning with a 0–0 draw with Uruguay so tedious, uninspiring, leadenly predictable, and utterly, irredeemably devoid of promise or hope, that I did a very silly thing. I gave my Cup Final ticket to Bill Oddie.

Yes, I know. But I calculated that the furthest this England team could get (with the help of miracles) was the semi-final. I therefore called Graham, told him I would be returning sooner than expected to start writing—which helped to alleviate a growing sense of guilt over playing truant for so long—and (a glutton for punishment) returned to Wembley for the next ordeal: a game against Mexico, who began the match in an original way. At the kick-off, their centre forward touched the ball to an inside forward, who promptly kicked the ball sixty yards, straight to the English goalkeeper, Gordon Banks. The Mexican team then retreated to a man into their last quarter of the pitch and defiantly twiddled their moustaches. After just ten seconds, a goalless draw was staring us in the face! Stare, stare, stare, it went, for thirty-seven minutes and then . . . Bobby Charlton! He gathered the ball in the centre circle, swayed left, accelerated right and smashed a glorious thirty-yard shot into the top left-hand corner of the Mexican goal, releasing scenes of transcendent joy, and above all . . . RELIEF. The whole stadium was on its feet, leaping about, arms waving, hugging, screaming ecstatically, and as I cavorted, I suddenly felt my knee bump someone. Glancing down, I was startled to see the only two people in the stadium still in their seats, right next to mine: a nicely dressed middle-aged couple smiling happily. I'd barged into the husband.

"I'm so sorry!" I said. "I'm afraid I got rather carried away."

He smiled sweetly at me.

"Don't worry," he said, "I'd like to be on my feet too! But I'm afraid my wife doesn't approve."

And they looked at each other lovingly.

Ten days later I was sitting in the same seat when the wondrous

Bobby Charlton scored both the goals that sent England to the World Cup Final against Germany. That night I was on the plane back to Ibiza. Silly me.

And so Graham and I finally got down to our first film script, and I can say with complete confidence that we had absolutely no idea what we were doing. Of course, we had no idea that we had no idea what we were doing, and that meant that our enthusiasm stayed intact. We had also not done much research, so we knew little about how either pollsters or British politics worked. But we raced ahead anyway, starting at Scene One, confident that from a score of decent three-minute sketches (or scenes) we could construct a hundred-minute film, and so displaying an optimism similar to that of two youths who, having put up a garden shed, now decide to build a cathedral. If this sounds a bit hard on the two of us, it's because I wish to be honest (and realistic) about the many screenplays that I have set eyes on. With one exception (Michael Frayn's *Clockwise*) I've *never* been offered a top-class comedy role, although there have been a handful of screenplays which contained well-written, smaller parts for me. It used to puzzle me why there were so many clueless comedy film writers making a living, until I realised that the producers who were commissioning them had no idea whatsoever how dreadful the screenplays were. Talk about the blind leading the blind . . .

Anyway, Graham and I steamed ahead, with me sitting inside at the typewriter, and Graham lying on the balcony outside, sunbathing and helping out in his inimitable way. It was a lop-sided arrangement but one that never bothered me, because I was such a control freak I liked Graham not being able to see what I was typing. Sometimes I let him win one of our occasional arguments—which were very seldom heated—but then I would actually type out the version I preferred, safe in the knowledge that he would never remember what had been agreed in his favour.

Far more important, I had tracked down a little cafe in the next village, with a television set that was going to show the World Cup

Final on the Saturday. I arrived there mid-morning when it was still deserted, had a couple of beers, ordered a sensational *conejo au Franco,* and then sat, drinking coffee, and watching the room fill up.

With Germans. I was expecting plenty of locals and a sprinkling of tourists, even in an obscure little outpost like this, but not half the population of Dortmund. In fact, I came to the slow realisation as they poured in and sat around me . . . that I was the only English-man there. They were very friendly, but there were many of them, and all my exits were cut off. What strategy could I employ? It was too late to pretend that I was German. I'd greeted the early arriv-als with *"Guten Tag! Ich liebe Deutschland,"* but within a few seconds found myself conversing in English, in which they were all fluent. Perhaps, I hoped, they would think that I was an English-speaker but *not* actually English. A Rhodesian, possibly, or a Canadian, there just out of curiosity, to try to pick up the rules of this so-called "Beauti-ful Game." But I knew that I lacked the self-control to fake an atti-tude of benevolent detachment while watching what was arguably the most important event since the Crucifixion, so I plumped for the role of the ultra-sporting, frightfully decent Upper-Class Twit, and consequently found myself shouting "Oh, well played, Germany!" when Helmut Haller opened the scoring in the twelfth minute, and managing to restrain myself, when Geoff Hurst equalised, to "Good show! Bit lucky though!" My fixed grin and easy manner did not be-tray the writhing contortions of my hands and legs beneath the table, however, and when Martin Peters put us ahead twelve minutes from the end, I clapped a little too violently; I tried to compensate with "Come on Germany! Give us a game!" but that seemed to strike the wrong note. The most testing moment, though, came in the last min-ute of normal time when Uwe Seeler fouled Jackie Charlton, and the pig-dog dolt of a Swiss referee, finally revealing his Nazi credentials, had the gall to penalise England, and then ignored Schnellinger's blatant handball, allowing a Prussian swine named Weber to draw the game. I sat there applauding warmly, as a horde of fat, arrogant, sausage-eating Krauts capered around me, spilling beer and celebrating their racial superiority.

Still, we nailed them in extra time, didn't we? Disputed goal, my *arse*! When the final whistle sounded I rose slowly to my feet, shrugging apologetically, smiling wryly and nodding, and managed to get clear of the cafe and its complaining "Never crossed the line!" Bosch clientele without actually saying that I, personally, never thought that they'd lost the Second World War either.

After this interruption, Graham and I continued work on the script. He had, it turned out later, just met the love of his life, a young fellow called David Sherlock, but he didn't tell me this for another twelve months. When he did, I understood why he'd spent such a large proportion of our writing sessions sunbathing. I, for my part, also met a lifelong friend: a delightful tall blonde (surprise!) called Pippa of whom I became very fond.

I have one last memory of Ibiza. There was a very pleasant and competent open-air restaurant an easy walk from our house. It became our default diner. But the service was slow. Usually it didn't matter because we were happy to sit outside for hours in the balmy evenings sipping sangria, but one evening Alan Hutchison arrived late and hungry, ordered the rissoles (which were always delicious) and then sat at the table with his stomach rumbling, quivering in anticipation. Well, he quivered for a very long time; he politely asked every few minutes when his rissoles were coming, and was assured "dos minutos." After an hour or so, the quivering increased, and was supplemented by suppressed rage, of a kind I had never before observed in this mild-mannered man. Finally, as I was becoming worried that bits of him might start shaking loose, or that, worse still, he might kill and eat our waiter, he stood up, announced, "Right!" and strode off with great resolution into the indoor section of the restaurant. We sat, poised for the sound of shouts or blows, but . . . nothing. Ten minutes later, he reappeared, carrying a plate of his designated rissoles, and tucked into them. When it was safe to speak to him, I asked for details. Nobody, he informed me, had taken any notice of him when he stalked through the restaurant, nor when he arrived in the very busy kitchen. He was expecting to be challenged, so that he could air his grievance, but the various chefs ignored him. Then he saw a large plate of uncooked rissoles. He took down a frying pan, poured in some oil, added a lot of rissoles and started frying. Occasionally the other chefs glanced at him, but nobody seemed put out and so when the rissoles were cooked, he flipped them on to a plate and carried them back to his table. I loved Alan for this: he may be the only person in world history who has responded so effectively to slow service.

13

I flew back to London a couple of days later, and handed in to David Frost the first draft of *The Rise and Rise of Michael Rimmer*. At that moment, however, he had a much bigger fish to fry: his new, three-times-a-week show *The Frost Programme*, which was due to start in less than a month. It was an attempt to create a new format with a much wider mix of ingredients than had ever been tried on British television before: serious political interviews mixed in with entertainment items, occasional sketches, light-hearted pieces which sometimes involved the guests (I remember ringing hand bells with Jeremy Thorpe, the leader of the Liberal Party at that time); the odd singer; stunts (I once tried to see how much Mandarin I could learn in a week; answer: not a lot); very occasional film items; no show-business chit-chat that I can remember, but otherwise only the kitchen sink was omitted. Once when the singer Shirley Bassey was a guest, Terry Gilliam was invited to the studio to sketch her. David then panicked, racing into the wings during a commercial break to make sure Terry's portrait was not too unflattering. Fortunately, it wasn't. (Terry must have needed the work.)

Once *The Frost Programme* had bedded down a little, it evolved into a very interesting hybrid and became the talk of London town. It did not, however, become the talk of the country, because it was only shown in certain regions. Its absence from television screens in Weston-super-Mare alarmed my parents (even though they could still hear me every week on *I'm Sorry I'll Read That Again*). Dad therefore wrote me a letter asking me if I had ever considered applying for a job in the personnel department of Marks & Spencer. I was able to reassure him I was not destitute, but I still treasure the moment when, after telling this story on the radio several years later, I opened a letter with Marks & Spencer on it, and found that someone there had sent me an application form.

I took on various small roles in the programme. Occasionally I would write a short, generally slightly satirical duologue, which I would perform with David at the start of the show. From time to time I'd perform a short monologue. I might also join in a light-hearted group item with guests. If required I'd come up with something a bit more bizarre, like getting everyone to sing the Clifton College school song:

> . . . For working days or holidays,
> And glad or melancholy days,
> They were great days and jolly days
> At the Best School of All!

My other function was to act as a "minder" for one of that evening's guests, making sure they were happy and were given a drink (just one) before a floor manager came to take them on set for their appearance. And it was while performing this rather easy job that I made my one near slip-up of that autumn.

It was a particularly unfortunate cock-up because it came on the back of something of a breakthrough for the show. When *The Frost Programme* started, the one problem we had was that David found it impossible to secure "serious" guests. Because he had presented the cutting-edge satirical shows *That Was The Week That Was* and *Not So Much a Programme, More a Way of Life* (which had achieved a pinnacle of irreverence never before reached by British entertainers), followed by a *Frost Report* series that was at least a bit cheeky now and again, the bigwigs (politicians, generals, ambassadors, top civil servants, professors, bishops, tycoons and suchlike) wouldn't touch David with three bargepoles fastened together with something a lot stronger than Sellotape. So for the first few programmes David was unable to do any "serious" interviews at all, and because he couldn't do them he had no way to *prove* to VIPs that he *was* intending to do proper duologues with them (and *not* sit them on whoopee cushions or send them up rotten).

And then . . . we hooked one. Not a big fish, but at least a hake: a *former* Cabinet Minister in the Macmillan government, called Ernest Marples, who had been Minister of Transport. There was great excitement; careful preparations were made; and we went out of our way to ensure that when Mr. Marples arrived at the studio to talk to David about Japanese business methods, which he had been studying in Tokyo for a couple of months, he would be greeted in a suitably sober and respectful way by lots of fifty-and-over men in dark suits, nearly fawning on him. When he entered the green room, where I was sitting on the sofa, guarding the guest I had been allocated, everyone jumped to their feet and half-bowed, stood respectfully for a bit, and then, not wanting to bother the ex-Minister, sat down and made sure that they didn't stare at him. And it was at that moment I realised my guest had disappeared. He had blindsided me and now there he was bearing down on Mr. Ernest Marples (the *ex–Cabinet Minister*) with his hand outstretched, and beaming.

"Good evening, Mr. Marples!"

"Oh! Good evening . . ."

I was paralysed. I could see what was coming.

"My name is Martin Braithewood. I'm on the show with you."

"Oh really . . . er . . . what are you doing, Martin?"

"I'm playing the spoons."

I wish I had a sculpture of Marples's expression: I would contemplate it whenever I felt melancholy. It was the look of a man who had prepared himself for the worst, and had badly underestimated. He, *an ex–Cabinet Minister,* was about to appear on national television with a spoon-player. So much for *his* chances as the next Chancellor of the Exchequer.

Fortunately, he went on anyway, the interview turned out well, word went round, and within a couple of weeks the Pillars of Society were queuing up to talk to David Frost. And what a remarkably fine interviewer he was. Sharp, agile and yet empathetic, he could get people to say more than they had planned, which paradoxically often redounded to their credit, and he could also forensically take apart a weak case. His spontaneity proved far more effective with audiences than the usual clichéd current-affairs minuets; and some of his now largely forgotten interviews—for example, with Major Mike Hoare, the Congo mercenary, and Emil Savundra, the con-man—were (along with Melvyn Bragg's wonderful conversation with the dying playwright Dennis Potter) among the very best I've ever seen.

As for me, although my contribution to the show was small, and sometimes absolutely minute, being involved in it proved an extraordinarily valuable experience. The three-times-a-week live performing of material, sometimes written only six hours before, forced upon me a different mindset from the one I'd had in *The Frost Report*. There I could *aim* to give "perfect" performances, and the knowledge of this put extra pressure on me. Now I had to accept that everything I did was going to be a bit under-rehearsed, that perfection was way out of my reach, and that I should just go with the flow and not get uptight about the boo-boos. And I learned that when you stop concentrating on avoiding mistakes, you relax a bit, and consequently . . . you actually make fewer.

MEANWHILE, DAVID had informed me at the end of the summer that he wanted to give me a show of my own. I was both flattered and very scared, but came to the conclusion that since I could surround myself with a team of hand-picked people, I wouldn't have to carry too much responsibility myself and would therefore be able to cope. I always strongly believed in safety in numbers.

So, it turned out, did Tim Brooke-Taylor. When David had earlier asked *him* to do a series, he too had said he wanted to work with others—and he had proposed that he and I team up (unfortunately I'd been too busy at the time on other projects). Now the two of us bowed to the obvious and proposed to David that we should work together. David sensed that even as a duo we were a little apprehensive about the new venture, but comforted his two scaredy-cats by explaining that we wouldn't have to worry about a large audience because the show would go out late at night, and that, in any case, expectations were non-existent. Then he dangled what for me was the perfect carrot: he encouraged us to do the zanier, wilder, off-the-wall, madcap, out-of-left-field, oddball and wackier material that Gra and I used to suggest in the *Frost Report* script meetings, the material that had always met with the response: "Very funny, boys, but they won't get it in Bradford." So we said, "Yes, please . . ."

Involving Graham in the new venture was a no-brainer, but our other suggestion was, on the surface at least, rather bizarre:

"David, you'll be a bit surprised at this."

"Go on . . ."

"Marty Feldman . . ."

"Marty? But he's not a performer!"

And David was correct. Marty hadn't performed since his arrow-firing days on Margate Pier. He was, first and foremost, a writer. But we wheedled away, telling David (who knew what fine scripts Marty would provide) that Marty was extraordinarily funny, not just when he was fooling around, but when he spontaneously went into character—as a cockney barrow-boy, or a Hollywood film producer, or an oleaginous men's outfitter, or a wily Gypsy fortune teller—until David, almost convinced, finally raised his real objection.

"But . . . what about the way he *looks*?"

Having had his say, David let us get on with it. So Tim, Marty, Graham and I sat down to put together a pilot to convince a TV executive we all liked and trusted—Cyril Bennett of Rediffusion—to commission a short series, to be called *At Last the 1948 Show.*[1] The four of us worked harmoniously: Gra and I still wrote mainly together, Tim therefore joined Marty, but the two writing teams spent a lot of time in the same room. We knew, of course, that we were going to do a show with zany sketches. The question that remained, though, was: how were we going to link the sketches? We were all tired of the musical numbers that punctuated *That Was The Week That Was,* and of the traditional linkman à la Frost programmes, and, of course, the *Monty Python* approach lay a little way in the future. What were we to do? Was there another method? And then we had a breakthrough: what about a link *girl*?

What sort of a girl? Funny . . . dappy . . . pretty . . . bubbly . . . adorable . . . But who?

You have to know that throughout my first few years in British television, there was a constant search among male comedians for girls who were funny (and, if possible, pretty, too). Our perception was that there weren't many *very* funny women around: that somehow even talented comediennes didn't ultimately want to make fools of themselves—they always seemed to be holding something back. It wasn't until Dawn French and Jennifer Saunders came along in the 1980s that I saw female comedians on television who whole-heartedly "went for it." It was wonderful that for the first time the best women were funnier than the best men. I was genuinely thrilled.

As we planned our show, therefore, few if any names came immediately to mind. Then, out of the blue, someone said, "Oh, you should take a look at Aimi MacDonald." She had, apparently, done some

---

[1] The title was intended as a joke about the slowness of programme planners making a decision.

very good stage work, and was currently appearing at a nightclub in Mayfair. Tim and I therefore secured the necessary funds from the Frost organisation to go along to watch her in action. We took our seats, the show started, a chorus line capered on to the stage, and right there on the end of the line was someone who we immediately decided would be perfect for the role we had in mind—we just prayed that she would turn out to be Aimi. Once the floorshow had come to an end, and the owner of the club, Davy Kaye, had done a really hilarious and rude half-hour routine, he joined us at our table, bringing with him our pick from the end of the line, the lovely Aimi MacDonald (as she was always henceforth known).

We soon decided that we shouldn't get Aimi to link the sketches; instead we would write her silly little quickies, at the end of which she would say, "And now . . ." I suppose we were trying to send up the whole idea of "links." Her delivery was perfect: a little high-pitched and pedantic (Pythonesque shades of Anne Elk) but wonderfully cute and happy with it.

One of my favourite Aimi interludes started with her holding a newspaper.

> Hello! I'm the lovely Aimi MacDonald! Do you read your horoscope every day? I do! I'm Scorpio. That's the same as Burt Lancaster. I wonder what it says today . . . (*She consults the paper and reads, carefully*) "Scorpio. Your name is Aimi MacDonald and you are reading your horoscope out on television . . ." (*After a moment, her face lights up*) Ooooh! That's really good, isn't it? (*Pause*) It's not so good for Burt Lancaster, though . . . And now . . .

With Aimi in place, we wrote the pilot script and started rehearsals in early December. They were particularly enjoyable because Tim, Gra and I had performed together so often that we immediately fell into a shared style and working method. I'd always thought Gra a fine performer, but even so, when the two of us performed together, I never felt quite the connection with him that I had with Tim. We two watched and listened to each other like hawks, which sometimes led to felicities of timing that wouldn't have happened with Gra and me. I suppose I always felt that Gra was ever so slightly away on his own. But then that was Gra.

Marty was the unpredictable quantity. We all knew he had the potential to be hilarious, but because he hadn't had the chance to pick up much in the way of acting technique he was erratic: in the early rehearsals he might do some lines or visual business wonderfully well, and then get it all wrong the next five times, or suddenly manage to perform brilliantly a part of the sketch he'd always flubbed before. He needed an immense amount of rehearsal, and this we were happy to give him until his performances were so "grooved" that he could reproduce them reliably (I never forget that the French word for rehearsal is *répétition*). And Marty was up for it: he was excited he was at last going to be in front of the camera and worked away tirelessly, as we made him run some sequences seven or eight times in a row. Nevertheless, to be on the safe side, we kept his roles fairly small in the pilot episode.

The net result was that when the day for the recording came, and we were placed in front of a studio audience for the first time, we all produced quite polished turns and earned a decent amount of laughter. Given that the material was a bit, or a lot, wackier than people were used to seeing on television, we were more than satisfied with the reaction we received.

A few days later we sat in a darkened room in the Rediffusion building on Kingsway and watched the tape of the show. Ten seconds after it finished, the door opened, and Cyril Bennett looked in. "Pure gold!" he said. "A series of six, please." We were both elated and excited: we instinctively knew we were going to be producing something slightly different. So we started beavering away at the scripts that we would start recording in February, because the Christmas break was almost upon us.

I'd suggested to Connie that we could see each other over the holidays, so we met in Barbados and stayed in the Blue Water Beach Hotel, just outside Bridgetown. We hadn't spent any time together for about six months, and because in those days international phone calls seemed very expensive and oddly daunting, we had stayed in contact mainly by air-mail letters (printed on amazingly light paper, so they would not tax the plane's engines too greatly). There was no question that we loved each other, but I think we both felt a little tentative about where the relationship was going. Being 3,000 miles apart, with our careers rooted in different countries, made the future very uncertain. But we enjoyed our beach holiday—I managed to avoid waterskiing—and were both stunned by seeing *Dr. Zhivago* one evening; watching Geraldine Chaplin and Julie Christie, I seemed to receive some intuition of the deep importance of my relationship with Connie: I'd never before taken a message like that away from a cinema.

On our last evening, God gave us a present: we were sitting under the stars when Harry Secombe sat down next to us. I'd never met him before, but had adored him in *The Goon Show,* and always sensed that he was, as we say in show business, wonderful. In the flesh, however, he scored comfortably higher in wonderfulness than I had ever expected. I think "warm" is the best (if inadequate) word for the man. Connie and I sat chatting to Harry and his wife and we laughed and laughed and then I found myself in deep conversation (with a man best known for blowing raspberries and singing loudly) about theories of time, about which he knew an alarming amount. I came to the conclusion that although he was bonhomie personified, he had a very astute mind. (He told me once that at the Palladium he used to get a great reception with all the funny material, but when he sang a bit of opera at the end of the show, he could sense they were fidget-

(Above) The cast of *At Last the 1948 Show: (anti-clockwise from top)* Aimi MacDonald, Marty Feldman, me, Tim Brooke-Taylor, and Graham Chapman; *(below)* recording the "Rhubarb Tart" song.

(*Above*) The *1948 Show* team trying to amuse ourselves;
(*below*) with Peter Cook on the set of *The Rise and Rise
of Michael Rimmer.*

(*Above*) Peter Sellers, Ringo Starr, and me, enjoying a joke;
(*below*) *The Goon Show* team and a bit of me.

(Above) The Pythons; *(below)* "And now for something completely different."

(Above) "Upper Class Twit of the Year"; *(below)* taking a break from "Hell's Grannies."

A choice of uniforms.

(Above) Terry Jones and me impersonating Alan Whicker;
(below) inspecting a parrot.

Guess who.

ing, yet at the end of the aria, they went wild and clapped frantically. Then one day, he realised they were applauding themselves ...) Finally, Connie and I went back to our hotel, both thinking that the world seemed a much better place than it had a few hours before. What a man!

The next day I flew back to London, thinking how difficult it seemed to foretell the future (I was still naive enough to think it was possible). But, of course, the moment I arrived in London such speculations were swept aside by the urgent writing requirements of *The 1948 Show*. We had five weeks to write five episodes, *and* to rewrite the pilot, making six altogether. Just the four of us, with some help from three of the *Frost Report* team, Dick Vosburgh, Eric Idle and Barry Cryer (all of whom also appeared regularly in both series).

But ... there's a problem chronicling them. The Frost organisation *wiped* all thirteen tapes. Really. They no longer exist.

You see, back in those Palaeozoic times TV shows were recorded on enormous reels of videotape, which were expensive and also took up a lot of storage space. So, unless a repeat was on the cards, TV companies liked to reuse the tape. (A by-product of this was that they didn't like you to edit the programme you'd made, because to do that you had to cut the tape with a razor blade, and that rendered the tape unfit for future reuse. And for some reason the companies didn't want the public to *know* that shows were edited—don't ask me why—so tape editors were never allowed a credit.)[2] By the 1970s the storage problem had become so acute that the BBC destroyed several

---

[2] On *The 1948 Show* we had a great editor called Johnny Fielding, who had once worked on *The Goon Show*. When the powers that be persisted in refusing to roll his name at the end of *The 1948 Show*, we gave him a credit nevertheless, but for "Choreographing the underwater chariot race." This went through unchallenged. Each TV edit Johnny did for us took about eight minutes, as the audio and video tracks had to be parted, and then cut separately, before being blended again. Interestingly, this was precisely the same system as the one employed by the Romans.

priceless series, which means that Alan Bennett's *On the Margin,* and episodes from Peter Cook and Dudley Moore's *Not Only . . . But Also* and from *Hancock's Half Hour* no longer exist: acts of vandalism that, for me, equal the burning of the library in Alexandria.

David Frost's hatchet man, a Mr. George Brightwell, not wanting to be thought a laggard in this artistic carnage, ordered the wiping of thirteen episodes of *At Last the 1948 Show* starring Marty Feldman, Graham Chapman, Tim Brooke-Taylor and John Cleese, so that he could *free up four and a half cubic feet of shelf space.* George had a reputation as a hard businessman. Very hard, the Vinny Jones of British television executives (except that his suit fitted him better). So hard, in fact, that an immensely well-liked agent called Sonny Zahl, at the end of a meeting with George, actually jumped out of George's office window and fell several floors to his death. There were rumours that George used to leave it open for this express purpose.

So . . . suddenly there were no tapes of *The 1948 Show.* It was no more. It was an ex-series.

Then . . . a Swede found five reels in the vaults of a Stockholm TV station. Much rejoicing followed, slightly dampened by the discovery that there were not five episodes, but five half-hour compilations of *1948 Show* sketches, chosen with an eye to Swedish comedy sensibilities. Then, in 2010, when Marty Feldman's widow Lauretta died, *two* more shows were found in her attic. At the time of the Python O2 Arena shows, Wilfred Frost (David Frost's son and my godson) happened upon another pair, somewhere in the Frost Archives. In addition, my old PA Howard Johnson combed the internet and found shards of the show out there—thirty seconds of this, a minute of that, so, with the help of the splendid Dick Fiddy, a consultant for the British Film Institute, we are beginning to put them back together. Recently I've been able to view about eight and a half *1948 Shows* . . .

And because I really liked what I saw when I watched the series, and because it's generally regarded as half a step in the direction of

Monty Python, I propose to demonstrate the sort of comedy we were doing by presenting you with extracts from the better sketches.

"Lazy bastard!" I hear you cry. But I believe I can justify my behaviour, for several reasons.

1. The sketches are really funny (in *my* opinion and it's *my* fucking book).
2. The two series were transmitted just *once, decades ago,* and even then, *not in large areas of the UK,* so it's unlikely that you will start thinking, "Oh God, not *this* again." (That's why some of the extracts are longer than usual.)
3. I know this book is supposed to be an autobiography, but the fact is that most of you don't give a tinker's cuss for me as a human being or feel for the many different forms of suffering that make me so special. No, you are just flipping through my heart-rending life story in the hope of getting a couple of good laughs, aren't you?

So I'll start with some of the sketches where I'm an authority figure. In the first I'm a psychiatrist and Tim, a first-time patient, is having trouble confiding his problem:

> TIM BROOKE-TAYLOR: Well, I was saying, I've started to meet girls in the course of our business and at parties and socially, and well, I don't like to tell them about, well, it's not a thing you can tell people about . . .
>
> JOHN CLEESE: Come on, come on! Spit it out!
>
> TBT: Sometimes I think . . . sometimes I really . . . (*He mumbles inaudibly*)
>
> JC: What?! You come in here, you won't say what's up, it's all bloody mumbling! I can't hear a word, you're all tensed up like all the other nuts that come in here. You know

how much fun this is, listening to loonies eight hours a
day? It's so boring! (*louder*) So will you please tell me, in
God's name, what's the matter with you?!

Long pause

TBT: I think I'm a rabbit!

JC: You stupid loony! 'Course you're not a rabbit! Pull
yourself together!

TBT: I'm a rabbit! (*imitating*)

JC: Look, if you were a rabbit, you'd have big long ears,
wouldn't you?!

TBT: They dropped off when I came in!

JC: Look, if you say you're a rabbit once more, I'll smash your
face in! Now, what are you?!

TBT: I'm a . . . I'm a . . . dog. (*panting*)

JC: Right, that's better! Here's a bone, we'll take it from there
next week.

Standard Cleese bullying but Tim was wonderfully good at being
frightened. The terror he summons up before he blurts out "I think
I'm a rabbit" has to be seen to be believed.[3]

Here's another version of me as an authority figure, this time at a
zoo, where I discipline Tim:

JOHN CLEESE: (*on phone*) I'm seeing the governors for lunch
to discuss buying a new tiger, I'm seeing the giraffe
keeper at three, so I'll see you at half past.

VOICE: (*on phone*) Oh, and sir, the reptile keeper's outside to
see you.

JC: Bring him in. (*Hangs up. Several keepers bring in a large
snake with a keeper-sized bulge in it*) Lay it down there.
(*They put it on a table and leave*)

---

[3] And it can be—it's on the DVD of salvaged footage.

JC: Morning, Lotterby.

TIM BROOKE-TAYLOR: Morning, sir. Sorry, sir.

JC: Fourth time he swallowed you this week, Lotterby.

TBT: I think he's acquiring a taste for me, sir.

JC: I'm getting fed up with this, Lotterby.

TBT: I don't do it deliberately, sir!

JC: I know you. You like loafing around in there.

TBT: Oh, no, sir, I don't, sir!

JC: Any time you feel like taking an afternoon off, you just pop along to the boa constrictor and climb inside.

TBT: No, sir! Swallowing me I think is a sign of affection, sir.

JC: I'm not having the boa constrictor treated as a rest room.

TBT: I'm sorry, sir!

JC: Sorry's not enough! It's an expensive business! It costs us fifty pounds every time we operate to get you out.

TBT: Couldn't you put a zip on it, sir?

JC: No. I'm going to teach you a lesson. We're not going to operate this time. We're just going to let nature take its course.

TBT: (*screams frantically*) But that'll take years, sir! What shall I eat?!

JC: Second-hand mice.

Now that there was no one to warn us that our stuff might not be fully appreciated in Bradford, we were able to push the envelope a little further, but we liked always to set the extra silliness in a familiar context—even a rather bland and reassuringly normal one. It seemed to enhance the lunacy, by making it stand out in contrast. Parodies often provided that familiar framework.

As Gra and I always loved writing sketches where some flawed logic prevailed, which someone was trying urgently to figure out, we hit upon a parody of a popular BBC radio show where schools competed against each other in general knowledge:

JOHN CLEESE: Good evening, and welcome to another
edition of *Top of the Form*. And this evening, we're at the
semi-final stage, and tonight's contest is between the
boys of the King Arthur's Grammar School, Podbury,
and the girls of the St. Maria Kangarooboot the Second
County High School and a half. And so without further
ado, let's go straight on to Round 2. David—what is the
name we give to the meat we get from pigs?

MARTY FELDMAN: Pork?

JC: Good, good, that's two marks to you. Marcia, what is
the name of the metal alloy that we get from zinc and
copper?

GRAHAM CHAPMAN: Brass?

JC: No, no, I'm afraid not. The answer is pork. Malcolm,
what is the capital of Australia?

TIM BROOKE-TAYLOR: Sydney?

JC: No, no, I can see you're not going to get this one. The
capital of Australia is pork. Arthur, who wrote *A Tale of
Two Cities*?

MF: Pork?

JC: Good, that's two marks for you. And so, on to Stig's
question. Stig, what was the date of Captain Cook's
discovery of Australia?

GC: Pork?

JC: Good, two marks. And the last question of this round to
you, Lust: can you quote the first two lines of Thomas
Gray's "Elegy Written in a Country" . . .

TBT: Pork!

JC: Good, and the score at the end of Round 2—please, Joan
Sharp.

JC: (*in wig*) Well, the score at the end of Round 2 is the
boys of King Arthur's Grammar School, Podbury,

3, and the girls of Mildenhall Grainboiling Institute
Salmontooth, 4.

Card shows score tied at 4–4.

JC: Thank you, Joan, and so on to Round 1. Tell the
difference. David—what is the difference between a
monsoon and a mongoose?

MF: Um, well, a monsoon is a long plastic pole you hang out
of windows at an angle to keep the birds away, and a
mongoose is a box you lock books up in for Easter.

JC: No, I can only give you a half for that, but I can offer it to
you, Marcia.

TBT: Pork?

JC: No, no, you're guessing, aren't you? Well, a monsoon is a
wind, and a mongoose isn't.

In the context of the familiarity of the TV interview format, we
also wrote a two-hander where the interviewer has an odd reaction
to certain words.

INTERVIEWER: Good evening. Tonight we're taking a look at
beekeeping, and here to tell us all about it we have in the
studio a man who has been keeping bees for over forty
years, Mr. Reginald Prawnbaum. Good evening, Mr.
Prawnbaum.

PRAWNBAUM: Good evening.

INTERVIEWER: Tell me, what first interested you in the bee
world, Mr. Prawnbaum?

PRAWNBAUM: Well, even as a child I used to . . .

INTERVIEWER: Shh!

PRAWNBAUM: I'm sorry, shouldn't I have said that?

INTERVIEWER: No, of course you should. Pay no attention.
When I say, "Shh," it's just a nervous mannerism

I've picked up. If I want you to keep quiet I will say, "Shoosh." You were saying?

PRAWNBAUM: Oh, I see. Well, even as a child I used to wander around . . .

INTERVIEWER: Shh!

PRAWNBAUM: . . . in the fields near my house, watching bees fly from flower to flower . . .

INTERVIEWER: Shh!

PRAWNBAUM: . . . and, er, taking note of the flowers that they visited.

INTERVIEWER: Shoosh!

PRAWNBAUM: Was that wrong?

INTERVIEWER: I'm so sorry. Did I say, "shoosh"? I mean, "shh." Do go on, it's most interesting.

PRAWNBAUM: And so I have grown to love the little, er . . .

INTERVIEWER: Shh!

PRAWNBAUM: . . . creatures. You know nature really has produced a little masterpiece in the life of the bee.

INTERVIEWER: Quark! I'm sorry I'm afraid that's a reflex action too. I squawk whenever someone mentions the word "life." Quark! You see, even when I mention it myself. I should have told you. Please go on.

PRAWNBAUM: Oh, very well. Bees, as you know, are divided into . . .

INTERVIEWER: Shh!

PRAWNBAUM: Different categories . . .

INTERVIEWER: Shh!

PRAWNBAUM: . . . The queen bee and the worker bee, whose life span . . .

INTERVIEWER: Quark!

PRAWNBAUM: . . . whose living expectancy is only one year.

INTERVIEWER: Shh!

PRAWNBAUM: The worker bees, on the other hand, have a
    much longer . . .
INTERVIEWER: Shoosh!
PRAWNBAUM: Do you want me to stop?
INTERVIEWER: Yes, you were about to say "life." Quark!

And so on. I rate this as one of the ten best sketches I have written in my entire life. Quark! If you don't agree . . . Shoosh![4]

You see what I mean about the "logic"? Here's one more, where Marty slowly drives me mad when he enters an old-fashioned train compartment, where I am sitting alone.

MARTY FELDMAN: Excuse me, is this seat occupied?
    He points to the seat next to JC in the otherwise empty, spacious carriage.
JOHN CLEESE: No.
    MF puts case overhead and sits down as close as possible to JC and fidgets. Pause.
MF: Excuse me, would you mind if I changed places with
    you?
JC: What?
MF: Could I sit there?
JC: Yes, I suppose so.
    JC stands and moves to the opposite seat. MF moves his overhead case, then sits across from JC.
MF: Do you mind if I smoke?
JC: No, not at all.
    Pause.
MF: . . . I wish I had a cigarette.

---

[4] There's a good performance of it on iTunes, when Rowan Atkinson and I reprised it for an Amnesty concert.

JC: . . . What?!

MF: I wish I had a cigarette.

JC: Do you want a cigarette?

JC holds out a cigarette for him.

MF: Oh, oh, oh—no, I don't think I will.

JC: Please take one.

MF: No, no, I mustn't, no.

JC: Take one.

MF: No, no, really.

JC: All right.

JC puts them back in his pocket. Pause.

MF: I wish I hadn't refused that cigarette. How I wish I hadn't
refused the cigarette that nice gentleman had offered
me, because I . . .

JC offers again.

MF: Oh, thank you! (*takes one*) Thank you very much!

*JC pulls out a lighter and prepares to light it, but discovers
MF has put the cigarette in his pocket.*

JC: Aren't you going to smoke it?

MF: Oh, no. See, if I smoke it now, I won't have one for after.

JC: After what?

MF: After I smoke this one. If I had two cigarettes now, it
would be plain sailing.

JC: Have another cigarette.

MF: Thank you!

JC: Keep the pack!

MF sits for a moment and then starts talking quite quietly.

MF: Once upon a time there was a fairy prince, and his name
was Arthur Aldridge. And he got on a train, and a magic
wizard gave him some cigarettes. Magic cigarettes . . .

JC: What are you talking about?

MF: I'm telling myself a story. To pass the time . . .

JC: Well, will you please tell it quietly?

MF now tells the story to himself. We are aware only of his
lips moving. Then . . .
MF: . . . happily ever after. The end.
    He starts looking carefully all round the carriage. After a
pause . . .
MF: I spy, with my little eye, something beginning with B.
      Or J. B or J.
JC: How could it begin with a B or a J?
MF: For various reasons, none of which I am at liberty to
      divulge. B or J. Easy . . .
JC: What's the answer?
MF: Ectoplasm.
JC: Ectoplasm?
MF: Mr. B. J. Ectoplasm. He works in my office.
JC: But I can't see him!
MF: You can if you have an appointment.

While some of the *1948 Show* skits were still fairly conventional,
we were slowly getting bolder about being wilder and sillier. But it
was a slower process than one might think. In the first series we did
at least seven sketches that had been performed in *Cambridge Circus*.
There were even a couple of reworkings of sketches from Footlights
days: a martial arts skit which Tim, Gra and I had done in the 1962
revue, and Gra's one-man wrestling bout. Using well-tested material
here and there boosted our confidence at a time when we were still
unsure of ourselves.

We also did a fair amount of physical comedy, which had been
largely absent from the various Frost programmes. Here the humour
was in the action: Marty constantly falling asleep while appealing for
funds to help fellow-sufferers from narcolepsy; policemen chasing a
burglar in a library as quietly as possible; a minister falling apart during a TV party political broadcast (later rewritten for *Monty Python*);
a dentist having so much trouble with getting at a back tooth that he

has to climb into the patient's mouth (created on a separate set, of course); and—a very surreal idea of Marty's—an escaped criminal taking refuge under an opera singer's vast skirt while she's singing an aria. ("We know you're in there, Murphy!" say the armed police who surround him. "Come and get me, you dirty rats!")

The team got on well during the six shows of the first series: we laughed a lot, there were no heated, edgy arguments of the upcoming Cleese–Jones variety, we all liked our director, Ian Fordyce, and the staff were sweet and helpful. It also helped that I was becoming more relaxed as a performer about making mistakes. I remember, for example, tripping up on the following four-line quickie (written by Eric Idle) that I was performing straight to camera:

> Are you bright, hard-working, ambitious, intelligent and quick-witted, with a good personality and a smart appearance? Do you get on well with people and find that they look on you as a natural leader? Do you feel that you're being held back in your present position and that with a go-ahead firm, you'd get right to the top? Cocky little devil, aren't you?

The second take went fine, but afterwards, in the green room, I was taken to task by a friend. "How could you get it wrong?" she said. "It was only *four* sentences." I started to explain, but she was on the attack and became quite seething about my lapse. I had already invited her to a dinner party at my place later that week, so I said, "Here's a bet. If you can do it correctly at Friday's dinner, I'll give you £20." And I gave her the script.

On Friday, she arrived, and wanted to do it immediately, but I stalled her and introduced her to my friends and announced that dinner was served. Towards the end of the meal, I explained the bet, everyone got a bit excited, and I asked her if she wanted to leave the table to practise it. She declined, so I prolonged dinner by serving extra drinks (although she'd hardly drunk at all, of course), and then we went into the living room to get ready for her performance, and I remembered I had forgotten to make a phone call, so I ran off, and the "call" took some time, and when I got back I asked her if she was ready, and she was, so I outlined the bet one more time and then said, "Cue!" And, of course, she got about five syllables out before she fluffed. As she left later, I gave her my most saturnine smile and said, *"Now* you know why I screwed it up. And there are only five people here."

Performing sketches, then, could still cause a little stress from time to time. So, too, could censorship problems—at least for the nice, late-middle-aged lady called Jane whose job it was to worry about these things. Tim and I were nominally in charge of the script (we had some sort of vague titles), so when there was an issue with it we were the ones who went to see Jane. She was very nice, but she worried about *everything*.

> JANE: You've set this sketch in a town hall in Richmond.
> TIM BROOKE-TAYLOR: Yes?
> JANE: Well, there are two towns in Britain called Richmond.
> JOHN CLEESE: And?
> JANE: One of them might complain.
> JC: But there's nothing rude about the town.
> JANE: No, but . . . I am concerned.
> TBT: OK! Let's call it "Goolie."
> JANE: Thank you!

As for the rest of us, our anxieties were almost entirely script-related and arose because our pattern of rehearsal was as follows:

First day: Read-through. Everything looks fine, so afterwards write for next week's show.

Second day: Rehearsal. On second thoughts, two sketches feel a bit weak, so the evening is spent rewriting them. One of them now much better.

Third day: Rehearsal. One sketch still not working, so rewrite in evening, but by now we have lost all confidence in it, so start thinking of new sketch to replace it. Eventually think of one. Write it.

Fourth day: Rehearsal. New sketch doesn't work. We stop rehearsing early so we have extra time to come up with new sketch. We are feeling tired and a bit anxious, and don't like any of our new ideas as they all seem derivative. Write two new sketches.

Fifth day: Rehearsal. New sketches stink. Panic looms. Depressed as well as tired. Devoid of funny thoughts.

Sixth day: Rehearsal. We borrow a sketch from *next* week's script. But it doesn't feel very funny either and we don't have time to rehearse it properly.

Seventh day: Bad night's sleep. Recording in front of LIVE audience. Show goes rather well so suicide pact put on hold and we celebrate instead.

Eighth day: New script doesn't feel as good as last night's and we are already a sketch short. Spend evening trying to write but too tired and stressed.

And so on and so on. Panic, anxiety, loss of sense of humour, insomnia, depression, bleeding from ears, migraines, vertigo, loss of appetite, blurred vision, nocturnal enuresis, etc., etc. But . . . no tensions within the team. Just fear the show would be *bad.*

Writing and performing in these six shows taught me an important creative principle: the more anxious you feel, the less creative you are. Your mind ceases to play and be expansive. Fear causes your thinking to contract, to play *safe,* and this forces you into stereotypical thinking. And in comedy you must have innovation because an old joke isn't funny. I therefore came up with Cleese's Two Rules of Writing Comedy.

First Rule: Get your panic in early. Fear gives you energy, so make sure you have plenty of time to use that energy. (The same rule applies to exams.)

Second Rule: Your thoughts follow your mood. Anxiety produces anxious thoughts; sadness begets sad thoughts; anger, angry thoughts; so aim to be in a relaxed, playful mood when you try to be funny.

We all thought the reaction to the shows would be all right, because the studio audiences liked them, but the response was better than we expected, especially from the TV critics. They were paid a lot of attention in those days (some of them were worth it then) but there was one in particular, Philip Purser of the *Telegraph,* whose opinion we cared about *a lot.* So when he wrote a review in which he criticised ITV for not showing the programme nationally ("If I lived in the Midlands, say, I'd be mutinous by now") and argued, "if it weren't for Alan Bennett we'd be hailing it as the funniest thing for years," we were over several astronomical entities, some of them very distant. On the whole, the critics tended to pick me out, while missing Marty. They spotted him in the autumn, though.

Before I develop the narrative further . . . One more favourite sketch! (The cost of which is included in the price of the book, so you can skip it without feeling cheated.)

JOHN CLEESE: Come in! Ah, good morning. Come in, thank you. Do sit down. What can I do for you?

GRAHAM CHAPMAN: Well, I'm interested in your memory training programme.

JC: Oh good, well, a lot of people feel that they'd like to improve their memories. The wonderful thing is, improving them is not as hard as, uh, as hard as, uh, nails.

GC: I beg your pardon?

JC: As hard as nails. It's word association. You see, it's the basis of my system . . . You remember things by associating with . . . uh . . . with, uh . . . people like that.

GC: People like what?

JC: They like to improve their memory. Now, what can I do for you?

GC: Well, I'm interested in your course.

JC: Good! You remembered that. You see, you have learned to associate your interest in my course with my asking why . . . association of ideas, it's the basis of everything we do to acquire a better memory. But it's not as hard as . . .

GC: I think?

JC: No, hard as nails. Remember? Never mind, never mind, you'll soon pick it up. Now, take a common object like this.

GC: A saucer.

JC: Good! Well done. Now what does it make you think of?

GC: Well, uh . . .

JC: What would you like to think of?

GC: Like to think of?

JC: A nude woman!

GC: A nude woman?

JC: Well done! You're getting it! What is the nude woman doing?

GC: Drinking tea?

JC: Good! And what's she drinking tea out of?

GC: A cup?

JC: Quite right! A cup and . . . saucer! It's a saucer! Are you getting it?

GC: I'm not sure . . .

JC: One of the association ideas is that the basis of our method, indeed, the whole, the whole, hole in the wall—what do I see through the hole in the wall? A nude woman! Every time!

GC: Every time?

JC: Of course! It's such a strong image, you can't forget it.
You associate that with anything you want to remember,
anything—numbers, dates, names, anything—try again.

GC: Battle of Trafalgar?

JC: Ah, Trafalgar, Trafalgar Square, square, hole in the wall,
look through the hole in the wall, what do I see?

GC: A nude woman?

JC: Excellent! Excellent! Who is this nude woman?

GC: I don't know.

JC: The Empress Josephine, 1815. See? Josephine, 1815.

GC: 1815 was Waterloo. Trafalgar was 1805.

JC: Wait a minute, I haven't finished. Josephine's wearing
boots, Wellington boots, you can't see the toes, so
deduct the ten you can't see from 1815, 1805. Simple!

GC: All right, the date of Waterloo.

JC: 1815!

GC: Yes, but how do you do it?

JC: Ah, wait a minute, ah . . . Waterloo, Waterloo Station,
train to Brighton, Brighton Pier, peer through the hole
in the wall, and there's the Empress Josephine in the
nude, 1815.

GC: But she's got Wellington boots on.

JC: No, Battle of Waterloo, Duke of Wellington, in he comes,
wants his boots back, so he sees her toes, no need to
deduct ten, Waterloo 1815. See?

GC: Fire of London?

JC: What?

GC: The date of the Fire of London.

JC: Oh. Let me think, let me think . . . date of the Fire of
London . . . Fire, fiery, diary, Samuel Pepys, yes, Pepys
wrote in his diary about the Fire of London, Samuel
Pepys, peeps through the hole in the wall, what does
he see?

GC: A nude woman?

JC: No. Three nude women. By the light of the fire, he sees three stunning, gorgeous nude women, sex, sex, sex, sexteen sexty-sex.

Despite the success of the series, the feeling of *responsibility* was killing me, and when *The 1948 Show* was finished, I fell in a heap and lay there for a week. Once I had recovered, Gra and I settled down to start writing the new *Frost Reports*.

THE CHINESE have a blessing: May you live in uninteresting times. So I was blessed to be doing this second series with David. For three months there was calm, order, predictability, not a hint of a crisis or anything else "interesting." The show ran smoothly, David was genial, Jimmy charming and well organised, I was less stressed, the writers had all become good pals and the two Ronnies were . . . funny. Just funny, whatever they did. Ronnie C's timing was still an education for me but I also began to notice Ronnie B's supreme competence. This sounds like faint praise, but it's his own fault because he made *everything* look so easy.

Gra and I wrote a sketch we particularly liked, because it was rather wilder than the Frost norm. Ronnie B played the big part, with Ronnie C "feeding" him.

Adrian Wapcaplet sits in his luxurious advertising agency office. The client, Mr. Simpson, enters and Wapcaplet rises to greet him.

WAPCAPLET: Ah! Come in, Mr. Simpson. Welcome to Follicle, Ampersand, Goosecreature, Eskimo, Sedlitz,

Wapcaplet, Looseliver, Vendetta, Wallaby and Spong, London's leading advertising agency. Do sit down. My name's Wapcaplet, Adrian Wapcaplet.

SIMPSON: How do you do.

They both sit.

WAPCAPLET: Now, Mr. Simpson—I understand you want us to advertise your washing powder?

SIMPSON: *String.*

WAPCAPLET: String, washing powder—what's the difference?! We can sell anything.

SIMPSON: Good. Well, I have this large quantity of string—112,000 miles of it to be exact—which I inherited. I thought that if I advertised it . . .

WAPCAPLET: Of course, a national campaign! Useful stuff, string, no trouble there.

SIMPSON: Ah, but there's a *snag,* you see. Due to bad planning . . . the 112,000 miles is in three-inch lengths.

He gives Wapcaplet a sample three-inch length of string.

SIMPSON: So it's not very useful . . .

WAPCAPLET: Three-inch lengths, eh? . . . That's our selling point! Simpson's *Individual* Stringettes!

SIMPSON: . . . What?

WAPCAPLET: The "Now" string . . . pre-sliced, easy-to-handle Simpson's Individual Emperor Stringettes. *Just* the right length!

SIMPSON: For what?

WAPCAPLET: Er . . . a million household uses!

SIMPSON: Such as?

WAPCAPLET: Tying up very small parcels, attaching notes to pigeons' legs, destroying household pests . . .

SIMPSON: Destroying household pests?

WAPCAPLET: If they're bigger than a mouse you can strangle them with the string, and if they're smaller you can

flog 'em to death with it . . . Buy Simpson's miracle
  Stringettes *today*!

SIMPSON: Miracle? It's only *string*!

WAPCAPLET: *Only* string? It's everything! It's waterproof!

SIMPSON: No it isn't.

WAPCAPLET: All right—it's water-resistant, then.

SIMPSON: It isn't.

WAPCAPLET: . . . All right! It's water-*absorbent*! It's . . .
  *super*absorbent string. Absorb water today with
  Simpson's Individual Water Absorbitex Stringettes.
  Away with floods!

SIMPSON: You just said it was waterproof . . .

WAPCAPLET: Away with the dull drudgery of workaday
  tidal waves! Use Simpson's Individual Space-age Flood
  Preventers!

SIMPSON: You're mad.

Not that zany, I agree, but we were getting there.

WITH THE final *Frost Report* under our belt, Graham and I spent a few days on the *Rimmer* script, and then jumped in a limo with Tim and Marty to be driven up to Manchester for an appearance on the big chat show of those days, *Dee Time,* hosted by Simon Dee. My first television interview, back in the early days of *The Frost Report,* had been a grim experience, but this time I really enjoyed myself, not least, I fear, because the four of us behaved rather badly.

We had never met Simon before we walked on to his show, which was live, and I'm not sure he quite knew which one of us was which. And he certainly had no idea as to the identity of the fifth member of our group, since this was the guy who'd driven the limo from London and whom we'd decided to invite on with us. Once our driver had sat down he decided to take off his shoes and socks and began eating a sandwich he'd brought with him. Dee was understandably bewildered, but wisely didn't risk an introduction and the interview proceeded without any clarification. The moment Simon turned away from us to introduce the first commercial break, we hid behind our sofas so effectively that when the poor man turned back from his announcement, he thought we'd left, and a panic ensued.

The reason we were feeling naughty was because we were all just about to go on holiday. Graham was due to spend a month in Mykonos, which slightly surprised us, as it was an island known for its gay lifestyle even in 1967, so it didn't strike me as being his kind of place. And Tim and I were flying to Brussels the next day, to link up with Alan Hutchison, so that the three of us could travel together down to Italy by car, to take a beach holiday in Elba.

Strangely enough, given that I didn't have a driving licence, the car we were driving was mine. The success of my television ventures had inspired me to acquire a rather beautiful and expensive old Bentley, which I'd fallen in love with not just because it was decked out in British Racing Green but because it was *big*: with child-bearing hips, and a big walnut dashboard, and big walnut trays built into the back of the front seats, so that people could sit in the back and have picnics while being driven about in Oxfordshire. I'd started to learn to drive, and in the meantime had acquired a provisional driving licence that allowed me to drive my car along the road, provided I put "L" plates up and had a qualified driver sitting next to me; and I'd also bought a chauffeur's cap, to confuse people who'd seen the "L" plates.

Once Alan had picked Tim and me up at Brussels airport we began driving south (they wouldn't allow me behind the wheel), all three of us full of high spirits, playing up the role of young English gentlemen abroad. We wore Panama hats, I had on a cricket shirt and a cravat, and as Alan drove the first leg of our journey, Tim and I did a lot of "royal" waving out of the windows, smiling and nodding graciously to the Belgian people, and blessing them. An hour later we retraced our journey. This time all three of us were sitting in the back of the Bentley, and we were still waving and behaving regally, but the car was slanting graciously backwards with the front wheels a couple of feet off the ground, suspended from the rescue truck that was towing us. Alan had put our car under a juggernaut (or, for American readers, a large truck) at a roundabout, while I was reading the map, and Tim in the back was unavailingly crying *"Priorité à droite! Priorité à droite."*

We left the Bentley and Tim at a garage, and Alan and I travelled back to Brussels to hire a much less magnificent vehicle. When we picked Tim up the next morning, he told us that he'd spent the night in his room with a "bird." Intrigued, we questioned him closely, and learned that he had been woken in the middle of the night by a strange, rather alarming noise and that when he had put the light on he had discovered a turkey vomiting on the mantelpiece. He'd thought of complaining but found that his phrase book did not cover this contingency.

So, in reduced circumstances, the three of us drove down to Pisa airport and collected another bird, called Christine. Tim had met her at the first *1948 Show* recording in mid-February and I'm pleased to report they married in 1968.

When I got back from Italy I found a message from Harry Secombe asking if we could meet between shows at the London Palladium, where he was headlining their big summer production, with help from my *Frost Report* friend Nicky Henson. My God, they worked hard, somehow managing to do *three* shows *each* Saturday. Nicky enjoyed the experience of playing the huge Palladium theatre with its packed summertime audience; the only bit he found difficult was the moment the curtain went up at the Saturday matinee, when he was hit by a smell of sweaty armpits from the audience that would have felled a camel. Nicky also told me a typical Secombe story: a few weeks after their show opened, Harry found out what all the dancers were being paid; he immediately insisted the show's accountants put an extra £5 in each dancer's wage packet, and deduct it from his own salary. There were a lot of dancers, and they never knew.

It's unusual to meet a man who is truly loveable, but Harry was one of those men, and that is probably why I felt so angry for him during our first meeting in his dressing room. (I'd arrived after the matinee and still remember an autograph hunter at the stage door asking me, "Are you anybody?" I was tempted to answer him on-tologically, but instead told him a white lie, and denied my own existence.) When Harry greeted me, he immediately presented me with a beautiful coffee-table book—a copy of J. B. Priestley's *Man and Time*. He'd remembered our conversation in Barbados! He then asked me if I would write some sketches for him to perform in a big TV special he had planned and I was genuinely thrilled. We chatted about ideas, and then his agent, Jimmy Grafton, arrived and handed Harry a script he had written for him—a big set-piece to end another show. Harry started to read it and I made some notes of the sketch ideas we'd just come up with. However, I slowly became aware that Harry was looking very worried by what he was reading. He clearly thought it wasn't funny, but being so good-natured he was terribly uncomfortable about making any sort of critical comment to Jimmy, who by now was immersed in a conversation with someone else. Eventually Harry cleared his throat a couple of times and said, "I think this still . . . needs a little work, Jimmy."

Jimmy looked round, almost irritated that he'd been interrupted. "What?"

"Er . . . well, Jimmy . . . I don't think this is . . . *quite* right yet."

"It's *fine,* Harry! You'll make it funny . . ."

And he turned back to a conversation that was clearly of more interest to him; and Harry just sat there, looking quite dejected, and rightly so, at the prospect of labouring his way through unfunny ma-terial in front of countless silent audiences, while his agent, having treated Harry's query with something approaching contempt, raked in the royalties without needing to make any further effort.

Being so low in the pecking order, and a yellow-belly by inclination, I said nothing. I felt impotent. But that this lovely man should be so callously exploited by a lazy, soulless agent made my blood boil. And I vowed to myself that I would never, *NEVER* be so "nice" and agreeable and co-operative that bullies and slackers could walk all over me and force me to do things that I might be ashamed of. And I think I can claim that I've usually managed to curb my placatory tendencies, and go toe-to-toe *when necessary.* This, as it happens, is seldom required, and when it is I don't exactly enjoy it. Nevertheless, as a therapist once said to me, "If people cannot hear you, you may need to raise your voice." For any *Daily Mail* journalist reading this, I should explain he was speaking largely metaphorically.

Fortunately Harry liked the sketches I wrote for him, and so did the audience. All, in fact, went very smoothly with our collaboration. The only slight hiccup I can recall occurred when he was reading a monologue off the autocue, and one of his new contact lenses started to rotate, and he had to take it out. I'd never seen one like it: it looked as though it had been part of a milk bottle. He must have had to put his eye in it, rather than vice versa.

MEANWHILE I had been asked to perform in my first movie: a film called *Interlude.* It was a straight part, with only a couple of slightly humorous lines, but I was very excited nonetheless. The role was that of a PR man at a TV company who is looking after a young woman journalist who has come to the company's studios to interview a famous Austrian conductor. An affair ensues between the conductor and the journalist.

Filming took place in the same Wembley TV studio where a few months before I'd done all the *Frost* programmes, so the setting could not have been more familiar, especially as my very first scene took place in the canteen. As I settled in to my first ever day on a feature film, several things surprised me: the sheer size of the crew—there must have been thirty-five in the canteen, all carrying out various jobs; the length of time between each camera set-up; the charming old-fashioned courtesy of the crew (everyone called me "sir"); the number of takes it required before anyone decided we could move on. I was also deeply impressed by the sedate, polite atmosphere, and the sheer efficiency of the crew. (An actor once told me the difference between British and French film crews: the former are great craftsmen who seldom go to the cinema, and never discuss "Film"; the French argue passionately all the time about "Cinema," but aren't that hot at their jobs.) This efficiency, I later discovered, was partly down to the director, Kevin Billington, a man of immense energy, but also calm and effortlessly friendly, who thought and spoke with unusual clarity. Thanks to him, the crew always knew what they were doing, and what they would be doing *next*. Later I was to work with many directors who operated in a very different way, substituting a mood of hushed panic for Kevin's calm progress.

So my first experience of filming was hugely positive. I even got on well with the star, Oskar Werner, although he had viewed me suspiciously for the first couple of days (he was much shorter). Then we got talking about food, and we never looked back.

UNKNOWN TO me, while I was beavering away on my various projects, a lot was happening on the Chapman front. When he got back from Greece, he called and invited Pippa and me to a party in

Hampstead. We went, found it very crowded, and after we had all greeted each other I drifted off with some other friends to watch a nail-biting football match on the TV. When it finally ended, Pippa was standing there.

"Graham's gone."

"Oh! Well, I'll see him on Monday."

"He wanted to talk to you."

"What about?"

"I'll tell you in the taxi."

(In the taxi.)

"He had to go, but he gave me a message for you. He's come out."

"He lives in Hampstead."

"No, he's . . . he's decided he's gay."

"What?"

"He's homosexual."

"Who are we talking about?"

"Graham!"

"Graham who?"

"Graham *Chapman*!"

"Yes, I know! But who does Gra say is gay?"

"*He* is!"

". . . I'm sorry. I'm lost . . ."

"Graham Chapman . . ."

"Yes . . ."

"Has decided he's a homosexual. He wants you to know he has a boyfriend."

"What is this all about?"

"It's true!"

"But why is he trying to wind me up?"

"He *isn't*!"

"Is it a bet?"

It's a good thing the taxi ride to Kensington was a long one, because Pippa needed every minute of it to convince me. While in Mykonos, Gra had met an impressive Swede called Stig, and Stig had convinced him that when he got back to London he should tell all his friends he had been living with his boyfriend, David, ever since they had met in Ibiza over a year before.

As we got out of the cab:

"Graham wants you to tell Marty."

So I telephoned Marty and we had an identical conversation, except that I was now doing Pippa's lines, and Marty was doing mine. The only difference was that Marty got quite irritated.

"John, it's eleven o'clock. Why are you calling me?"

"I just told you!"

"Please, don't mess me around anymore. It's not funny . . ."

Graham always used to say that I was shocked when he came out. That implies some sort of moral objection. Untrue. I was not "shocked," I was very, very, very, very, very, very, very, very, very, very, very *surprised*.

I had known Gra for over five years and he had always worn brogue shoes and cord trousers and a sports jacket with leather patches on the elbows, and he had been a beer-drinking, pipe-smoking, rugby football–playing medical student. In the '60s, if you were wondering if someone might be gay, these habits were not thought of as dead giveaways. Unless, of course, the person in question was female.

Gra now organised a coming-out party, and all Gra's friends met David, and a good time was had by all. In retrospect, the most surprising thing (after the news) was how little anything actually *changed*. It certainly didn't affect our writing relationship. But I think our material was getting better as we became more experienced and confident.

★

THE SECOND series of *The 1948 Show* was due to start in late September, so Tim, Marty, Gra and I settled down to write. We saw no need to make alterations to the format or the style of the show, but we now had a much clearer idea of what we were trying to accomplish, and that, combined with greater confidence, and the fact that we no longer had old material to fall back on, led to scripts that were more zany, madcap and off the wall—and therefore getting closer than ever to *Monty Python*.

As the series progressed it became obvious to us all that Marty was growing stronger and stronger as a performer: his technique had improved remarkably quickly, and the need for intense rehearsal sessions with him became much less frequent. Vocally he was not the finished article, as his odd voice production meant that he sometimes lost the rhythms of sketches that were heavy on dialogue, but if he could just respond to questions, rather than taking the lead in a sketch, he could be hilarious.

> *John Cleese, in a suit, sitting at an office desk. Marty Feldman*
> *enters, as Spriggs.*
> MARTY FELDMAN: You asked for me, sir?
> JC: Ah, Spriggs, it's you.
> MF: Is that all, sir?
> JC: No, Spriggs, sit down, please.
> MF: It wasn't me, sir.
> JC: Last week, Spriggs, I had to investigate several serious
>   complaints against you . . .
> MF: Oh, sir . . .
> JC: About forty thousand . . .
> MF: Sorry, sir.
> JC: That's a lot of complaints, Spriggs.
> MF: It is, sir, lots.
> JC: About Monday's incident.

MF: Oh, sir . . .

JC: Last Monday, Spriggs, you were scheduled to drive the
10:15 to Bristol. But you didn't, did you, Spriggs? You
took a cattle train, didn't you?

MF: Yes, sir.

JC: Why, Spriggs?

MF: I like animals, sir.

JC: You like animals?

MF: Yes, sir. Especially cows.

JC: So you took seven hundred of them. The entire London
to Brighton cattle train. To Manchester.

MF: Yes, sir.

JC: Why Manchester, Spriggs?

MF: I've been to Brighton, sir.

JC: But you ignored all the signals!

MF: I was out of the cabin, sir . . .

JC: Sitting on the engine, flying your kite—yes, I've seen the
photographs. What are you laughing at, Spriggs?

MF: I'm trying to break the ice, sir.

JC: Don't push me, Spriggs. Now, about Manchester
Cathedral . . .

MF: I forgot to stop, sir.

JC: Yes, I know, Spriggs. The traffic police have told me. So
has the Archbishop. He has described the arrival of you
and your locomotive in the nave during the 49th Psalm
in no little detail. Seems to have been an unnerving
experience for the entire congregation, Spriggs.

MF: I said I was sorry, sir.

JC: He goes on to say, Spriggs, that when he tried to restore
calm by mounting what was left of the pulpit, you
started shunting operations in the east transept . . .

MF: I was in his way, sir . . .

JC: Then why did you release all the cows?

MF: I panicked, sir, I couldn't see in all the steam!

JC: Nor could the congregation, Spriggs, that's why all the
    cows came as such a shock! The organ and the clanking
    and the hot steam all would have been alarming to an
    agnostic, let alone those who believe in the wrath of
    God. Even the Archbishop said he thought it was the end
    of the world.

MF: I can pay for the damage, sir. I took a collection . . .

JC: Yes, the Archbishop's told me. No, Spriggs, I'm going to
    punish you.

MF: Oh, sir . . .

JC: You are to write out fifty times, "I must not drive my
    trains into Manchester Cathedral." Now get out!

MF: Yes, sir.

JC: Oh, Spriggs?

MF: Yes?

JC: Where are last week's lines?

Finally, I want to present to you part of the best sketch Marty and
I ever did together. This time he was leading the dialogue as Mr. Pest,
but he was word-perfect, and pitch-perfect.

*A quite spacious bookshop. A customer enters and approaches
the counter, behind which stands an assistant.*

ASSISTANT: Good morning, sir.

MR. PEST: Good morning. Can you help me? Do you have a
    copy of *Thirty Days in the Samarkand Desert with a Spoon*
    by A. E. J. Elliott?

ASSISTANT: Um . . . well, we haven't got it in stock, sir.

MR. PEST: Never mind. How about *A Hundred and One Ways
    to Start a Monsoon*?

ASSISTANT: . . . By . . . ?

MR. PEST: An Indian gentleman whose name eludes me for
the moment.

ASSISTANT: I'm sorry, I don't know the book, sir.

MR. PEST: Not to worry, not to worry. Can you help me with
David Coperfield?

ASSISTANT: Ah, yes. Dickens . . .

MR. PEST: No.

ASSISTANT: . . . I beg your pardon?

MR. PEST: No, Edmund Wells.

ASSISTANT: . . . I think you'll find Charles Dickens wrote
David Copperfield, sir.

MR. PEST: No, Charles Dickens wrote *David Copperfield*
with two "p"s. This is *David Coperfield* with *one* "p" by
Edmund Wells.

ASSISTANT: (*a little sharply*) Well, in that case we don't have it.

MR. PEST: Funny, you've got a lot of books here.

ASSISTANT: We do have quite a lot of books here, yes, but
we don't have *David Coperfield* with one "p" by Edmund
Wells. We only have *David Copperfield* with two "p"s by
Charles Dickens.

MR. PEST: Pity—it's more thorough than the Dickens.

ASSISTANT: More *thorough?*

MR. PEST: Yes . . . I wonder if it's worth having a look through
all your *David Copperfields* . . .

ASSISTANT: I'm quite sure all our *David Copperfields* have two
"p"s.

MR. PEST: Probably, but the first edition by Edmund Wells
also had two "p"s. It was after that they ran into
copyright difficulties.

ASSISTANT: No, I can assure you that all our *David
Copperfields* with *two* "p"s *are* by Charles Dickens.

MR. PEST: How about *Grate Expectations?*

ASSISTANT: Ah yes, we have that . . .

He goes to fetch it and returns to the counter.

MR. PEST: . . . That's *G–r–a–t–e Expectations*, also by Edmund Wells.

ASSISTANT: I see. In that case we don't have it. We don't have anything by Edmund Wells, actually—he's not very popular.

MR. PEST: Not *Knickerless Nickleby*? That's K–n–i–c–k–e–r . . .

ASSISTANT: No!

MR. PEST: Or *Quiristmas Quarol* with a Q?

ASSISTANT: No, *definitely . . . not.*

MR. PEST: Sorry to trouble you.

ASSISTANT: Not at all.

MR. PEST: I wonder if you have a copy of *Rarnaby Budge*?

ASSISTANT: *(rather loudly)* No, as I say, we're right out of Edmund Wells.

MR. PEST: No, not Edmund Wells—Charles Dikkens.

ASSISTANT: Charles Dickens?

MR. PEST: Yes.

ASSISTANT: You mean *Barnaby Rudge.*

MR. PEST: No, *Rarnaby Budge* by Charles Dikkens . . . that's Dikkens with two "k"s, the well-known Dutch author.

ASSISTANT: No, no—we don't have *Rarnaby Budge* by Charles Dikkens with two "k"s, the well-known Dutch author, and perhaps to save time I should add right away that we don't have *Carnaby Fudge* by Darles Tikkens, or *Stickwick Stapers* by Miles Pikkens with four "M"s and a silent "Q"; why don't you try the chemist?

MR. PEST: I did. They sent me here.

The character of Mr. Pest suited Marty so brilliantly that we reprised it several times, but now making him more physically destructive, leaving behind vandalised sets as well as broken psyches. Marty was so funny in these sketches that people rightly recognised his emergence as a real star.

Meanwhile, there was one incident, quite unrelated to Gra's new lifestyle, which in retrospect seems significant in terms of the light it sheds on my collaboration with Gra. At the end of the filming of *Interlude,* my new friend Oskar Werner had given me, as a memento, the baton with which he had been conducting the orchestra. I really treasured it. Gra noticed it on my desk one day, I told him the story of how I'd acquired it, and he asked if he could pick it up. I said, "Yes, of course," and he started flexing it, bending it in an arc, but doing so a little harder each time. I nearly said, "Careful," but it felt unnecessary. Then Graham flexed it very hard, and it snapped. And what was so odd was that he didn't seem at all surprised or put out. He just said, "Oh," and then put the pieces back on the desk, and then in a completely neutral voice added, "Sorry." I was bemused, but in the tradition that became so much a part of Monty Python, said nothing.

Looking back on this with the benefit of hindsight, what Gra treated as the most trivial matter, comparable to dropping a biscuit on someone's carpet, might have been a sign of some competitiveness between us that was never acknowledged. I say this because I intuitively connect the baton story with something that happened quite early on in the Python era. Gra arrived for rehearsal and immediately (and untypically) started telling us all about a dream he'd had the night before. He found that he'd been made Chancellor of the Exchequer. He was sitting at his desk, issuing orders and signing important papers, and lording it over his civil servants and having a wonderful time being king of the castle, until he discovered that the Prime Minister . . . was me. The way he told it was quite painful: the news about my status really did shatter his dream. The glory of being the second most powerful man in Britain had vanished without a trace . . .

BY NOVEMBER 1967 I was beginning to feel I badly needed a break. Between March 1966 and then I'd done:

> *Frost Report*: 27
> *1948 Show*: 13
> *Frost Programme*: 40+
> *I'm Sorry, I'll Read That Again*: 41
> Film scripts in production: 2
> TV pilot scripts: 1
> TV appearances: 12
> Film appearances: 1

But now, I seemed at last to have a bit of time to myself, and I found my mind turning to some unfinished business.

SOMETIME DURING the course of the second series of *The Frost Report* in the spring of 1967, I received a "Dear John" letter from Connie. She felt that our geographical separation meant that it was not possible for the relationship to develop naturally, and she wanted us to become "just dear friends." It was a sweet and affectionate letter. It was also a shock. I could understand her decision—and when someone wants to break up, it has always seemed to me futile to try to prolong the agony—but I also felt very sad. I have the clearest memory of sitting on a park bench on Shepherd's Bush Green, just fifty yards from the beautiful old converted theatre from which we used to transmit the show every week. There'd been a break in camera rehearsal, when I'd wandered outside to gather my thoughts, and I found myself quite seriously considering whether I should just give up show business and go to New York to live, and perhaps earn my crust as a writer, or even a banker. After all, two of my Cambridge friends were banking away happily in Manhattan . . . and the relationship with Connie could blossom naturally there.

I also meditated on whether I required a change of personality— or perhaps just a change of name would do. I'd always thought "John," though very popular in England since King John's reign (and despite it, too), was rather dull and tame: worthy and honest, but not at all sparky. Of course, in the old days Johns were often called Jack, which is a much better handle: a bit cheeky, cheerful and, let's face it, sexy. Whoever heard of a "Dear Jack" letter? A Jack would tear the damn thing up. In addition, I'd always preferred "Cheese" to "Cleese," which is, quite simply, not a proper name. So, I thought, if had been Jack Cheese, I could have gone to live in Monterey and started a bank, and written in the evenings and had children with Constance Cheese, who would never have been able to resist Jack's advances.

Because my relationship with Connie had been so on and off (and was now off), I had become ever closer to Pippa, whom, as you will recall, I had first met in Ibiza. She was kind, cheerful, fun, and just plain easy to be around. Ultimately, though, I came to the rather hackneyed conclusion that, although I was incredibly fond of her, I wasn't actually in love with her. I would have liked to have been, but I wasn't, and that seemed crucial. What's more, I realised that I was not able to extinguish my feelings for Connie, despite the "Dear John" letter, and that I was still, probably, on average, taking things overall, at a conservative estimate, in love with her. Even though she wasn't, almost certainly, in love with me. However, one thing I knew for sure was that I felt unsettled in a quiet but all-important way.

So I phoned Connie and gave her some cock-and-bull story about having to come to New York for work reasons, and said it would be nice to see her while I was there. When she didn't tell me to drop dead, I jumped on a plane, and, once at my hotel, called her. She told me that she had arranged a small party for me the following evening—just friends of hers whom I knew from my time in New York—and at that my heart sank: I realised that by having friends there she was making sure that emotions would be kept under control, and so was clearly indicating how she viewed my visit. I thanked her and rang off. Oh well . . .

The next day I went to the party, and set eyes on Connie for the first time in several months. She was very friendly, we chatted, and I came to the reluctant conclusion that there was nothing between us any more, absolutely *nothing*. Nevertheless I acted all cheerful and optimistic, and after a couple of hours was able to make excuses about jet lag and slink back to my hotel, as bereft as an artichoke. Except that halfway there I suddenly thought, "What is the point of this silly pretence that I'm here for work, when I want to fly back home first thing tomorrow?" So I turned round, trudged back to Connie's apartment, rang the bell, confessed my pathetic plan, apologised, and found ten minutes later that we were getting married.

I have no idea what happened during those ten minutes, but happen it did, and the two of us then went out for a celebratory dinner. Later that night, back in her apartment, we talked about practicalities and, for the very first time, about money. Connie explained that she was fairly comfortably off, while I had to reveal that I wasn't—that whereas in America there was much money to be made in television, working for the BBC was akin to taking a vow of poverty, and that for *The Frost Report* I had received a grand total for the series of about £1,400, on which I then paid eighty-three per cent income tax. I think I'd mentioned this before our engagement but Connie must have thought I was joking. (Only two years later, when I told an old Footlights friend who worked a lot in American television what I was paid per episode of *Monty Python,* he laughed so much that he fell off the sofa.)

Fortunately it did not take long to reassure her that there was plenty of work for me in London and that we would have a reasonable standard of living there. We decided to marry in New York, though, and we agreed it would be a very small and simple affair; we both liked the idea of a proper ceremony, and so we chose a Unitarian church where all sorts of religions were embraced, and where I would be allowed to go through the service, carefully removing all the references to God. The Church of England had certainly worked its magic on me.

Connie had a lot of arrangements to make, so I flew back to London to look for a flat, and to face the awful bit. There are few feelings worse than the mixture of dread and guilt that grips you when you are about to dump someone who doesn't deserve it. It's much easier when things between you have been difficult for some time; it's much, much easier when it's unpremeditated and the natural denouement of a really appalling row, with accusations and recriminations and long-standing resentments (and a few freshly minted ones) and high-octane screaming and savage insults, because then the dumping process brings immediate relief and a delightful sense of easy, glowing self-justification—at least, until seventy-two hours later, when separation anxiety begins to kick in. But to dump someone, albeit ceremoniously, when she has been nothing but kind and cheerful and thoughtful and affectionate, just because she fails to tweak some obscure part of your unconscious . . . well, it makes you wish you were a sociopath or, better still, a banker.

To make things worse, Pippa took it very well. But she wanted to leave London for a time, decided on Johannesburg, and off she went. Two years later we bumped into each other again and we have been great friends ever since. It's typical of Pippa that she has also got on so well with most of my wives.

14

On February 20, 1968, Connie and I were joined together at the Unitarian church in Manhattan, at a warm, friendly little service, with about fifteen friends present. The only moment of disappointment came at the very end of the service when I discovered that I'd failed to excise one particular mention of the word "God." I can still remember how Connie looked just as the minister gave us his permission to kiss. Everything felt very right.

We decided to travel to London by boat, and it was the tranquillity of life on board the *Queen Elizabeth* that made me realise just how frantic my life had become over the past couple of years. I had experienced being lived by my life, as they say, rather than living it. It was a busyness that made me feel out of control. I had never thought of myself as particularly driven, yet I was now working on something every day, and the little spare time that remained was then immediately filled by a mass of petty obligations that I resented but seemed powerless to control. When I'd first been in New York, at Square East and then in *Half a Sixpence,* I'd spent most of my time reading, going to art galleries, taking exercise, seeing films, exploring the city, eating with friends. I always had great chunks of time for myself. Now, in London, I had to plan a week ahead if I wanted to get my hair cut. I had to adapt Edmund Burke: the price of free time was eternal vigilance. I felt that if I turned my back, someone would write an appointment in my diary.

I could see (though not as clearly as I do now) that one of my biggest problems was me. Because I wanted everyone to like me and to approve of me, I tried to be nice to everyone all the time and this proved a remarkably efficient way of losing control over my life. Connie noticed this very quickly. After we'd been in London a few months, she gave me some good advice. She said, "Don't feel like you have to greet every waiter as though he is a long-lost friend, and when we go for dinner at someone's house, don't take over the role of the host." What's more, being very nice was pretty tiring, so I often became tetchy—in as nice a way as possible of course—which meant I had to be twice as nice the next day, to prove how nice I really was. Consequently, I hardly ever dared to say a polite but firm "No" to anyone. And this brought me a second problem, because when the only people who are going to ask you for time-consuming favours, or invite you to boring events, are your friends and relations, it's possible to control things; but when you become even a minor celebrity you are faced with a constant deluge of requests for autographs, photographs, personal effects that can be auctioned, mementoes, locks of hair, speeches, advice on how to get into show business, money for charities, money to help people through university, money for operations, money for people who are down on their luck, quick chats over coffee about comedy, messages to children to encourage them before their exams, requests from student magazines for interviews, and for lists of my top ten books, films, songs, comedians, holiday resorts, wines, footballers, ways to be happy, most embarrassing moments, cocktails, walks in the Lake District, national flags, cheeses, cars and operations; also for help with finding an agent, for meetings with seven-year-olds who are my biggest fans, jokes for best-man speeches, recommendations of speech therapists in the Weston-super-Mare area, introductions to Ronnie Corbett, confirmation that I used to know a particular person, that it really was me in Beccles Town Hall snooker room on February 23, 1959, and for explanations of why a sketch in *The 1948 Show* had used the phrase "one up the jacksy," why my parents had chosen to send me to Eton, why I was such an ardent Quaker, how it was that I had stopped collecting death masks, why I had climbed K2 so frequently, and why I had finally agreed to play Othello.

By now I had a six-hours-a-week secretary, and when we had conscientiously worked through these requests and questions, we had to turn to deal with the invitations I had received: to speak at school sports days, at university unions, at Rotary luncheons, at retired railwaymen clubs, at drama colleges, at police dinners and political meetings; and to judge essay competitions, Weston-super-Mare beauty pageants, fancy-dress outfits, student plays, tug-of-war contests and carved-vegetable competitions; and to attend weddings, anniversaries, prize-givings, birthday parties, centenaries, summer fêtes, Labour Party rallies, Conservative Party rallies, Liberal Party rallies, Plaid Cymru rallies, car rallies, art gallery openings, amateur-theatrical first nights, Barrow-in-Furness Methodist Pigeon Fanciers' Wine and Cheese family evenings, short film festivals, medium-length film festivals, crematorium openings, children's parties, brass band galas, water-sports conventions, local history exhibitions, coronations, and my personal all-time favourite, an invitation to go to Melton Mowbray to attend the christening of somebody's cat.

And I want to emphasise that every single request or invitation came from really nice, polite, friendly people. (Mind you, I've only ever seen one rude invitation: it was from the Dundee Students' Union to Her Majesty the Queen, informing her that they had decided to invite her to visit Dundee University by thirteen votes to nine.) So I agonised over every single response, never saying, "Sorry, I'm too busy," because it might seem rather rude, but instead explaining how busy I was *at present,* but that *perhaps* in a few months I *might,* etc., etc. . . . thus merely postponing the decision and piling up half-promises to the point where simply doing away with myself seemed the easiest solution.

A lot of these requests came from charities. Now, I never met a

charity I didn't like. (I used to look askance at the Association for
the Aid of Distressed Gentlefolk, but was eventually persuaded of its
vital importance.) The problem was that there were over 60,000 active ones in the UK. So, seriously, how do you say "Yes" to cancer, and
"No" to spina bifida? Every day, opening my post presented me with
a series of Sophie's choices. And all this agonising—this ridiculous
time-wasting—was because it took me another thirty years to learn
that if you say "No" in a friendly, chatty way, people accept it with
great grace and goodwill, and do not hate you, or send death squads
after you, or report you to the *Daily Mail*. And until I realised this, I
found myself resenting perfectly amiable requests—simply because
I was incapable of a guilt-free "No." Nowadays I have a simple rule:
you can ask me anything you like, provided I can say "No." I have
also learned from nightclub bouncers that there are just as effective
ways of refusing people's demands that are less personally confron-
tational. When a bouncer is told, "I am a close personal friend of
Mick Jagger, and he invited me to his birthday party this evening,
but I have mislaid my invitation, and I have a couple of tickets for the
Wimbledon final that his wife gave me just now to give to him personally, will you let me in?" he will reply, "I'm afraid that isn't going
to happen, sir." This impersonal style presents the "No" as though it
is a law of physics: "I'm sorry, sir, but unfortunately entropy—that is,
microscopic disorder of a body—cannot ever decrease, and there's
nothing I can do about it. Sorry!" So I use a variant of this ploy when
people suddenly appear at my elbow, asking for a photograph with
me. I'm really not sure why this "Sorry to interrupt you but can I
have a picture with you?" irritates me so much. Perhaps it's the idea
of providing photographic proof for the rest of eternity of the moment I stood next to someone I'd never set eyes on before. In the past,
I have to confess, I sometimes responded to the request by saying,
"What, to commemorate the fact that we met four seconds ago?"
But now I have taken to replying, "I'm sorry but I'm afraid I don't do
that," delivering the line with a fatalistic smile that hints that the in-

terloper is asking me to betray some deeply held religious principle, and that the matter is consequently out of my hands. This has failed only once, at a South African airport in 2013, when it infuriated a fellow passenger so much that he wrote to the *Cape Argus* about it.

In the old days people would ask for a photograph of you, but now it's always, *always . . . with* you. Presumably so they can show their friends, "Look there's *me* with . . . what's-his-name." I truly believe that the worst aspect of the whole celebrity merry-go-round is the belief that your life becomes more meaningful because you have touched the hem of Simon Cowell's garment, or that true wisdom involves knowing the name of Steven Seagal's nanny's dog.

I feel a lot better for that.

Where was I? Oh yes . . .

On the *Queen Elizabeth* with Connie, thinking about why my life had become too busy. So far as work was concerned, I knew I was not driven by some great ambition. My horizons were, in fact, surprisingly constrained. I wanted to gain increasing artistic control over the television programmes I did, but I did not yearn for *The John Cleese Show;* I much preferred to be an influential member of a small team so that I had a lot of control over the material and how it was presented, but not total responsibility. And I wanted the shows to be as funny as we could make them because I had, by then, realised that it was much easier in comedy to be clever than it was to be funny. And, as my experience of performing in *Half a Sixpence* had shown me, I had no ambition to act in the theatre (between *Half a Sixpence* and *The Alimony Tour*—forty-six years—I only performed on stage in the Amnesty and *Monty Python* shows). So far as films were concerned, they weren't on my radar screen at all. They existed in a separate universe from mine, and never the twain would meet. So I was myopically focused on British television, of which I was inordinately proud, since it was clearly the best in the world (or, as somebody said, "the least bad in the world").

Anyway, after five days of an enticingly tranquil voyage, Connie and I landed at Southampton, made our way to London and moved into a flat I'd found for us in Knightsbridge. It was on the fifth floor of an attractive '20s apartment block, between the Knightsbridge Fire Station and Harrods, on Basil Street. Yes, Basil Street. When people hear this, they quite naturally say, "Oh, that's why you called him Basil." I'm sorry, but I don't think so. By the time we started writing *Fawlty Towers*, we were long gone from Knightsbridge, and I know we never made the connection consciously. Believe me, it is quite possible that these things are coincidental. For example, everyone who worked for Sir Charles Forte assumed that Fawlty was a reference to Trust House Forte hotels and restaurants. Had that occurred to you? It didn't to me. And take Basil's initials: "BF" for my father's generation was one of the rudest things well-mannered people could say about a man—it meant "bloody fool." Again, it never crossed my mind. A final example: it only dawned on me when I started to write this book that two of my most successful appearances have been in shows with circus in the title. Now if you say, "Oh, come on, you must have been *influenced* unconsciously by Basil Street—admit it," I will reply, "Well, if I was influenced unconsciously, then by definition I wouldn't know about it, would I? But I don't think so, and it's my life we're talking about, not yours, and if it *were* yours, I would defer to you, because you know a lot more about it than I do. And perhaps I'm writing this book because 'book' begins with a 'b' and so does Basil, which was a success, so unconsciously I'm hoping a book will bring me success, whereas screenplay begins with an 's,' like Sybil, and Basil's relationship with her was a disaster, and that pushed me towards television." And you will say, "No, that's not a fair example." And I will say, "Yes, it is! Now will you stop interrupting me and let me get on with writing the fucking thing?"

Our new flat was superbly located, two minutes' walk from Knightsbridge tube station, and a fifteen-minute taxi ride from almost everywhere we wanted to go. Gradually we settled into married life, and I introduced Connie to my friends, and they all took to her immediately. She, however, found one thing about them rather puzzling. She kept it to herself until one evening, when we were returning from a dinner party, she asked me why, although they were perfectly at ease answering her questions about them, they never asked her any questions about herself. It took me a while to figure this out. Then I had an epiphany. The reason was that the English middle class was so terrified of embarrassment that they never dared to ask a question about something unless they were absolutely certain that they were not prying into areas which might cause emotional distress. My friends knew nothing about Connie, and felt therefore that they had to be careful what they said just in case it turned out that her father had been eaten by wild pigs, or that her mother was a Jehovah's Witness, or that her brother thought he was the Duke of York, or that she herself had attended a Nazi Confectionery College, or had just started an affair with my uncle. The middle-class mind was endlessly creative when imagining potential pitfalls. So I explained to Connie that she needed to send a green light by, for example, talking about her father in a relaxed manner for a few seconds; then, I said, the queries about him would start flooding in. But what struck me as so odd was that I had been acting on this understanding all my life without ever having brought it to consciousness. As the French (and the Paraguayans) say, "A fish does not know the water that it swims in." And eighteen years later, when I was writing *A Fish Called Wanda*, I used this realisation, when Archie is trying to explain to Wanda the social straitjacket from which he is desperate to escape:

> Wanda, do you have any idea what it's like being English? Being so correct all the time, being so stifled by this dread of, of doing the wrong thing, of saying to someone, "Are you married?" and hearing, "My wife left me this morning," or saying, "Do you have children?" and being told they all burned to death on Wednesday. You see, Wanda, we're all terrified of embarrassment. That's why we're

so . . . dead. Most of my friends are dead, you know; we
have these piles of corpses to dinner.

So Connie spent time trying to get to grips with English ways,
learning to navigate London, going to auditions, practising an English accent, and cooking me delicious dinners while listening as I
read out what Graham Chapman and I had written earlier in the day.

I'd linked up again with Graham once I'd got back to London and
we were immediately contacted by the producer of Marty Feldman's
new TV show. Marty had attracted a great deal of attention in the
television world during the second series of *At Last the 1948 Show,* and
had now been offered his own series by the BBC. In retrospect it surprises me that I cannot remember experiencing any feelings of envy
or competitiveness at his rapid promotion: perhaps it was because
I'd done so many programmes in the previous year and a half, and
wanted a break from all that stress and responsibility; perhaps it was
because, as Marty seemed so much older than I was, I didn't feel competitive in the way we usually do with our contemporaries; perhaps
it was because I totally understood why Marty wanted a show over
which he had overall artistic control, and felt that I, too, could probably get one when I was up for it; or perhaps it was because Marty's
producer, Dennis Main Wilson, now craved an audience with Graham
and me, and, taking the art of flattery to unprecedented heights (or
depths), cajoled and beseeched us to write for the show, which without our material, he assured us, was certainly doomed to failure (this
was Dennis's standard MO).

Sometimes I find that taking a break from writing makes me
more fecund once I return to it; and now Graham and I wrote Marty
thirty minutes of material in record time, which was received ecstatically (how else?) by Dennis Main Wilson. Our package included
what we thought was an outstandingly funny skit with Marty, as a
disorderly Archbishop of Canterbury, badgering passengers in a railway carriage. Graham and I attended the first recording of the show,

and it was a great success, due in part to some spectacular film sequences. Marty's cast included Tim Brooke-Taylor, and a very suave former schoolteacher called John Junkin, who played the Cleese-type cold-blooded authoritarian swine roles.

Meanwhile, I had a meeting with David Frost, who seemed to have become my patron, guide and chief employer. And at one stroke he removed all the financial anxieties that normally accompany a freelancer's life. I explained to him that I hoped to spend most of the year writing, rather than in TV studios, because I did not want to leave Connie alone for long periods until she had found her London feet, and I knew that this would suit Graham well because he had decided to take a break from his medical studies, so that he could get enough money together to pay his previous year's tax bill. David then asked me how much I thought I needed to earn, and I rather cheekily suggested £10,000, a sum that I reckoned would be more than sufficient to allow Connie and me to trot along very comfortably. David's response to this was to commission two programmes on the spot. The first was a film idea Graham and I had cooked up about a detective agency that would feature Ronnie Barker, Ronnie Corbett, Marty, Tim, Graham and me. The other, which was David's suggestion and which I jumped at when he said he was happy for Connie to perform in it, was to be a special for American TV.

With my finances now secure for the next year, Graham and I settled down to write. We decided to focus on the special first, and soon came up with a title we liked: *How to Irritate People*. We swiftly established that, because of his *Marty* commitments, Tim was not going to be available, so Graham and I gravitated instead towards using Michael Palin (for reasons I can't recall: certainly neither of us had ever acted with him before). He accepted our invitation and then provided the story for one of the first pieces we wrote, about a garage owner who had sold him a car, and who had a wonderfully evasive way of dealing with the numerous complaints Michael made about it. This Mr. Gibbons (odd that the maiden name of Helen Palin, Michael's wife, was Gibbins) assured Michael that the reason the gearbox was a "bit sticky" was because the car was new, and he explained that the "bit sticky" gearbox was in fact characteristic of a high-quality car (for the first 2,000 miles)—indeed, one of the sure-fire ways to tell that you had not been sold a "lemon." When Michael later had trouble with the brakes, Mr. Gibbons told him that this was, again, because the car was new, but that if he had any brake problems he should bring the car in. Michael pointed out that he was having such problems, which was why he had brought the car in, to which Mr. Gibbons retorted, "Well, if you have any further problems, Mr. Palin, you be sure and bring it in." Graham and I adored this man's cast of mind: it reminded us of Lloyd George's observation of the Irish Republican Eamon de Valera that arguing with him was "like trying to pick up mercury with a fork." We wrote a concise sketch around Mr. Gibbons, which we had to film as it involved car doors falling off on cue. The occasion of that filming was the first time that Graham and Michael performed together.

It's well known among Python fans that this piece was later re-written as the "Dead Parrot" sketch. What happened was this: *How to Irritate People* was never intended to be transmitted in the UK. So when *Monty Python* started, and I happened upon a copy of the script in a bottom drawer, Graham and I decided that something should be made of it, both because no one in Britain had seen it, and be-cause we still loved the Gibbons character. We also felt, though, that having him as a car salesman was very clichéd. So we rummaged among other possible locations for him, and up popped a pet shop. Obviously someone had bought a pet and there was something badly wrong with it—it was dead! What animal, then? A cat? No, dead kitties are not funny. A mouse? Wouldn't work: too small, and too vulnerable. Something big? A dog? Could work, but people are fond of dogs. Imagine banging a dead dog against a counter to wake it up—you could get lynched. A parrot . . . ? Yes! Nobody's going to get upset about the death of a cartoon creature like a parrot—except, perhaps, its owner; the rest of us couldn't give a monkey's . . .

So out came *Roget's Thesaurus* (which should have had a co-writer's credit on several of our sketches) and we were away. Except that when we'd finished, it didn't quite work. Why? Something wasn't right with the pet-shop owner's responses: the balance between his evasions and his outright lies didn't build properly, so it wasn't convincing. We had to rewrite his lines twice more before we were happy with them. Strange to recall, when Michael and I performed the sketch in front of the *Monty Python* studio audience in 1969 the reaction was quite subdued. I believe about five years elapsed before it mysteriously morphed into a "classic." I suspect it was performing the "Dead Parrot" on stage at Drury Lane in 1974 that somehow started its elevation to iconic status.

Where was I? Oh yes, writing *How to Irritate People* . . . it's funny how I drifted off that subject. Possibly because, to be quite honest, it was not a good experience. Or, to be completely honest, it was a dreadful experience. But not when we were writing it. For in the early stages of its gestation Graham and I revelled in the freedom of being in charge of a script for the first time.

We particularly enjoyed writing a sketch based on our favourite Indian restaurant, the Naraine, just off the Earls Court Road. The owner, Bill Naraine, had taken to greeting the two of us in an absurdly grandiloquent manner: Graham was always "the Good Doctor," while he insisted on addressing me as "My Lord." He combined this extravagant fawning with self-abasement, apologising for his humble establishment and the ineptitude of his staff and the inadequacy of his chef, lamenting some imaginary problem with our last meal and promising to redouble his efforts on this visit, while ushering us to our table with flamboyant gestures and cries of delight. Had we asked him to carry us to our chairs he would have obliged instantly. When our triumphal procession finally reached the table, we would manage to seat ourselves despite his frenzied assistance and laudatory exclamations, at which point he would suddenly discover a grain of salt on the tablecloth, emit a roar of fury and despair at this latest assault on his guests' sensibilities, launch elaborate but savage denunciations at the waiters cowering around us, encomiums of praise for the Good Doctor's and My Lord's gracious forbearance, heart-rending prayers for our forgiveness, and bloodthirsty threats of vengeance against one poor waiter who was now scuttling, terrified, towards the kitchen, bearing the offending molecule of salt. Then there would be just a moment's pause in this extraordinary hullabaloo as he gathered himself for yet another outburst of frantic toadying, only to realise that he had forgotten to give us the menus. The consequent howl of despair would have frightened a banshee, and the waiters had to restrain Bill as he tried to commit suicide by beating himself about the head with the drinks trolley. (Perhaps I am exaggerating a little—though only towards the end.)

Graham and I were initially embarrassed by Bill's displays, but after a time we agreed to enjoy and indeed encourage them, to the extent that one evening, as we made our way to our table, Bill so surpassed himself in his outrageous fawning that half the restaurant stood up in acknowledgement of our apparent aristocratic status. As we wrote the sketch we felt that we were creating only a pale shadow of the original.

> DINER (GRAHAM CHAPMAN): Would you recommend the
> madras chicken curry?
> BILL (MICHAEL PALIN): Oh, yes, it is wonderful. For you it
> will be *mmmmm*!
> DINER: Ah, is that hot?
> BILL: Yes, yes, very hot.
> DINER: Ah, I don't want it too hot.
> BILL: No, no, not hot at all, it's extremely cool.
> DINER: Only I want it medium.

BILL: Oh, medium, that's what it is. Very, very, extremely
medium! Medium beyond belief! (*He kneels beside diner's
chair*) What a thing I told you that it was hot! Your
Grace, let me wash your feet.

DINER: No, thank you.

BILL: Let me lick them, then!

Later, a spot of dust is discovered on a chair. Bill lets out a cry of total despair and orders the waiter to burn the chair immediately.

I suspect that nowadays Michael's portrayal of dear Bill would not be allowed. It's OK to portray Germans as militaristic, the French as snotty, the Italians as histrionic, the English as uptight and asexual, the Swedes as depressed or the Swiss as money-grabbing, but political correctness deems some nations too vulnerable to tease, an attitude which strikes me as rather condescending. Perhaps when there are a few more Asian billionaires, Indians too will be regarded as permissible comedy fodder. (Incidentally, Bill's food was the best we ever found—and there was no charge for the cabaret.)

The one and only sketch Graham and I wrote for the show that, judging from internet viewings, has stood the test of time concerns two airline pilots who become so bored on a long-haul flight that they decide to amuse themselves by making ambiguous announcements to frighten their passengers:

CAPTAIN (JOHN CLEESE): (*over intercom*) "Hello, this is your
captain speaking. There is absolutely no cause for
alarm." (*to First Officer*) That will get them thinking.
(*First Officer reaches for the microphone*) No, no, no, no.
Not yet, not yet. Let it sink in. They're thinking, "Er,
what is there absolutely no cause for alarm about? Are
the wings on fire?" (*over intercom*) "The wings are not
on fire." Now they are thinking, "Er, why should he say
that?" So we say . . .

Steward enters the cockpit.

FIRST OFFICER (GRAHAM CHAPMAN): Oh, how are we doing?

STEWARD (MICHAEL PALIN): *(looks down the aisle)* They've
stopped eating; looking a bit worried.

CAPTAIN: Good.

STEWARD: Hang on, one of them is going to the washroom.

CAPTAIN: Is he there yet?

STEWARD: He's just closing the door . . . NOW!

CAPTAIN: Right. One . . . two . . . three . . .

FIRST OFFICER: *(over intercom)* "Please return to your seats
and fasten your safety belts immediately please."

In a couple of cases Graham and I opted to reuse sketches from
The 1948 Show: one a game-show spoof, with me as a heartless host
called Nosmo Claphanger haranguing an old crone; the other a send-
up of a current affairs interview about freedom of speech, where the
interviewer never stops talking, so that the interviewee, unable to
get a word in edgeways, goes berserk.

When I watched the whole show on DVD recently I was startled to find that the performance Graham and I gave of "Freedom
of Speech" was far weaker than the one Marty and I had done the
year before. I was also surprised by the naturalistic style of the whole
programme: much closer to *The Frost Report*, I felt, than to *The 1948
Show,* and without a trace of anything Pythonesque. Considering the
artistic control that we had, this may seem very odd, but I suspect
it was simply the result of having the theme of "irritation" from the
start, which encouraged us to remember what irritated us in ordinary life rather than to indulge in wilder flights of fancy.

In addition to the sketches Graham and I wrote for the show, Connie helped me with a couple, the first time we had ever worked together. One of them drew on her amusement at the way in which the
English upper class avoided the pronoun "I," as though there were
something vulgar about using it. I'd already noticed that using "one"

instead of "I" seemed to convey a sense of magisterial detachment and imply that any person not in total agreement with one's personal view must be dreadfully common. I therefore wrote a sketch in which a young upper-class couple on a date achieve the highest degree of verbal intimacy considered permissible by their class:

> *A fashionable Knightsbridge restaurant. At a romantically lit*
> *table sit an upper-class pair, Simon and Fiona, deep in conver-*
> *sation. Simon takes Fiona's hand tenderly.*
> SIMON: When one's with one, darling . . . one feels one's . . .
>   one.
> FIONA: One won *what?*
> SIMON: No. One's *at* one . . .
> FIONA: Oh! At one with *oneself.*
> SIMON: No, at one with . . . *one.*
>   *Fiona smiles.*
> FIONA: One so agrees.
>   *Simon looks deeply into Fiona's eyes.*
> SIMON: . . . One loves one, darling.
> FIONA: One loves one, too.
>   *She kisses his hand.*
> SIMON: . . . Where was one, darling?
> FIONA: One was saying one's wife didn't understand one . . .

Apart from the naturalistic, distinctly non-Pythonesque tone of *How to Irritate People,* there were other surprises for me as I watched the show for the first time in many years. I had no idea, for example, that I would discover another nascent Python sketch, this time in a far more recognisable form than the "Dead Parrot"—the "Job Interview," which appeared, slightly rewritten, in the fifth show of the first *Python* series, as an interview for a place on a management training course. Then I was astonished to find some proto-Python Pepperpots! These were Graham's creation: women who hooted and squawked and made pensive chicken-like noises, and in *Python* tended to discuss Jean-Paul Sartre or Mrs. William Pitt the Elder or the provenance of escaped penguins perched on their TV sets. He called them "Pepper-pots" because he felt that their shape resembled that of the cheap pep-perpots to be found in workplace canteens. In *How to Irritate People* we had them talking during a film—not very funny at all.

But the biggest surprise of all—in fact it was a shock—was to re-alise just how poor the show was. And then I remembered in ghastly detail the truly horrendous day we recorded it. Up to that moment there had been no sign of danger: we thought the script was pretty good, and Michael Palin remembers the read-through, on the first day of rehearsal, as being a bit of a riot. But from the instant we ar-rived in the studio that morning, everything went wrong. There were endless technical problems, which put the crew under such pressure that they never laughed at any of the sketches, and we there-fore found ourselves rehearsing to total silence—never an encour-aging experience, especially when you're performing new material. Worse, we got only halfway through the dress rehearsal before time ran out and the audience started arriving. Things didn't improve when the warm-up man went on stage: he failed to get a titter out of the audience; and when I went out to thank them for coming to the recording I was struck by their resemblance to the people in Weston on the day George VI died. My solar plexus tightened; I could feel the cold sweat coming. Then we started recording the show, and it was quieter even than a matinee I had once experienced in Dunedin—at least there they had had teacups to rattle. And now it really began to go downhill. Within five minutes none of the sketches *felt* funny, and this spells D-I-S-A-S-T-E-R for a performer. You just can't sense how to make the material funny, because it has suddenly become clear to you that it *isn't* . . .

One moment stands out as being especially appalling. Connie and I have sat down and started doing the "Ones" sketch, and I sense a stirring in the audience, just as though they have all awoken from a thousand-year sleep. A tiny flicker of hope flashes through my central nervous system. "Hold it!" cries the director. Why? We aren't told, of course. Silence. A minute passes. "From the beginning, please!" So Connie and I start it again, and just as we reach the same point, the audience stirs again, we even get a tiny laugh . . . and the director intervenes. "Hold it, please!" Connie and I stop and sit there for *seven* minutes while they *relight*. By the time we start a third time, we can feel the audience's boredom and *irritation* . . . So I tighten up, the sketch lays a complete egg, and we have to cut it from the show.

It's a nightmare once comedy stops feeling funny. I remember that when we did our first Python stage shows in 1973 (on our tour of the UK), the first two performances in Southampton and Brighton went really well; but when we moved to the Bristol Hippodrome the matinee audience there proved so unresponsive that they reminded me of the story of an actor who, pausing by a fishmonger's while doing his shopping one morning, and surveying the fish lying on the slab, with their open mouths and dead eyes, suddenly exclaims, "Oh my God! I've got a matinee today!" You can sometimes console yourself with the thought "Oh, it's just a bad house," but the complete silent apathy of this particular Bristol audience rattled me. Maybe it was because we'd only done the show twice before, but I now started to think, "Oh my God. It's not funny!" and for the rest of that performance I stood in the wings, or listened to the PA system in my dressing room, with a sinking feeling, becoming ever more convinced that our show was a flop, and dreading the humiliating tour that still stretched ahead. That night, however, the audience laughed from the first and my fears disappeared like a rat up a drainpipe. What *had* I been thinking? Of *course* it's funny. Listen to the audience reaction.

Unfortunately, there was no moment during the recording of *How to Irritate People* when it felt funny. It was an awful experience, and I felt bad that Connie had had such a terrible television baptism. I crept back to my burrow vowing that I'd never take on such a project again. *Ever.*

15

While I lay low and stitched my wounds, Graham and I were able to turn our attention to a wide selection of writing: our new private-detective film, which was great fun to work on, as its farce-like quality allowed us to indulge in humour at the wilder and sillier end of the spectrum; another draft of *The Rise and Rise of Michael Rimmer;* a TV special for the actress and comedienne Sheila Hancock, which Graham and I wrote with Eric Idle (we had, of course, worked alongside him on *The Frost Report,* but that was our first—and very harmonious—collaboration with him); and . . . an invitation, right out of the blue, to write some sketches for (fanfare of trumpets) . . . Peter Sellers.

Peter was at this time the world's leading comedy actor. He'd achieved this status in his *anni mirabiles* of 1963–64, when he created the role of Inspector Clouseau in *The Pink Panther* and played three different characters in one of the greatest comedies of all time, Stanley Kubrick's *Dr. Strangelove.* I'd worshipped him since the days of *The Goon Show,* where he did the majority of the voices, and I'd seen him grow into a superb character actor in very English movies like *The Ladykillers, Two-Way Stretch,* and *The Mouse That Roared.* During this time he also came up with three of the greatest comedy albums ever made, produced by George Martin, the best being *Songs for Swingin' Sellers;* while his appearance as a trade unionist called Fred Kite in *I'm All Right Jack* showed that he could also be a fine straight actor. It had to be admitted, though, that by the time Graham and I went to meet him in the spring of 1969, we'd heard he was getting a reputation for being difficult. (During the filming of *Casino Royale* in 1967, the director Joe McGrath told me, Peter had said to him that he did not want to do his close-up shots the same day that Orson Welles did his: he wanted to wait until he had seen Orson's close-ups in rushes, so that he could work out how to "top" him when he shot his own.)

The Peter that Graham and I met, however, couldn't have been friendlier. We showed him some of our sketches and, to our delight, he laughed a lot. And when he laughed he really bust a gut: he fell about and hooted. You could see him suddenly become animated by a joyous comic energy, of the kind that possessed Graham and me when we discovered a great comic idea. (It was never a single great *line* that set us all off—it was always the first perception of a great comic potential, prior to it being worked through.) It seemed to me that when Peter experienced this glee, he became for a moment a bigger person than his normal, sociable, lower-key self.

His first job for us was to come up with some sketches for an American "special." I can only remember one of the pieces, where Peter played an enterprising Scottish cloth manufacturer who had discovered some hitherto neglected tartans to sell to Americans: ones from clans such as the McRoosevelts, the McJPMorgans and the McGoldbergs. He was pleased with the way the sketches were received, and, to our amazement, immediately promoted us: he invited us to write a new draft of a screenplay based on Terry Southern's *The Magic Christian*. Gra and I therefore now found ourselves writing *three* movies.

Peter started by explaining that there had been several drafts of the script up to that point, and he showed us the most recent—the *fourteenth* draft, which contained quite the most exquisite stage directions I'd ever read: in the very first scene, an ornate clock on the mantelpiece was dwelt on in extraordinary detail. It was only when we read further, in search of dialogue, character and plot that the ghastly truth emerged: the script was just terrible. Graham and I were astounded. We yearned to ask one question: how could the writer of this material ever have been hired?

However, the screenplay's bottomless ineptitude was very liberating in that it left us with nothing to defer to, so we went back to the Southern novel and found it a talented, if lazy, mess, with a great premise: an immensely rich but principled man, Sir Guy Grand, plays large-scale practical jokes on people for the sole purpose of revealing to them, and to others, the baseness of their real motives. It may sound a bit prissy, but its mood wasn't: more satirical than didactic. Gra and I had a wonderful time inventing new pranks, including a sky-writing plane that left very rude words above the crowds at Ascot, forcing the authorities to send up another sky-writer to bowdlerise the vulgarities, resulting in a sky filled with words like "ARSENAL," "THE PENIS MIGHTIER THAN THE SWORD," "SCUNTHORPE," "PRICKLY" and "MISHIT." We came up with one other absurdly expensive idea: on the huge cruise liner which Sir Guy has hired to host and ridicule his most powerful victims, there is a very expensive restaurant where, if you want a steak, you are escorted to a huge below-decks paddock where you can choose your own cut from a large, heavily bandaged herd of steers.

Each morning we would arrive at Peter's flat at ten o'clock and give him the pages we had written the previous day, and he would say, "Less of this" or "More of that." It was all remarkably relaxed, the temperature in the room rising only if Britt Ekland walked through in her dressing gown (I think even Graham enjoyed this). After a time we began to socialise with Peter on an occasional basis. He took us to *Hair,* where I felt too shy to go up on stage with him to dance with everyone (typical!). He sent us to the theatre, to see *There's a Girl in My Soup* by Terence Frisby, to advise him whether he should do the film of it. (Snotty young know-it-alls that we were, we advised against it—sorry, Terry—but he ignored us, thank God, and made a very successful adaptation with Goldie Hawn.) And a lot of the time we just sat around while he told wonderfully funny stories of his music-hall days, and of his time with the Goons. Of course, we already knew he was a truly great "voice-man," but we marvelled privately at his ability to "do" people, effortlessly. He only needed to listen to someone for a few minutes to be able to impersonate them perfectly. Indeed, many of his most famous "voices" were inspired by entirely chance encounters.

He told us, for example, that once at the end of a theatre show, he had been accosted by a very boring fan, a scoutmaster in full gear, and was about to flee when he heard the man speak. He immediately invited him back to his dressing room, gave him a drink and kept him talking. Peter had found the perfect voice for the wonderful *Goon Show* character Bluebottle. When Stanley Kubrick asked him to play Clare Quilty in *Lolita,* he was wondering how he would speak the role until he bumped into an American with an unusual style of speech. Peter then chatted to him for twenty minutes, after which he had the guy off pat. But the best story came from George Martin. While he had been producing the *Songs for Swingin' Sellers* album, he'd fallen in love with one of the tracks in which a heartless agent is talking on the phone while auditioning an elderly Shakespearean actor who is trying to remember (unsuccessfully) a monologue from *Richard III.* To hear the poor old fool bumbling in the background while the agent chats up a girlfriend was absolutely hilarious, if somewhat cruel. When he played the edited album to Peter, George asked, "The sketch about that bastard agent. I know his voice from somewhere. Whose is it?" Peter replied, "It's yours."

Then, one day, we both got a first-hand insight into this extraordinary ability. We arrived at Peter's flat, to be greeted by his heart-of-gold chauffeur Bert. "He's overslept, boys. I'll make you coffee. He won't be long." So we sat there, reading through our "pages," and soon Peter appeared in his dressing gown, apologising for keeping us but doing so in a quite unfamiliar voice, which a few seconds later became a rather plummy upper-class accent, before lapsing into recognisable cockney. When he sat down on the sofa opposite, he morphed into a rather odd Eastern European dialect for about ten seconds, before he finally reverted to speaking in his usual manner. Gra and I pretended not to notice, but when we compared notes later we both realised that each morning Peter Sellers had to find his own voice.

It is a truth universally acknowledged that the greatest impersonators often have strangely colourless personalities. Perhaps their very lack of a strong identity means they have little of themselves to get in the way when they try to assume someone else's personality. I'm a poor mimic because I can't drop my own characteristics much, so when I impersonate someone, it sounds like them trying to impersonate me. As it happens, I greatly admire first-class mimics' super-sensitive powers of observation, the extraordinary accuracy with which they observe vocal production, inflexions, rhythms of speech, facial expressions and body language, all those tiny, unique traits which they can then reproduce so precisely. But I also can't help wondering whether they are, unconsciously, observing others closely in the hope they can find something there that they can "borrow" and incorporate into their own personality structure, to strengthen their sense of self. Perhaps it's an extreme form of the desire most people display early in their lives to find role models. Of course, once impersonators have developed this ability, they are rewarded by the delight they produce in an audience, whether they are at a party with friends, or earning a living on television, so they have no reason to stop, even though its original purpose has never really been accomplished. One thing is for sure. In Peter's case, his weak sense of his own identity did not lead to a very stable existence. Graham told me once that he had been talking to Peter, when he was summoned to an important phone call. A few minutes later, Graham glanced up as someone else entered the room, and it took him some time to realise that this someone else was, in fact, Peter. He had been so altered as a result of the (obviously very difficult) phone conversation that Graham had not recognised him.

That said, Peter's behaviour towards us was invariably kind and generous. He was a delight to work for, and though I'm aware he had a darker side, I never glimpsed it. He and David Frost—our two main employers—worked at opposite ends of the producer spectrum. Peter discussed our work, criticised it and offered suggestions every time we had new scenes to show him, which was most weekdays; we loved this as it's always a thrill to work with someone who's better than you are (an experience I repeated twenty years later with Charlie Crichton on *Wanda*). David, by contrast, would discuss the general theme of the film a couple of times, and we'd see him again when we had finished the first draft a few weeks later, but essentially he left things to us, trusting our talent. This is a rare quality. Most film executives believe that because they have been given an office with a big desk, they must simultaneously have received, by some mystical process, an understanding of comedy which its practitioners often find it takes twenty years to acquire. So they interfere all the time, not because they have anything useful to say, as Peter did, but because they are very anxious. A few years ago, at Disney, a producer who had never written, performed or directed any comedy was telling me how to make my screenplay worse, and I remember thinking that their office was the only place on earth where such a person could manage to sustain an illusion of expertise.

So Graham and I revelled in our good fortune in working for two great bosses on three screenplays: *The Magic Christian, The Rise and Rise of Michael Rimmer* and *Rentasleuth*. We were to work on these for most of the next year, with very few diversions. We had become, by choice, full-time writers, and we loved it.

I think it was a very happy time for both of us. Now that Graham had "come out," David Sherlock was properly integrated into his social life. And he was finding writing a lot more fun than endless medical studies. He had always been very serious about becoming a doctor, and did eventually qualify, but I suspect that this was the year when he realised that comedy was his real passion.

As for me, I was more content and relaxed than I had been at any time since I had left New York. I was, after all, married to Connie, and although I remained extraordinarily naive about the psychology of women, we loved each other's company, and enjoyed endless visits to restaurants, the cinema (there were lots of great films in those days for people over twenty-five) and, best of all, the theatre. It was a golden age of British playwrights. When I was not struggling to understand Pinter (even with Connie's help) I was discovering Peter Nichols, Alan Bennett, Tom Stoppard, Alan Ayckbourn and Michael Frayn, all of whom for several decades to come were to provide some of the greatest theatrical comedy ever written: that was in addition to some Feydeau farces at the National which transported me to a brand-new level of bliss. It was now that I realised that farce—acted with real seriousness—was my first love.

I was also much more at ease now that I was free of the nerves I had experienced whenever I had to stand in front of an audience. The rhythms of a writer's life were congenial to me. If I was anxious about anything at this time, it was an absurd (but at that time inerad-icable) worry that I ought to be soaking up information about every-thing on the planet so that I would be as well informed as Leonardo da Vinci or John Stuart Mill or Mr. Bartlett. I was always in a state of awe when I found myself among highly informed people. Con-sequently, even when I was enjoying writing with Graham, there would be a part of me that wanted to finish as soon as possible, so that I could resume reading about ancient Egypt, or precious stones, or the history of anaesthetics, even though I knew that I read slowly (a hangover from studying science and law) and had a distinctly aver-age memory. The only thing you learn when doing comedy is how to do comedy, so I always experienced a sinking feeling late on Sunday afternoons as I reluctantly put my books aside and started focusing on the work week ahead. I called it "putting on my blinkers" (in the USA, "blinders").

That's not to say that I didn't greatly enjoy writing with Graham. It was always quite difficult for us to get down to work in the morning, and we developed many strategies to postpone doing so; but as someone said to me recently, "It's hard to start writing, but it's hard to stop." Once I'd become absorbed, the desire to get the damn thing right conflicted with my other desire to settle down to that book about the Syrian Orthodox Church. Perfectionism is a good trait professionally, if unhelpful to the quality of your private life.

Graham and I no longer worried so much when we had an unproductive session: we were experienced enough to be confident that we would soon be compensated by a fertile one. Our average rate was about four minutes of screen time a day, which may not sound much, but if sustained would theoretically have given us a movie script every six weeks. When we started *Python*, our average dropped a little as we had no overall story to guide us each day—every morning we had to come up with a fresh idea, not just continue on from yesterday. Even so, we could still produce at least fifteen minutes of sketch material each week, which, with fifteen from Mike and Terry Jones, and eight from Eric, plus Terry Gilliam's animations and opening and closing titles, meant we could edit all the weaker stuff out and still have enough material for one show (and often a bit to spare for the next).

The great joy was the laughing. There would be a moment when a really funny, wild or zany idea popped into our heads and we would both erupt. David Sherlock tells how there would suddenly be shrieking and howling and "the drumming of feet like a child having a tantrum, only this was the sheer delight of the lunacy of the idea" and how the screaming and howling with laughter would go on for some time before we actually settled again to write it down. I think Gra and I, more than the other Pythons, would suddenly be possessed by this bolt of gleeful energy, and in such huge quantities that we could fully discharge it not through plain laughter but through physical pyrotechnics: we would howl and hoot and drum. Some years later when I was being briefed to write a Video Arts film on some aspect of selling, an expert salesman told me that closing a sale was, for him, the next best thing to an orgasm. Clearly, he'd never written comedy.

Graham and I led very separate social lives. We always had done, since Cambridge days. I can scarcely recall us having dinner together, except as part of the Python group, usually when we were away from home, filming. But when we wrote in those days, we nearly always went out for lunch together. Our conversation was typically male: it would not have occurred to us to talk about "private" matters. Occasionally Gra would say things that seemed rather strange: for a time he would get quite angry about the "selfishness" of Buddhism, where people "sat around" meditating when they could be helping other people; he often expressed a strong dislike of gays who were effeminate; once he became quite insistent about the idea that touching someone's genitals was really no different from touching their arm; sometimes he would talk interestingly about medical matters—I can remember his telling me about iatrogenic diseases (illnesses caused by doctors). But mostly it was politics, TV, comedy and suchlike. My abiding memory of those times is that when we were not chatting (but often when we *were* writing) he could drift off into a reverie, stroking his sideburns while peering at his watch.

Sometimes I couldn't resist taking advantage of this tendency to daydream. Once, when we were strolling together through a Knightsbridge arcade and he was miles away, I stopped him, grasped him firmly by the shoulders, turned him ninety degrees to the right, and shoved him very firmly into a posh jewellery shop. At first he was so inattentive that he offered no resistance. Then, realising what was happening, he tried to decelerate. Instead he tripped as he passed through the doorway of the shop, picked up speed and, with arms outstretched to soften the blow, ran full-tilt into the counter. The salesman standing right behind jumped backwards and fell over. Gra now behaved with impeccable politeness, explaining to the poor cowering man why he had sprinted at him, and pointing outside at a man who was laughing so much that passers-by had stopped to watch and figure out what that individual was laughing at.

On another occasion I had booked a table at one of our favourite restaurants, the German Food Centre, in the *1948 Show*–style name of Mr. Hyaena-Explosion. It had taken some time to re-pronounce and spell it on the phone, since the German Food Centre took these matters seriously, but eventually the reservation was agreed. When we arrived there at one o'clock I made sure Gra was alongside me as I approached the maître d'. "Mr. Hyaena-Explosion!" I announced loudly. The maître d's face lit up. Something that had clearly been on his mind all morning was now satisfactorily resolved. *Alles in Ordnung!* Beaming, he replied, "Of course! Zis vay please . . ." I strode after him, and then turned back to see Gra simply standing there with his mouth open. It took a lot to get his attention at times.

Gra was always mildly irritated by any display of decorum, or good taste, if he felt it was a direct challenge to his deepest beliefs. When I mentioned once that Connie and I had guests coming to dinner that evening who were a bit formal and stuck-up, he carefully cut out some very small pieces of paper, wrote an obscenity on each one, and then hid them round our flat in all the rooms our guests were likely to visit. Connie found one of these just ten minutes before they were due to arrive: a moment of pure panic that set off a frenzied paper chase, as we raced around the apartment trying to find them all before the doorbell rang. We missed one, which he had placed on the basin in the visitors' loo. It simply read, "Anus." I've always wondered whether our guests speculated why we might have put it there.

Our enjoyment of practical jokes—and our slowly growing reputation as writers—came together one day when we were phoned by a Hollywood director called Sidney Salkow, who was visiting London and wanted to meet us. The day of our rendezvous we checked him out and found he had a string of films to his credit, every one of which sounded distinctly "B-movie." We therefore decided that the room in which we were to meet should be decorated in a manner that would honour the importance of the occasion. I have always had an extensive collection of soft toys (I buy them pretending they are for children), so now we raided this, placing the animals all round the room, partly hidden, with each one looking at the chair Mr. Salkow would be sitting in: a squirrel behind that lamp, a leopard up on the curtain rail, a raccoon under this chair, an ostrich behind the television, a warthog on the windowsill, two badgers peering from the filing cabinet, an asp on the anglepoise, a tiny lemur peeping out of a tissue box, a giraffe hiding at the top of the curtains, a crocodile outside the window (taped to the ledge), looking in at Mr. Salkow's chair three feet away, two zebras watching from a waste-paper basket, monkeys in the light shades, all concealed as best we could, so that our Hollywood director would spot them only one at a time. Our hope was that a slow, gradual realisation that he had an audience of fauna would rattle him more than one huge, simultaneous zoological revelation.

But Mr. Sidney Salkow was not the rattleable type. He entered the room like a typhoon, pumping our hands, exclaiming with great enthusiasm, congratulating us on all things British, and generally establishing his credentials as a high-end extrovert. And within seconds he was perched in his chair, gesticulating wildly as he launched into a description of the opening scene of the movie he was so excited about us writing.

> SIDNEY SALKOW: There's this huge castle in the middle of a plain, and it's got a huge front gate.
> JOHN & GRAHAM (*variously*): Where is this, Sidney?
> SS: Er . . . doesn't matter! And a huge army is besieging this castle, right?
> J & G: Yes. Who . . . ?

ss: It's been besieging this castle for months, right?

J & G: Right. Who . . . ?

ss: And the front gate of the castle bursts open (*SS claps his hands*) and these three hogs run out! What an image! Wow!

J & G: *Hogs?*

ss: Yeah! How about that?

J & G: You mean big pigs?

ss: Huge! The biggest you've ever seen! *Three* of them!

J & G: Sidney . . . Why . . . ?

ss: And strapped to the first hog is Ernest Borgnine!

J & G: *Ernest Borgnine?*

ss: Ernie and I go way back. He's committed to the movie. He's huge.

J & G: Why is he . . . ?

ss: And strapped to the second hog is . . . *Guess!*

J & G: Sir Laurence Olivier?

ss: No! Charlton Heston! And guess who's strapped to the third hog.

J & G: Sean Connery?

ss: No! Sophia Loren! She's huge!

J & G: But why . . . ?

ss: And the hogs run out towards the army—

J & G: Sidney, Sidney!

ss: What?

J & G: Why are they strapped to the pigs?

ss: *Hogs!* Because it's a siege.

J & G: . . . And . . . ?

ss: They're showing the army how much food they've got left.

J & G: *What?*

ss: They've got *so* much they don't even need three hogs!

J & G: OK, but why have Ernest Borgnine, Charlton Heston
and Sophia Loren been *strapped* to them?

By this time, our minds were reeling. But I promise you, this is a
pretty damn accurate account of what happened when we met our
first Hollywood director.

As for our animals . . . we'd both assumed he'd missed them. But
as we shook hands when we parted:

SS: Anyway, boys, think about it, OK!
J & G: Yes! Yes, we will, Sidney.
SS: Great! And by the way . . . nice animals!

Maybe the joke was on us. I just wish I could remember why
Sophia Loren was going to be fastened to a pig.

ONE WAY and another Graham and I wrote together almost full-
time from the *How to Irritate People* recording in May 1968 to the
taping of the first *Monty Python* show on August 30, 1969. The only in-
terruptions were the handful of days I spent in front of the camera in
tiny roles dignified by the courtesy title of "cameo." The first of these
was on one of my favourite TV shows, *The Avengers,* with the third
Emma Peel, Linda Thorson, in which I played a man who registered
the copyright of the unique make-up of every single circus clown by
painting it on to a real hen's egg (this, believe me, is how it really used
to be done). I was duly surrounded by multiple racks of these eggs,
and of course the pay-off was that I ended up knocking them all over.
Since by now I fancied myself at physical comedy, I told the direc-

tor I thought I could floor every egg in one take, which would have helped as this was the last shot of the day and everyone wanted to go home. It turned out, however, that I couldn't. So the whole crew had to spend the next two hours putting the eggs back on the racks and trying to hide the bits that were cracked. Under massive pressure, I got it right the second time.

Then the wondrous Denis Norden (one of the half-dozen people I would choose to join me on a desert island) somehow finagled me into appearing in two films he had written. The first, *The Bliss of Mrs. Blossom,* had me playing a clerk in a post office, supporting Freddie Jones and the great comic and cartoonist Willie Rushton. It was a fairly unremarkable experience, though I remember being struck by the care with which the director arranged an amusing sticker on a noticeboard behind me: perhaps it was there in case the audience got bored watching us act.

The other Norden gift, though, was rather more memorable because it gave me my first experience of filming with a big Hollywood star. George Sanders was a super-suave English actor who, along with James Mason, had cornered the market in elegant-British-swine roles. Our scene together required me to play the manager of a tea plantation in the Far East having dinner with my employer during a "native uprising," and the humour stemmed from our very different reactions as the plantation villa was attacked: Sanders sitting there quite unconcerned, drinking his soup, while bullets whizzed everywhere, hitting the candlesticks and crockery; me frozen and terrified, vacillating between trying to mimic his calm, and diving for cover (and instant dismissal from my job). In those days before CGI, the action was for real: crockery and cutlery were sent flying about, propelled into the air by jets of compressed air, and I had to hold a (wax) drinking glass full of red wine steady as it was shot out of my hand by a stunt man with a .22 rifle resting on the back of a chair, just out of view. (I was, however, allowed to hold the glass at its base.) I was touched when, at one moment, George Sanders actually stopped them shooting my close-up as it was becoming too dangerous for me. I was also impressed a little later when he insisted that some water that was to be thrown on him should be really cold, to help make his reaction to it as genuine as possible. We all watched him surreptitiously throughout the day as he gave the crew a master class in languid elegance. Some years later I learned that he had committed suicide because he was "bored." I admire insouciance greatly; this, however, seemed to be taking it a bit too far.

It was Peter Sellers who was responsible for my next cameo appearance. At the end of one of our script sessions, he mentioned that Thames Television had decided to make a radio-style recording of a famous old Goon show, *Tales of Men's Shirts,* as a TV special, and then casually asked me whether I would like to play the announcer (the part originally played by Wallace Greenslade) when they recorded the show the following week. My mind reeled, but I said as languidly as I could that I thought I could fit it in (I'd been watching Mr. Sanders very carefully); then I made Peter laugh by saying that I needed to agree the fee, as I wasn't sure I could afford to pay it (an old joke, but a very appropriate one).

What was wonderful about performing the Wallace Greenslade role was that there was no pressure on me to get more than the odd smile; what was even more wonderful was that as the programme was being shot as a radio show, and we all therefore had scripts in front of us, there was no possibility of my forgetting any lines. So I was able to stand next to the trio I had worshipped since the age of fourteen, occasionally reading a paragraph when the red light blinked, and feeling both thrilled and slightly numb. I didn't screw up; it all went very smoothly; and suddenly it was over and there I was, back home on the sofa, trying to decide whether it had really happened. I checked the next day, and it had.

Meanwhile Graham and I were steaming ahead with our three film scripts. Our second draft of *The Magic Christian* (the film's sixteenth so far) was deemed good enough to secure financing for the enterprise; but to our disappointment Terry Southern was then invited to do the final draft, and proceeded lovingly to reinstate the mess we had first been presented with. We both hated the end result (you'd expect that, if you knew writers as well as I do). Graham wondered whether a Mr. Jack Daniels should have been credited as Southern's co-writer. Even so, it was hard to resist when Peter Sellers offered me a small part opposite him in a rather good scene where Sir Guy Grand purchases a "School of Rembrandt" portrait and then cuts out the nose of it with a knife, explaining to my character (a snotty young art dealer) that he only collects noses. I, of course, have to react with horror, and I exclaim "Shit!" This was quite a naughty word in 1968—so naughty, in fact, that when, some months later, my scene was shown on television to promote the movie I became, as far as I know, the first person ever to say "shit" on British television. (This, incidentally, is one of my three claims to fame: the others are that I have a species of lemur named after me, and that I was once French-kissed—on camera—by Tim Curry.)

While *The Magic Christian* was trundling along, David Frost managed to secure financial backing for the *Rimmer* film. We all agreed that Peter Cook would be great as the brilliant pollster who manipulates the results so that he ends up as Prime Minister, and I was delighted when I heard that Kevin Billington was to be the director: I'd been hugely impressed by his clarity and bright, enthusiastic energy when I'd worked with him on *Interlude*. Since he and Peter were so much better informed about the British political scene than Graham and I, it seemed the perfect plan for the four of us now to work together on the script until we started shooting at the end of June. And since Gra and I knew nothing about the actual process of putting a film together it was a relief to have someone like Kevin to explain how it all unfolded, and what had to be decided when. For his part I think that Kevin found Gra slightly disconcerting. During our first week working together, the four of us were walking up to a Polish restaurant we frequented when Kevin dropped his voice and asked me, "Does Graham always say as little as this when he's writing?" The funny thing is that I was surprised: I'd got so used to Gra that his behaviour no longer struck me as odd.

Our meetings were held at Peter's house in Church Row, Hampstead, and the collaboration became a very happy one. A few weeks before, I had briefly appeared (both as Robin Hood and as a butler) in a show that Peter and Dudley were putting together, but as it hadn't involved individual scenes with either of them I hadn't got to know Peter particularly well. Now, though, I saw him regularly, and while at first I felt like a new boy in his presence, I soon relaxed: he was so welcoming, cheery and easy to write with. And he was effortlessly, brilliantly funny all the time. We'd be sitting there discussing some aspect of the plot and he'd slide into a five-minute monologue that he could easily have bestowed on a West End audience. As Frank Muir once said, "He could saw it off by the yard." His excellent biographer Harry Thompson relates that after Peter had been staggeringly funny one evening, he quietly lamented to a friend that none of it had been written down. It was lost forever.

Later, though, I began to see that there was a downside to Peter's superb talent: it flowed so easily for him that he never had to learn to grind it out like the rest of us. Consequently, when inspiration did eventually begin to fail him, he lacked a writer's cussed determination to keep at it until things began to flow again (and he really was the only genius I have ever worked with, except for the American TV director Jimmy Burrows of *Cheers* and *Frasier* fame). Not that this was remotely a problem when we were working on *Rimmer*: our sessions were always productive and enormous fun. By the spring of 1969 everyone was happy with the script, Kevin was able to start casting, and shooting began at the end of June. I had a small part, as a man called Ferret who is learning the tango.

With *Rimmer* well on its way, Graham and I were able to switch our focus to the *Rentasleuth* screenplay. Whereas *Rimmer* was a satire, albeit not a very sophisticated one, this was an out-and-out comedy,

and we thought some of it was really funny. There was a great scene
where the Ronnie Corbett character has trapped a bullion van and is
trying to force the Ronnie Barker character to unlock the doors by
filling up the driver's cab with water from a hose. In another scene
Marty Feldman steals an invalid carriage (which turns out not to be
very fast) and Tim Brooke-Taylor hijacks an ice-cream van (similarly
handicapped) to pursue him, so that during their furious race they
are passed on either side by cars, bicycles and, eventually, joggers.
And finally, in an extended sequence, Graham and I feed doctored
meat to a couple of Doberman pinscher guard dogs to render them
unconscious: the meat fails to have any effect, so we have to ply them
with more and more until after a time they become so friendly they
let us in anyway, following us everywhere, wagging their tails and
demanding more meat while we burgle the place; of course when
the supply of meat runs out, the dogs turn nasty. This was the kind
of material Gra and I loved writing best: one foot in a crime drama
where the consequences were theoretically serious, the other foot in
extreme silliness but with all the behaviour kept *just* believable—in
other words, more farcical than the usual heist movie. And the most
exciting thing was that we had lined up a cast that could do what the
very best comedians can manage: they can go "over the top" while
taking the audience with them; that is, they can make people accept
absurdity where many good comedy actors would fail.

With David Frost's approval, we started looking for a director,
and this led me to possibly the most embarrassing moment of my
life. First we approached Denis Norden, for us *the* expert on comedy
in the UK, but Denis simply had no desire to direct (I completely
sympathised with him). Next my agent asked me if I knew a director
called Jay Lewis. As it happened, I did. I'd met him on holiday and
liked him immensely. My agent read me his credits (not great, but
very good) and told me that Jay had looked at the script and really
liked it. Would I ring him? I was about to go away for a few days but
promised I would call the moment I got back, which I duly did. The

phone was answered by Jay's girlfriend, the actresss Thelma Ruby. I greeted her and told her that I was delighted to hear the news about Jay. "We buried him this afternoon," she replied. I stammered that I was not delighted that he was dead, just that I was delighted he'd liked the script before he died, but that, on the contrary . . . Then I said, "I'm sorry," put the phone down and killed myself. Several times.

Now we were asked if we knew a Charles Crichton. We looked him up, and leapt about excitedly when we discovered that he had directed for the Ealing Studios, which between 1949 and 1955 had made the greatest batch of comedy films England ever produced. Charlie had made my second favourite (after *The Ladykillers*), *The Lavender Hill Mob,* so we sent our script off to him—and then recalled that our ending was a complete and deliberate steal from that very film (or, let us say, it had influenced us greatly).

Fortunately we discovered when we went to meet him that he had not noticed. Even better, we realised after about five minutes that we had stumbled across a treasure, a man who knew so much more about film than anyone we'd ever met that it was almost embarrassing. We'd pack up for the day, having left some problem unresolved, and then the next morning Charlie would push a sheet of paper towards us, rather shyly, while puffing on his pipe, and we would glance at it and realise that he had not only come up with the solution but somehow also clarified a plot point and added a good joke. Under his tutelage the script improved rapidly, to the point when in August, just before *Rimmer* stopped shooting, *Variety* carried a story that David Frost's film company's second film, *Rentasleuth,* would be "helmed" by Charles Crichton (and written by Gra and me).

Sadly it never happened. David Frost quietly sold our script to a producer called Ned Sherrin who immediately refused to use Charlie, without giving us any reason why. We admired Charlie so much that we walked away from the project, followed by the rest of the cast. Sherrin then changed the film's title to *Rentadick* (he had a great fondness for smut) and proceeded to produce a stinker—such a stinker, in fact, that the film critic Alexander Walker memorably described it as "another nail in the coffin of the British film industry." He'd had it rewritten entirely, of course.

One way and another, it was just as well that Gra and I parted company with our script, as we swiftly came to the conclusion that Sherrin was tasteless, slimy and incompetent. Shortly afterwards he tried to cheat us financially, so we added "treacherous" to the list. He had a habit of turning up for meetings with us accompanied by a different young waiter each time, who would sit patiently some distance away while we discussed the film. We shuddered to think for what purpose he was waiting. Money, we assumed. The one thing I'm grateful for is that Sherrin was still alive and kicking when Charlie won his Oscar nomination for Best Director for *Wanda*. (Incidentally last week Graham conveyed, by Ouija board, his endorsement of this particular paragraph.)

Perhaps this is the moment to admit that although Gra and I had two films being shot and a third confirmed, and that although it's pretty rare for young screenwriters to have three out of three scripts actually made, the reality was that we didn't have much idea what we were doing. We could write good jokes and funny scenes, but we didn't know how to structure a full-length film. It's not that hard to get the hang of writing sketches, and by now Gra and I were capable of writing a very decent TV half-hour. (In fact during this whole period the best script we did was a pilot for Humphrey Barclay based on Richard Gordon's *Doctor in the House;* with Gra's medical-student background it proved surprisingly easy to create a funny and believable programme, and it gave rise to a long-running series.) But a feature of a hundred minutes is a different kettle of fish, a bird of another feather, a different ball game and a horse of a dissimilar hue. If a half-hour sitcom is, say, seven times harder to write than a sketch, then a movie is twenty times harder than a sitcom, *especially* if it is a *comedy* (if you think this is special pleading by a comic, just write down the names of fifty great dramas and then struggle to come up with fifteen great comedies).

Of course, film scripts are hard to get right in any case. My friend William Goldman, whom I regard as one of the greatest of all screen-writers (and author of the best book about Hollywood, *Adventures in the Screen Trade*), once told me that he found them more difficult than novels or plays. The need to keep the plot moving all the time is a hugely demanding one—the slightest moment of stagnation and a cinema audience is immediately bored (although a lot of explosions do help to sustain their attention). Add to that the following diffi-culty in comedy: you cannot make an audience laugh continuously for a hundred minutes—human psychology and physiology will not allow it—so you have to plan a sequence of alternating peaks and troughs in the laughter, while ensuring that you engage the audi-ence's attention fully during the passages that are not trying to be funny. In *Fawlty Towers* Connie and I were able to build the tension and the laughs continuously, but if you try this for more than about thirty-five minutes some kind of ennui infects the audience. I don't know why exactly, but it does. Sir Henry Irving was asked on his deathbed whether dying was hard. "No," he replied, "dying is easy. Comedy is hard."

You will now understand why I have managed to write only one really good film script in fifty years (though I contributed to *Life of Brian,* too).

While Graham and I were happily writing our three films, we knew to some extent that we didn't know what we were doing; we just didn't fully grasp the depth of our ignorance. Fortunately the people around were generally as clueless as we were, which is why the films got financed. But they all failed, by quite a comfortable mar-gin, *Rentadick* (producer Ned Sherrin) being by far the direst.

So it was probably a good thing that Gra and I at this point got involved in something we *were* good at. And it was all because every Thursday afternoon we'd taken to the habit of stopping work early in order to watch a children's programme. It was called *Do Not Adjust Your Set,* it featured Michael Palin, Terry Jones, Eric Idle and, latterly, some of Terry Gilliam's earliest animations, and it just happened to be the funniest thing on British television, morning, noon or night. After one particularly brilliant show I said to Graham, "Why don't I give them a call and see if they want to do a show with us?" Graham agreed, I rang Michael, we met a few days later and came to the conclusion that it felt like a good idea, and we then approached Barry Took, Marty Feldman's old writing partner, whom we knew quite well from *The Frost Report* and who was some kind of consultant with the BBC. Barry in turn arranged for us to see Michael Mills, the head of BBC Comedy.

On the appointed day we trooped into Michael's office. He greeted us and said he'd heard we wanted to do a comedy series, and we said, "That's right," and he said, "Well, tell me what you've got in mind"— and, of course, we couldn't. I know it seems incredible but we had had no proper discussion at all about what kind of show we were going to do. We just wanted to do one. Michael was obviously expecting some kind of presentation, so as the silence grew ever more embarrassing he began prompting us. "Will you have guest stars?" We looked at each other. "Probably . . . not." "Music?" "Er . . . maybe some . . . not a lot." "Film?" "Yes! Definitely some film, yes!" The six of us sat there looking clueless and unprofessional in front of the most important man in British television comedy. It was humiliating. And I was about to suggest that we should go away and discuss what sort of show we did intend to do, and then come back in a couple of months, or years, when Michael suddenly shrugged and in a resigned tone said, "OK, go away and make thirteen programmes."

He didn't even ask for a pilot . . .

As we thanked Michael and left his office, happy and excited, we had no idea just how lucky we had been—for the world of television would soon start to change and make a decision of the kind Michael had just made inconceivable.

But being nascent Pythons, we still delayed figuring out what it was we were going to do. We were given a production schedule, and Gilliam convinced various BBC financial folk that he really could produce animation at the tiny cost he claimed was possible, but otherwise there was no progress at all, because we were all heavily involved in other projects, and even when we did manage to meet, all our efforts went into coming up with a title for the show, which the BBC was now obsessively demanding. Each time we thought we had come up with one, we would then panic the next morning and cancel it, and so we worked our way through *A Horse, a Spoon and a Bucket; Owl-Stretching Time; Bunn, Wackett, Buzzard, Stubble and Boot; The Toad-Elevating Moment;* and *You Can't Call a Show "Betty."* Eventually the BBC gave up on us and started referring to it as *Barry Took's Flying Circus.* We liked the *Flying Circus* bit and nearly attributed its ownership to Gwen Dibley (Michael Palin's suggestion). Finally one evening somebody suggested Python (a great name for an untrustworthy impresario, I thought), someone else added Monty, which had connotations of our greatest World War II general, there was hysteria, and history was made.

A few nights later I happened to watch a new Spike Milligan comedy show called *Q5.* I was dismayed: it was brilliant. I rang Terry Jones. "Yes," he said, "I've just seen it, too." "But," I said, "I thought that's what *we* were going to do." "So did I," he replied.

Still, we now had to create *Python,* and we debated for some time what kind of style the show should adopt. Michael and Terry Jones, inspired by Terry Gilliam's animation, suggested a stream-of-consciousness approach. For our part Graham and I felt we needed to get rid of a lot of the conventions of TV comedy (without being absolutely sure of what they all were). When we actually met to plan the first programme, though, we floundered around, playing with a few ideas that nobody was excited by. Then we realised that nothing was going to happen until we all went home and started to *write* . . .

So the next morning Chapman and I sat down and stared into the distance for a bit, before, as usual, I picked up *Roget's Thesaurus* and started reading words out at random.

"Buttercup. Filter. Catastrophe. Glee. Plummet."

"Ah," said Gra. "I like plummet."

A couple of minutes passed.

"A sheep would plummet, wouldn't it?" one of us said.

"If it tried to fly, you mean?" said the other.

(I should explain that when you've written a piece with someone you can never remember afterwards who exactly contributed what.)

"But why would it want to fly?"

"To escape?"

A couple of months later the "Flying Sheep" became the first *Monty Python* skit to be recorded. I still vividly recall the moment, about two minutes before taping started, when I stood in the wings with Michael Palin, watching as the moment approached for Terry Jones to walk up to Graham to begin the dialogue. "Michael," I said, "do you realise, we could be the first people in history to record a comedy show to complete silence?" There was a pause, and then Michael responded, "I was having the same thought."

We had no idea at all whether people would think *Python* was funny. It really felt that risky.

But the sketch started . . . Michael and I strained our ears . . . a giggle . . . a small laugh . . . another giggle . . . a big laugh!

And we looked at each other and I thought, "Maybe it's going to be all right."

16

When I completed the last line of the previous chapter, I thought to myself, "What a neat way to end this book."

But as you will have realised by now, dear reader, it was not to be, because since I wrote that artful cliff-hanger, unforeseen Pythonic activity has taken place: namely the reunion show at London's O2 arena. To ignore that might be perceived as skimping. So . . .

What a huge success it was—although I say so, who shouldn't. I refuse to be modest. Ten audiences of 16,000 loved it and gave us ten great warm, happy standing ovations, and I've only heard three snotty comments altogether (apart from the *Daily Mail,* who panned the show, claiming we had "mixed reviews"—they were about as mixed as Hitler's reviews at Nuremberg, a reference which the *Mail,* as a formerly pro-Nazi paper, should easily get).

The funny thing about it all was . . . it happened by accident. Back in November 2013 the five surviving Pythons had had to convene a meeting to discuss a disastrous law case: one of the producers of our 1975 film *Monty Python and the Holy Grail* had claimed a share of some of the profits of *Spamalot* equal to that which each of the Pythons was getting, and we'd ended up with legal costs in the area of £800,000. Our meeting, then, was not for the happiest of reasons, but despite this we all felt it was great to be back together: enjoying each other's company, laughing a lot, and horsing around like sixty-year-olds.

And then someone said, "Let's do a show to pay our costs!" Within five minutes it was a done deal.

My original assumption was that we'd have sufficient die-hard fans to justify staging two or three shows, but we were all staggered when tickets for the first show were sold out in forty-four seconds, and a further four shows within a few hours. We were literally *world news* after our first press conference. Our breaths were taken away and not handed back for some time (the show's producer, Phil McIntyre, told us, "You've unleashed a monster"). Naturally, we were tickled pink: *Python* had been "old news" for thirty-five years and the media had certainly treated me as "passé" for decades, so it was so lovely suddenly to discover that there was this reservoir of affection and appreciation still out there. However, we soon realised we had no idea how the actual *show* might be received. There was much nervousness and uncertainty and, indeed, foreboding among the more gutless of the Pythons.

Months later, though, I was able to stand on the O2 stage and feel how *satisfactory* everything had been. And then it struck me that Graham should have been there to enjoy it with us.

He died of cancer in 1989, at the age of only forty-eight, and although he never enjoyed a major success outside *Python*, within it he played an absolutely crucial part in every aspect of its creation. It goes without saying that he was a very fine performer indeed (until alcoholism shackled him), but to my mind it was as a writer that he injected his unique contribution to the show: humour of a kind none of the rest of us could have provided—the inspired, off-the-wall line (or idea) that helped lurch a sketch into new, more fertile territory. Frequently, if I was getting bogged down in too much logical and predictable stuff, he would come up with some lunatic suggestion that would liberate us. And, as I've said before, it helped enormously that we shared such a similar sense of humour. We may have been different in many other ways, but what he hooted at made me howl: when I split a gut, his intestines opened in the same place.

In addition, he had a priceless, quite uncanny knack of knowing what the audience was going to laugh at. I trusted his judgement of this so implicitly that I never bothered to develop an idea that he didn't like. The other side of this was that sometimes his encouragement kept me working away at something in which I'd lost confidence. A good example from the *Python* era is the "Cheese Shop."

The genesis of this sketch was particularly odd. A few days before we wrote it we travelled down to the south coast to shoot a Mike-and-Terry piece set on a boat. It was a stormy day, and since I have a propensity to be seasick, I was apprehensive. However, when we arrived we were assured that things would be all right, as we were going to shoot inside the harbour. I was playing the part of a Python Pepperpot, and all I had to do was to come up on deck and screech some inanity or other. Easy, I thought, because the whole take couldn't last more than about six seconds. But the moment I stepped on to the boat, I knew things were not going to be "all right." I was conscious of a distinct rocking motion, and as the shot was set up I began to feel worse . . . and worse. Then our director, Ian McNaughton, said, "Right then, let's shoot," and I climbed down on to the lower deck to await my cue. I stood there long enough to recall that during the Second World War some British sailors on the ships taking supplies to Murmansk had actually died of seasickness, and reflected what a happy release that must have been. Then I heard Ian shout, "Action," and I clambered up on the deck, faced the camera, opened my mouth—and vomited over the camera. I'd heard of projectile vomiting before, but I'd never actually seen it, let alone done it.

"Cut!"

Costume and make-up raced over to clean me up and reapply lipstick, while the camera crew wiped the lens and removed small pieces of carrot from the operator's hair. The boat continued to rock. "Are you all right, then?" Ian asked. "Yes," I lied, and climbed back down the steps, thinking about all those lucky sailors.

"Action!"

I steeled myself, raced up the steps, forgot my line—and threw up again. "Fuck!" shouted the operator. There was less actual sick this time, but unfortunately it was better directed, so the cleaning-up operation took longer. Eventually, though, the make-up girls were satisfied, the camera glistened, the operator had found a sou'wester, and I was invited to slink down below for a third attempt.

"Action!"

I stumbled up the stairs and this time all went comparatively well, as I got the whole line out before the vomit.

"Print!"

Later that day, in the car that was taking us back to London, Graham noticed enough signs of life in me to advise that I should try to eat something. Was there anything I fancied? "I think I could manage some cheese," I replied. So we started looking for food shops, but couldn't spot one. Then we passed a chemist's. "There's a chemist's," Graham said. "I wonder if they have any cheese," I mused, to which Graham replied, "If they did it would be medicinal cheese." I laughed and said, "There's a sketch there."

So when we next sat down to write, we asked ourselves why anyone would go into a chemist's to ask for cheese. Obviously, because they'd been to a cheese shop that didn't have any. Hence the sketch. But as it consisted merely of a customer asking for a particular cheese variety, and the cheesemonger saying that he didn't have that one for some reason or other, I kept losing confidence in it, and asking, "Graham, is this *really* funny?" Then he'd take his pipe out and say, "Yes," and we'd go on for a bit—"Well, stout yeoman, four ounces of Caerphilly, if you please," "Ah! It's been on order, sir, for two weeks"—and I'd ask again, "Gra, are you *quite* sure this is funny?" and he'd grin affirmatively. This was repeated every time I got cold feet ("Cheddar?," "Well, we don't get much call for it round here"), which was about six more times. So if it were not for Graham, the "Cheese Shop" sketch would not exist, and I would be deprived of my happiest *Python* memory: reading it out for the first time and seeing

Michael Palin laugh so much that he actually slid off his chair on to the ground and just lay there rolling about.

Incidentally, Graham and I never got round to the medicinal cheese idea.

Now I've been trying throughout this book to convey to you some kind of portrait of the extraordinary being that was Dr. Graham Chapman. Having just told a tale of him at his wisest, therefore, I need to say there was another side to him that I felt was unknowable, at least to me. So here's a tale of Gra at his oddest.

During the first series, the Pythons were on the Yorkshire Moors one hot afternoon, filming a Mike-and-Terry piece about an upperclass shooting party, various of whom return home that evening with gunshot wounds. It was not an inspired piece, just a series of sight gags involving accidents, and Graham and I had managed to secure small roles, so we spent most of the time hanging around the wardrobe truck some distance from the filming. When we'd finished the crossword—it seemed to be the only vaguely constructive thing we could do while waiting to be called to perform—we tried to devise means to stop ourselves going mad with boredom, without much success. Graham decided to practise saying the name of a radio comedienne called Betty Marsden faster than anyone had ever said it before; I tried to balance an umbrella on my chin for a whole minute.

At one point I noticed that Graham had left his pipe on a chair, and I picked it up and put it in my pocket, without his noticing and without my having any clear idea how I could squeeze some entertainment from the situation. A few moments later, in mid-umbrella balance, I sensed Graham moving close behind me. And when I turned I was surprised to see how agitated he had become.

His searching was almost frenzied, and I felt a flash of alarm, mixed with puzzlement as to why the missing pipe was causing him so much distress. I felt it was time to confess. "I've got your pipe," I said, taking it out of my pocket and showing it to him. He glared at me for a moment, snatched it, stepped up to me as I reflexively started to apologise, and kneed me in the groin. Although he missed the testicles, he hit the pelvic bone pretty hard, but the pain was as nothing compared with the wave of utter astonishment that broke over me. I knew this man well! What on earth was this about? By now he was shouting at me. Then he strode off . . .

I realised I was slightly in shock, so I sat down slowly and carefully, but my mind was already casting around for possible explanations. Suddenly, a Freudian one became obvious. I had not taken his pipe. I had stolen his penis.

Some months later there appeared in the *Daily Mirror* a rather different version of the pipe incident, one which Graham had given to their reporter. As he told it, the whole thing had taken place in the studio where we recorded the *Python* shows. He recalled how, after he discovered I had purloined his pipe, he chased me across the studio, rugby-tackled me, repossessed the pipe, and sat on my head. I was bemused when I read—and reread—Graham's narrative, because it was not feasible that his version and mine could be different interpretations of the same event, *Rashomon*-style. Even allowing for the vagaries of memory, it was clear that one of us was, let's say, a bit hazier about the event than the other.

To sum up, Graham was kind, intellectually gifted and very talented, but some of the time he enjoyed only a tenuous relationship with reality. Fortunately, this never seemed to affect our professional relationship, nor did it have an impact on the affection I felt for him.

AND SO, at the very beginning of *Python,* when we all went off to write, it was business as usual for Gra and me: we just continued meeting and writing, usually at Basil Street. The only difference this time was that now we were writing for *Python.*

After a few days we phoned around and agreed to meet and to read out what we'd written . . . to try to find out what the hell we were doing. We met at Terry Jones's house, because it was large, and because it also gave us all a chance to see South London. It was worth the trip: there was much laughter, and we parted feeling we were heading in the right comedic direction. Roughly. So we settled into a simple routine. Every six or seven working days the five of us would get together for a read-through to assess the material, and see if we could construct a whole show from it. I say "the five of us" because Terry Gilliam didn't write for these sessions: when we assembled a show we'd indicate in the script where we wanted his animation, and whether it would be a longer or shorter piece, and this would guide him when he sat down to create his little masterpieces. We never saw these until the afternoon of the day we were recording the show, so there was no chance to make suggestions, as happened with the rest of us while we rehearsed together. I think Terry preferred it that way; and in any case no other process was possible, given the time restraints we were working to. Otherwise we were very much a team, constantly exchanging suggestions and ideas and, all this time, getting to know each other better. The read-throughs were almost always enjoyable: a lot of very funny stuff was being written, much of it quite original. Sometimes, of course, the writers of a particular sketch would be disappointed if it didn't earn many laughs, but some of it might be salvaged in ingenious ways. In general I felt that the discussions of how to improve material by cutting or rewriting were of a very high quality. As Eric once remarked, there weren't many other places where you could get advice of this level of comic expertise.

If you want to understand how the *Python* group operated, you need to grasp one essential fact: like Graham and I, Michael and Terry and Eric were primarily *writers, not performers*. So we never argued about the *casting*. If we had been actors at heart, we would, of course, have been fighting for the best roles. But we never did, because once we had agreed on a sketch it was always obvious to us, as writers, who should play which part to get the best out of it. In other words, who was least likely to muck it up. One result of this was that we never wrote parts which were intended to showcase our talents, as actors would have done.

Various Pythons. I am standing on Terry Gilliam.

But because we were writers, our passion (please excuse this word, but my publisher's marketing department asked that I should include it at some point) was invested in our scripts, and not in our acting. And sometimes this . . . *passion* . . . would lead us into very silly territory. *Very* silly . . .

On one occasion, for example, somebody had written a sketch that was set in a rather drab, moth-eaten dormitory. Someone else suggested that this should be lit by a magnificent Louis XIV chandelier. We liked this, but another Python said, "No, by a dead stuffed

farm animal with a light bulb in each foot." We liked this even better. Then one of us observed, "Obviously a sheep." And it was at this
point that the debate started.

"What do you mean, a sheep? It's got to be a goat."

"A goat?"

"Of course! The horns make it funnier visually."

"But sheep are stupid, and stupid is funny."

"Look, sheep are more rounded. Goats are angular."

"So?"

"Well, the angularity will look more incongruous."

"A farm animal hanging from the bloody ceiling looks incongruous enough already, without anybody bothering about how angular
it is."

"It's funnier with wool, though."

"What's funny about *wool*?"

"Well, it's soft and shapeless."

"Yes, but goats look more ridiculous, with those Marty Feldman
eyes and tufts of hair sticking out all over them."

"But people don't think of them as *dim*."

And so on, and so on, three pro-goat and two pro-sheep, with the
argument getting more heated, and also nastier, with ad hominem
comments about each other's parentage, and bizarre sexual practices,
until after about twenty minutes, I managed to detach myself from
the fray, regain my composure, consult a higher power, and ponder
philosophically on the absurdity of it all, the utter ridiculousness of
five Oxbridge graduates fighting ferociously over a simple choice
between a sheep chandelier and a goat chandelier, when it was obvious to the meanest intellect that it was funnier when it was a
fucking *goat*.

I think we cared too much about the scripts really and that's
why the arguments got so heated. Sorry! Got so *passionate*. When
this happened the dynamic of the group became very predictable.
Michael, who hated confrontation, would retire to a safe distance;

Graham would say even less than usual; Eric would try to be reasonable and constructive; Terry Gilliam would side with anyone else called Terry; and Terry Jones and I would lock horns and . . . not behave well. I would become very precise and cold and tight-lipped, with suppressed impatience and irritation seeping out of my ears. Jonesy's voice would get higher and higher and more and more insistent, and he would never, *never* shut up, or concede a point, or admit to a scintilla of doubt. I felt strongly about some points, and would fight for *them,* but Jonesy felt strongly about *everything,* and would go to the wire on all of them; and even if, at the end of the script meeting, the tide of opinion ran strongly against him and his opinion was overruled, the next morning, as we sat down with our coffees, he would announce, "You know, I was thinking this morning, and I *really feel* that . . ."; and we would be right back to half-past three the previous day. It seemed as though he had a fundamental belief that the merit of his argument depended on the strength of his feelings about the matter, and since he *always* felt uncontrollably passionate about *everything,* then clearly he was *always right.* This irrational claptrap, coming as it did from a swarthy, excitable, plump Celtic demi-dwarf, struck me not just as thoroughly impertinent but also as a noisy and ignorant attempt to undermine the most basic principles of the Enlightenment. What is more . . .

I'm sorry. I got a little carried away there . . .

Yes, Terry and I did argue regularly. But the dominant emotion was exasperation rather than anger, and I think we acted as useful counterweights to each other, enabling the group to make good comedic decisions. It was interesting in this regard that when the group was split over the merits or demerits of a particular script, the Cambridge trio often voted together, not for reasons of tribal loyalty, but because we were coincidentally more concerned with structure and logic, while the two Terrys and Michael were more interested in mood and in visual presentation. Thus they often felt constricted by our preoccupation with left-brain issues, while we were genuinely puzzled by what seemed to us an almost careless, and certainly cava-lier, attitude to logical connections and clarity. The Cambridge trio, I think, believed these two qualities were essential, because no matter how wacky the premise of a sketch was, once it had been established, its rules had to be followed, or else the sketch would lose coherence and, thus, "believability." It may seem bizarre to use the word "believability" about a *Python* sketch, but in some mysterious way the audience will accept *any* premise, no matter how weird, and then allow it to set the rules for what is, and what is not, believable in *that* piece.

Take, for example, the "Buying a Bed" sketch, in which an ardent and newly married young couple dash into a department store to buy a double bed. Once we know that the salesman Mr. Lambert always puts a large paper bag over his head every time someone mentions the word "mattress," and that he will only take it off when everyone sings a verse of "Jerusalem," it's essential that those rules are followed. If one of the characters were to say "mattress" and Mr. Lambert did not don the bag, then the audience would immediately become puzzled by the inconsistency, and a puzzled audience will not laugh. This happens for two reasons: firstly, because at a ratio-nal level, they suddenly do not understand this arbitrary change in the rules, and instead of laughing are thinking, "OK, but what are the rules *now*?"; and secondly, because this slight puzzlement always causes a disconnect in their emotional involvement in the sketch, which diminishes laughter just as effectively.

But if Michael and Terry sometimes certainly felt that Graham and I adhered too strongly to our demand that every sketch should have a tight internal logic, that didn't matter, because disagreement within a team, and the expression of diverse opinions, is *creatively invaluable*. All the research shows that teams whose members share the same attitudes will enjoy the experience of working together, will have good opinions of the others in the team, and be keen to repeat the experience; but creatively they will produce bugger-all.

By contrast, teams whose members view things differently from one another will argue, but this creative conflict produces innovation. You *want* creative conflict: what you don't want is personal conflict, because that will complicate proceedings and can result all too often in deadlock. The *Python* team was very diverse—just look at the entirely separate directions our careers went in after our time together—but despite our disagreements, creatively we worked very well together. We all had shortcomings, but these were balanced by the others' different strengths.

Oddly enough, despite our sometimes heated disputes in the script meetings, there was extraordinarily little friction when we actually came to rehearse. Once a script was accepted, acting it out was a very straightforward process; and since any lurking weaknesses became obvious after a few run-throughs, brainstorming to find improvements in either text or performance was a relaxed and enjoyable experience. Over the years I had come to the conclusion that every single time I rehearsed something, it got better, and I always felt that when I worked on *Python*. The others didn't always feel the same way and rarely wanted to practise sketches as much as I did, but they usually indulged me.

I was always surprised when fans asked whether we ad-libbed because, as writers, we weren't interested in improvisation, which is, after all, much more a performance activity. But I suppose that technically what Gra and I were doing while writing *was* improvising different lines (until we found a combination that worked); and, obviously, if we thought of a new line during rehearsal, we'd try it. However, there was another reason we never ad-libbed during the actual recording of the shows. There simply wasn't enough time. We taped the show in front of an audience of roughly 300—there was our unwritten rule that an audience of fewer than 200 wouldn't laugh properly—and they would be let into the studio at 7:30 p.m. Once they were in their seats, there was a warm-up, the cast were introduced, we began recording at 8, and we finished at 10:00 *on the dot*.

We were never allowed to go past 10 p.m.—for reasons I never understood—so we had exactly two hours to get everything done and that meant that, what with all the changes of sets and costumes and the retakes when we or the technical crew made mistakes, we were constantly under time pressure. If the performance of a sketch was adequate but not excellent, we would proceed with the next sketch, hoping that there would be enough time at the end to go back and do it again. So every moment was valuable and we could never afford to take the risk of trying something that had not been tested in rehearsal.

As I sit here, trying to convey to you how the *Flying Circus* shows were put together, a wonderful irony strikes me. Everything I am writing about the TV series is the polar opposite of our experience at the O2.

To start with the obvious, there we all were in the studio, in 1969, wondering how this new kind of humour would go down with an audience of 300, all of whom, as the Aussies say, didn't know us from a bar of soap. In 2014 we were performing live, in a huge arena seating 16,000 people, the vast majority of whom were dedicated fans. No one at the O2 had bought tickets because they couldn't stand *Python*.

Next, I've emphasised the teamwork of the TV series. Well, nothing like that happened at the O2. The day after we decided to do the show, we realised that four of us had absurdly busy schedules. Eric was the only one with any time on his hands. So he volunteered to come up with a running order, based on the sketches that had worked for us when we'd done the stage shows between 1973 and 1980.

When we had a read-through a couple of days later, there was an encouraging development: we all liked the running order Eric had come up with, and after we'd agreed to some changes to the beginning of the second half, we asked him if he would take on the production of the whole show. Thank God he agreed, because the rest of us were about to depart in different directions: Michael was off on his travels, recording every moment of his exciting existence in exquisite detail, either on film or in his diary, or—usually—both; Jonesy was about to go into pre-production of his aliens movie (the one incorrectly described as "a Python reunion" by the British press for the past four years); Terry G had found a film to direct in Bucharest and was eagerly anticipating spending the arctic depths of the middle European winter there; and I was flying to sunny Sydney, where I was to spend four months at the splendid Four Seasons hotel, writing 45,000 or so words of this book.

And Eric . . . just put the reunion together.

The first two problems he had to solve were, firstly, that with only four main performers, how was he going to give us time to make costume changes between our appearances, and, secondly, how would he be able to create a show that would fill the huge O2 stage, when a procession of two- and three-handed sketches were clearly *not* going to cut the mustard?

It was lucky for all of us that he'd been working for years on various productions of *Spamalot*, because he'd acquired enough experience of musical comedy to be able to add to the mix of sketches (and film) . . . the vital and magical ingredient—song and dance!

Song and dance?! In the first three *Python* TV series I can't recall a *single* song or dance. So Eric turned his back brilliantly on a long-established *Flying Circus* tradition. Had he faltered, the reunion wouldn't have worked. Thank you, Eric.

Another vast difference between the TV series and the O2 shows: bad language. On television we were very constrained by the mood of the times. The BBC allowed us the occasional "bloody," "damn" and "bastard," but that was about as far as we could go. The most extreme word to appear in *Python* came at the end of the "Spanish Inquisition" episode, when, as one of the three cardinals trying to reach the Old Bailey but failing because the show ended before they could get there, Michael Palin exclaimed, "Oh, bugger!" To our delight and surprise, Michael Mills allowed it. "I would never have believed I would OK it," he said, "but when I actually saw it, it was so funny, I'm going to." However, when Graham listed one of his hobbies as "masturbation" in the "Summarising Proust Contest," there was a real rumpus, and it had to be removed at the editing stage.

I was never much bothered by this, because I had a rather unusual attitude to foul language: generally, I was opposed to it. My reasons, though, were not puritanical but purist comedic ones. Quite simply, I regarded swearing as a form of cheating, a lazy way of getting a laugh out of material that wasn't intrinsically funny enough. But as general standards have fallen, so have mine. The best advice I was ever given came from David Attenborough in the early seventies: he said, "Use shock sparingly." So I now permit myself a "fucking" here and there: maybe four in a two-hour show. But, deep down, I sense the best comedy should not rely on artificial stimulants.

This may seem a bit rich coming from someone who has recently performed in the Python reunion, and I must take responsibility for my part in this: after all, Michael, the Terrys and I all encouraged Eric to assemble and direct a show that, at the end of the production process, could accurately be described as an "Evening of Sketches and Musical Filth." Imagine sending his lyrics for approval by the BBC's first Director General, Lord Reith. Martial law would have been declared.

But while attitudes to swearing and vulgarity have shifted in one direction in the past forty years, another set of values seems to be threatening comedy by moving in the opposite direction. I refer to the life-denying force called political correctness. This may have started as a kind intention, but was soon hijacked and taken ad absurdum by a few individuals without any sense of proportion—which means, by definition, that they are without any sense of humour either. Fortunately, the TV series were made at a time before this half-witted posturing had taken hold; equally luckily, by 2014 we were so doddery and addled that we seemed to be given a free pass in this area. (Or perhaps our audiences agreed with us. After all, *Python* fans tend to be rather intelligent.)

One final, rather odd, contrast between 1969 and 2014.

The *Flying Circus* was always, despite its love of breaking comic conventions, and the originality of some of its content, recognisably a TV comedy show. The reunion at the O2 was not a television show on stage, but then neither was it a recognisable theatrical event. I'm not just referring to the audience knowing so much of the material, or the wonderfully affectionate reception we received throughout. For a start, what other comedy group has done a pop concert?

At the press conference back in November 2013, I'd tried to suggest something along these lines. The journalists' questions indicated that they were viewing it as a big theatrical production, so I ventured that it would be more of an interaction with the audience, a celebration, or even a party.

So what was it? I don't really know. I do know that on the second night, the orchestra played a silly intro to the "Spanish Loonies" sketch, and at the end they all stood up and shouted, "Olé!," which broke me up, and the audience went with me, and the whole arena laughed for ten seconds, *before a word had been said*. And I know that during the interval of the third night, when I was annoyed that I'd fluffed a line in the "Michelangelo" sketch, and confided this to Eddie Izzard, whom I bumped into backstage, he said, "John, they've seen you do these sketches right many times. It's more special for them when you get them *wrong*." What an insight! And . . . the opposite of the way I'd always worked on the TV shows.

In the last analysis, all I know is that the O2 provided the most fun audiences I have encountered in fifty years, and that *they* turned the evening into a joyous and touching melange of laughter, affection and mindless goodwill. No wonder the *Daily Mail* hated it.

The day after the final show, we all had lunch together. We agreed unanimously that we felt no regret of any kind. As Eric said, it had been a "sweet goodbye." We'll meet together now and again for a

meal, but otherwise we'll all go off happily in our different directions: Michael travelling, Eric writing songs, Terry G raising money
for another plotless extravaganza, Terry J to the anger management
classes that are beginning to transform him, and me to puzzle out an
experience I'd had at the O2.

On only our second night, while I was waiting to start a sketch,
in the few seconds before the spotlights were turned on me, when I
could therefore still see the whole, huge, packed arena stretching in
front of me . . . I found myself thinking: "How is it *possible* that I'm
not feeling the slightest bit excited?"

Perhaps I should stick to writing from now on.

PHOTO CREDITS

All images are from the author's personal collection, unless otherwise indicated.

p. 5 Bottom: Phillip Jackson / Associated Newspapers / Rex Features

p. 6 Top: © BBC / credit : Photo Library

p. 6 Bottom: Mirrorpix

p. 7 Bottom: © AF archive / Alamy

p. 8 © AF archive / Alamy

INTERIOR IMAGES

p. 79:   Clifton College

p. 175: Lord Crathorne

p. 240: Ben Jones / Rex Features

p. 366: © Rolf Adlercreutz / Alamy

Every effort has been made to trace or contact copyright holders. The publisher will be pleased to make good any omissions or rectify any mistakes brought to their attention at the earliest opportunity.

ACKNOWLEDGEMENTS

My grateful thanks to Jim Curtis for his extraordinary scholarship, his constant support, and his ability to clarify chronologies at a moment's notice; also to Howard Johnson for turning up masses of good stuff about *At Last the 1948 Show*; and to my publishers on either side of the Atlantic, in particular Susan Sandon, and not least Kevin Doughten, and my publicist Charlotte Bush.

I'd like to thank all the people who have been part of my life, and who have therefore helped me to write this book. I don't want to name them all, because there are quite a lot, and if I miss two out they will be very upset and never want to speak to me again, and I don't want to risk that.

Finally, a word of warning about my editor, Nigel "Spats" Wilcockson, who will try to take sole credit for this book when he only deserves three-quarters of it.

And . . . three cats and a Fish, who put up with me while I was, etc., etc.

INDEX

Italic page numbers indicate illustrations.